The Political Plays of Langston Hughes

The Political Plays of Langston Hughes

With Introductions and Analyses by Susan Duffy

Southern Illinois University Press
Carbondale and Edwardsville

Frontispiece: Photo of Langston Hughes courtesy of Peter Steffens

Library of Congress Cataloging-in-Publication Data
Hughes, Langston, 1902–1967.
The political plays of Langston Hughes / with introductions and analyses by
Susan Duffy.
   p.   cm.
   Includes bibliographical references (p.) and index.
   1. United States—Politics and government—20th century—Drama.
2. Afro-Americans—Politics and government—Drama. 3. Political plays,
American. I. Duffy, Susan, 1951–   II. Title.
PS3515.U274A6 2000
812'.52—dc21
ISBN 0-8093-2295-1 (cloth : alk. paper)   99-031502
ISBN 0-8093-2296-X (pbk. : alk. paper)

For Bernie and Elizabeth

Contents

Acknowledgments

Research projects that result in publication are never the product of a single person, even when an attribution of individual authorship appears on the title page. I have received invaluable assistance from many people in researching this area of Langston Hughes' career and in preparing the manuscript for publication. I would like to acknowledge them here and offer my sincere thanks to all of them. Without them, this book could not have been completed.

First and foremost, I must begin by acknowledging my husband and daughter, Bernard and Elizabeth Duffy. Bernie's suggestions and editorial comments invariably strengthened and helped polish the final product. Liz's interest and support revealed itself when she asked to take a copy of the whole typescript to her high school English class because her teacher refused to believe that Langston Hughes wrote plays. Through her efforts, the teacher and twenty-four other students now know Hughes wrote more than poetry. For their love, their unfailing support, and their quirky sense of humor that helped get me through many days, I offer my thanks and love.

I would like to acknowledge the financial support awarded by Cal Poly State University in San Luis Obispo. The State Faculty Support Summer

Fellowship allowed me to finish the research on the project, and a sabbatical leave in the fall of 1993 enabled me to begin writing this book. Additionally, I want to acknowledge Janice Stone and the staff of the interlibrary loan department of the Kennedy Library at Cal Poly. All of my projects in the last ten years have benefited from their efficiency and tenacity in locating materials I needed and securing them for my use. Thank you.

I would like especially to thank James Simmons, editorial director of Southern Illinois University Press. His interest and faith in this project allowed it to be published by SIU Press. I would be remiss if I did not thank the reviewers who offered commentary on this manuscript in its various permutations. The individuals at SIU Press who helped prepare the manuscript for publication also deserve credit for overseeing the technical aspects of publishing this book. To them I offer my sincere thanks.

Finally, I would like to thank the readers now engaged in examining this book. This project took several years to complete, and your interest in the subject is appreciated. I hope this investigation into one area of the political writings of Langston Hughes will open doors for further investigations. Within its pages you will find my interpretations of evidence regarding Hughes' participation in the leftist political arena of the 1930s. Any errors of fact or interpretation are my own. If you believe I am in error regarding fact or interpretation, I encourage your corrections. This study is intended as a beginning. Subsequent studies will, I hope, expand the investigation into the political uses of art during the 1930s.

The following individuals, organizations, and archival collections have generously given permission to reprint from the following copyrighted works or manuscripts. *Scottsboro, Limited* copyright © 1931 by Langston Hughes. *Harvest* copyright © 1999 by the Estate of Langston Hughes; with thanks to Pete Steffens. *Angelo Herndon Jones* copyright © 1999 by the Estate of Langston Hughes. *De Organizer: A Blues Opera in One Act* copyright © 1996 by the Estate of Langston Hughes, by permission of the estate of James P. Johnson and the James P. Johnson Foundation for Music and the Arts, Inc. All plays reprinted by permission of Harold Ober Associates, Inc. *De Organizer, Harvest,* and selected letters (written by Langston Hughes and James P. Johnson) courtesy The Yale Collection of American Literature, Beinecke Rare Book and Manuscript Library, Yale University. Letters, from Langston Hughes to Noel Sullivan, in the Noel Sullivan Papers (Banc Mss C-B 801), The Bancroft Library, University of California, Berkeley. Letter written by Ella Winter, the Joseph Freeman

Papers, Hoover Institution. Transcript of interview between Langston Hughes and Reuben Silver, May 1961, courtesy of James V. Hatch, Hatch-Billops Collection, Inc. "The Same" and "Chant for Tom Mooney," poems by Langston Hughes, courtesy Craig Tenney, Harold Ober Associates, Inc. The National Archives in College Park, Maryland; the Labor Management Documentation Center of the M. Catherwood Library at Cornell University; the Local History Department of the Harrison Memorial Library in Carmel, California; the Theater of the Thirties Collection of the Fenwick Library at George Mason University; the Federal Theater Project Collection in the Library of Congress; the State Department Records of the National Archives. I am indebted as well to the archivists and staff who work in these collections.

The Political Plays of Langston Hughes

Introduction:
Chasing the Dream

When examining the career of Langston Hughes and the corpus of his work, critics turn first to the nearly six hundred poems he composed during his prolific career that spanned half a century, from the 1920s to his death in 1967. His poetry receives the greatest attention, and while his position as a leader in the Harlem Renaissance rests primarily on his reputation as a poet, his prose writings, in the form of essays, short stories, novels, and autobiographical renderings, have also merited serious academic attention. Though most examinations of Hughes focus on his reputation as a literary artist, he was also a commercial writer. He made his living through commercial freelance writing, the sale and royalties of his prose works, and the occasional lecture honoraria. Edward J. Mullen makes the case convincingly that Hughes embarked on a literary career because of the success of his poems in the 1920s. During the 1930s, he turned to prose and drama to make his living.[1] Although Hughes wrote for newspapers—and the birth of Jesse B. Simple on the pages of the *Chicago Defender* is well documented—he was sustained primarily by his output of freelance essays, speaking engagements, and other contract work, in addition to the supplemental income provided by his patrons and friends. A dozen books—including novels, collections of short stories, an autobiography, and a five-volume series devoted to Jesse B. Simple—extend the genres included in his works to boundaries rarely matched by other writers. His success in these areas has been thoroughly researched by literary critics and biographers.

It was the theater, however, that proved to be Langston Hughes' dream deferred. One of his earliest published works is a children's play, *The Gold Piece,* published in *Brownie Magazine* in 1921. Biographers are quick to note Hughes' youthful infatuation with the theater nourished by his mother's dramatic recitations and aspirations for her own theatrical career and their trips to performances in Kansas. The Cleveland years, 1916 to 1920, are marked by Hughes' association with Karamu House, founded by Rowena and Paul Jelliffe as an artistic sanctuary and school for inner-city children. Here, he attended classes, taught art, and developed a love for the theater that would be sustained in a lifelong association with the Karamu Theater Company. Hughes' desire to see his plays produced was so great that when he was unable to find companies to produce his plays, he founded his own: the Harlem Suitcase Theater, the Los Angeles Negro Art Theater, and the Skyloft Players in Chicago. Throughout his career he wrote regularly for the theater, leaving behind a collection of forty plays authored independently and twenty-three written in collaboration with other writers and musicians.[2]

In addition to his poems and books, Langston Hughes authored or co-authored sixty-three scripts, which include among them one-act plays, two- and three-act comedies and dramas, children's plays, gospel plays, propaganda plays, operas, and historical pageants. Yet as a dramatist, playwright, and librettist, Hughes has gone unnoticed and unexamined. The few considerations of his dramatic works focus mainly on *Mule Bone* and the well-known feud over authorship it engendered between Hughes and Zora Neale Hurston.[3] Others receiving attention are *Simply Heavenly, Mulatto, Little Ham,* and *Black Nativity.* There are limited academic investigations of the musical works of the better-known scripts, like *The Barrier, Soul Gone Home,* or *Tambourines to Glory,* but Hughes' political plays are untreated. Not only have his political plays escaped notice, but also his satires, operas, historical plays, children's plays, and radio scripts have never been compiled or studied either by dramatic genre, subject matter, or production techniques. Webster Smalley's 1963 compilation, *Five Plays by Langston Hughes,* remains the only anthology of Hughes' better-known scripts. One finds others anthologized in collections occasionally, but the scholarship on Hughes as a playwright is sparse.

Any examination of Langston Hughes should begin with a reading of

Arnold Rampersad's two-volume biography, *The Life of Langston Hughes,* which offers a thoroughly researched and remarkable record of Hughes' accomplishments from 1902 to 1967. Rampersad provides the definitive chronology and primary evidence necessary to understand Hughes' personal life and how it was reflected in his works. Rampersad charts the course of Hughes' life brilliantly and indicates those areas that are in need of further investigation. Missing, however, in Rampersad's exhaustive scholarship is critical assessment of Hughes' works: his poems, prose, and, for the purposes of this study, his dramatic works.

The focus of this study is purposely narrow. My intention is to examine one segment of Hughes' dramatic scripts written in the 1930s—his labor plays. This study assumes some familiarity on the reader's part with Hughes' career. It offers no long explanations of Hughes' excursions, trips abroad, or rationales for such trips, nor does it launch into exhaustive explanations of Hughes' political and personal associations beyond what is necessary to understand the background to the plays presented here. Such detailed information is provided fully by Rampersad's biography, and the reader is directed there for reexamination of the extant evidence. The interpretation of the evidence may differ. Reading correspondence from Hughes to various friends and professional associates over a period of years led me to the conclusion that because of his dispute with Zora Neale Hurston over the authorship of *Mule Bone,* Hughes developed an obsessive distrust of non-contractual collaborations in theatrical endeavors.

There are two contrasting views of Hughes delineated in this study that should be identified at the outset. The first asserts that Hughes was foremost a professional writer who used the Left and the publication opportunities offered by well-placed leftist literary figures to advance his career. The second posits a purer idealistic commitment on the part of Hughes to champion the cause of the politically disenfranchised and write from a position of moral and political rectitude. Hughes was an artist, Hughes was a social critic, Hughes became a prominent public figure for political groups—but evidence suggests that Langston Hughes was not a political ideologue. An idealist, yes, an ideologue, no. One should not infer from the first view that he merely exploited leftist groups for his own professional and financial gain. Likewise, one should not infer from the second that Hughes had little or no interest in American political movements. The psychological profile of Hughes and his associations with groups and individuals throughout his personal and professional life is too complex to be subjected to simple labels that either glorify or vilify his motivations; nor is it the intent of this study to do so. The interpersonal struggles of the man are caught somewhat in Rampersad's biography. This work is not so much intended as a study of Hughes' personal ethos as it is an analysis of the plays that stand as part of American literary labor history.

One book cannot examine the whole range of Hughes' dramatic works as well as his involvement in the theatrical companies he helped found to produce his plays. Similarly, it would be beyond the scope and interest of most presses to publish all of his plays and collaborative efforts in one gigantic multivolume set. This study purposely employs a very narrow focus, yet it targets an important aspect of Hughes career as a playwright: his leftist-inspired scripts written during the decade of the 1930s. Published here for the first time in a collection are *Scottsboro, Limited; Harvest* (referred to in most books as *Blood on the Fields*); *Angelo Herndon Jones*; and for only the second time, *De Organizer*.

LEFTIST ISSUES AND LABOR PLAYS

"Perhaps Langston Hughes does not relish the title of Proletarian Poet, but he deserves it just the same," pronounced Margaret Larkin in her article "A Poet for the People" in 1927.[4] Although Larkin compares Hughes' poems to those of Robert Burns, a more apt comparison, considering his plays about labor, might be made to Byron and his defense of the Luddites. Alain Locke, writing in *Opportunity* six years later, called Hughes "a militant and indignant proletarian reformer."[5] Hughes himself recognized this tendency in his writing and also acknowledged it as one of the distinguishing features of his style that writers and publishers sought. In a 1934 letter to Noel Sullivan, Hughes details working on a revision for Knopf. "I think my real métier is protesting about something, so I now begin the first chapter by protesting about Paul Robeson's lawyer living in a hotel that doesn't want Negroes to use the front door. . . . So it gets off now with an emotional bang! that I trust Knopf's will feel 'sounds like me' . . . [s]ince that is what they desire."[6] A decade later, Hughes referred to himself as "a social poet." Towards the end of his career in 1961, he modified his self-appraisal, commenting in a radio symposium, "I am . . . primarily a . . . propaganda writer; my main material is the race problem."[7] While the arguments for social justice are evident in all of his works, they are particularly pointed in the dramas. "Agit-prop" (agitation-propaganda) was a label attached to his early theatrical efforts. Throughout the decade of the 1930s, Hughes' dramatic themes targeted sociopolitical issues employing a range of approaches. Plays such as *Mulatto* (1931); *Scottsboro, Limited* (1933); *Harvest* (1935); *Angelo Herndon Jones* (1936); and *De Organizer* (1939) were serious dramatic pieces. At the opposite end of the spectrum one finds his satiric parodies in *Em-Fuhrer Jones, Little Eva's End, Limitations of Life,* and *Uncle Tommy's Cabin,* all written around 1938.

Many of Hughes' works, including his plays, were translated and distributed in Russia during the 1930s. While not an overt political revolutionary, his actions, as well as the company he kept, were monitored by United States government agents. Hughes' embrace of Communism did not enhance his credibility with the FBI, nor did his association with prominent Communist and leftist political and literary figures in the United States. His controversial trip to Russia, attendance at the first Workers' Theaters International Olympiad, and questionable position as president of the League of Struggle for Negro Rights raised governmental suspicions. Finally, his speeches before the American Communist Party John Reed Clubs and International Writers Congress and his poems— especially "One More 'S' in the U.S.A," "Good Morning Revolution," and "Goodbye Christ"—caught and held federal attention for decades. These actions, among others, would come to plague him in his career and result in his being called in 1953 to testify before the Senate Permanent Sub-Committee on Investigations headed by Senator Joseph McCarthy.

When one considers Hughes' connections with the political Left, a symbiotic relationship begins to appear. Leftist groups, most notably the John Reed Club, used his growing celebrity status as a public relations ploy to attract black members, and Hughes, in return, used the artistic networks of leftist writers and artists to further his own career. As he candidly wrote in 1936, "I have come to the conclusion that Fate never intended for me to have a full pocket of anything but manuscripts, so the only thing I can do is to string along with the Left until maybe someday all us poor folks will get enough to eat including rent, gas, light and water—said bills being the bane of my life."[8]

Hughes' ties to leftist groups were close, but he gravitated toward the artistic and literary activities of successful and prominent individuals within these groups, more so than to an ideological involvement in politics. This association was carried on mainly through his interaction with members of the John Reed Clubs, which, as Eric Homberger has noted, "were an attempt to apply the Proletcult notion of literary studios to America." Despite the fact that they received no institutional recognition from the Communist Party, the John Reed Clubs served as an important impetus to the leftist movement in the United States. Operating under the motto "Art Is a Class Weapon," John Reed Clubs promoted the use of art for social and class liberation. The philosophical tenets of the function of art for political purposes found support in American intellectual and artistic circles across the country. In 1934, five years after its creation in New York, there existed thirty clubs with over twelve hundred members across the United States.[9] Homberger's contention that the "John Reed Clubs appealed to writers who were socially conscious, but not necessarily only those who were Communists" applies to Langston Hughes.[10] Hughes was active in these groups, his name appearing among those elected to the presidium at the first National Conference of the John Reed Clubs, though the extent of his activity is periodically labeled "honorary."[11] In the John Reed Clubs, Hughes sought and found support and artistic company on both coasts.

His play *Blood on the Fields* grew out of his well-known association with the John Reed Club in Carmel, California, which had only nine members. The main interest of this small but active group was the defense and support of migratory agricultural workers. It counted among its members and supporters not only Hughes but also noted leftist social critic Lincoln Steffens and his wife, Ella Winter, with whom Hughes collaborated on *Blood on the Fields*. The controversial nature of the JRC in Carmel manifested itself in local protests. Because of his involvement with the Carmel chapter, Hughes felt compelled to leave Carmel in 1934, fearing attack by resident Legionnaires.

While Hughes is credited with founding the Suitcase Theater in Harlem, what is not generally known is that this group grew out of the John Reed Club in New York. Hughes was one of four directors of the newly formed company that would be comprised of "a group of proficient actors who [would] travel with a minimum of equipment and a repertory of working class plays to be given before labor organizations." Startling about this alliance are the names of the other directors: Langston Hughes shared administrative and artistic responsibilities with Jacob Burck of the *Daily Worker;* Paul Peters, author of *Stevedore;* and most surprisingly, Whittaker Chambers, who later turned state's evidence against Alger Hiss in one of the most celebrated spy trails in U.S. history.[12]

Hughes played down his association with Communist groups in his autobiographies and statements made later in his career. He was one of the "fellow travelers," as literary historian Daniel Aaron dubbed them: individuals "who were in the 'movement' who sympathized with the objectives of the party, wrote for the party press, [and] knowingly affiliated with associations sponsored by the party" but who were not actually members. As Aaron points out, only a small fraction of left-wing writers were actually members of the Communist Party, but many writers were infatuated more with the *idea* of Communism than they were with the Communist Party itself.[13] Langston Hughes was certainly a "fellow traveler." The evidence of his involvement with such groups in the 1930s is clear. His motivations for involvement are open to speculation, but significant in such musings are two incidents, one personal, the other political, which coincide with his marked shift to the Left.

The first is his painful break with the philanthropic but dictatorial patronage of Mrs. Charlotte Mason. This incident, and the emotional havoc it wreaked upon Hughes, is chronicled vividly in Rampersad's biography. Hughes' forced departure from the security of Mason's New York apartment and his subsequent embrace of leftist figures may be viewed in terms of a professional, if not emotional, rebound. The leftist literati offered connections and outlets for talented individuals whose sole support came from writing.

The second incident places Hughes' shift on a higher, ideological plane. It was, as Rampersad has noted, "the driving public force in Hughes' move to the left . . . the Scottsboro controversy." The imprisonment of nine black youths in Alabama and the accusations leveled that they had raped two white prostitutes in a freight car became a national cause célèbre for leftist groups in the United States in the early 1930s. The tragedy of "the Scottsboro Boys" became the subject of artistic treatments for many artists and writers, including Hughes. The Communist Party's active involvement in the defense and appeals of the Scottsboro Boys turned the case into what Rampersad terms "a great opportunity" for the recruitment of blacks to party membership.[14]

Though Hughes attended meetings and rallies and contributed several articles to leftist publications, including *Opportunity, Crisis,* the *Daily Worker,* and *New Masses,* his leftist fervor of the 1930s waned in later years. His artistic legacy of this period, however, especially in his plays, merits renewed investigation. Hughes' labor scripts require examination from the standpoint of their political rhetoric, their depiction of various groups within the labor force of the 1930s, their use of documentary detail, and their potential to stand as propaganda within a movement. Hughes' coming-of-age as a playwright occurred in the 1930s at precisely the time when labor theaters, associated with the same leftist groups in New York with which Hughes associated, were hanging banners across their stages proclaiming "Theater Is a Weapon."[15]

The leftist theater movement in the United States spanned only a few years of a decade. By 1941, most of the leftist groups affiliated with the Communist Party had disbanded. Even the government-supported Federal Theater Project was closed in 1939 for alleged "Communist" leanings. Morgan Himmelstein maintains that audiences failed to patronize social drama because they preferred popular comedies. "The 111 showings of *Stevedore* fell disastrously below the 835 of *Three Men on a Horse* because the Depression theater-going audience preferred the escape of the Broadway farce to the serious problems of the American Negroes."[16] Hughes recognized the salability of comedy as early as 1935 with *Little Ham*. Just at the beginning of 1936 he wrote again to Noel Sullivan, informing him, "My life of late, creatively, has been entirely devoted to the Drama—such as it is—and if you see Steffy [Lincoln Steffens] you might tell him that I'm determined to be a playwright in spite of all." Still, he managed to alternate between comedic writing and social commentary. The same letter continues: "I did a play about Angelo Herndon in one act (in which Herndon doesn't appear except as a picture on a poster) which seems to have won the *New Theater* award of $50, although I haven't gotten the money yet."[17] The following year he wrote *Joy to My Soul*, produced by the Gilpin Players at Karamu House, which also produced *Little Ham*. A year later he would turn his comedic talents to writing political and social parodies: *Em-Fuhrer Jones, Uncle Tommy's Cabin,* and *Little Eva's End*. Interestingly, his dramatic writings follow trends in the rise and fall of leftist drama of the 1930s. Hughes tested a number of experimental dramatic forms—agit-prop, documentary, chorale recitation, and so on—before finding commercial success in his comedies and operas. His most overtly political plays of the decade of the 1930s remain, however, the focus of this study. One might guess what prompted Hughes to abandon his efforts in writing political dramas in favor of comedies, historical pageants, and operas: as a professional writer, his living, comprised of royalties and commissions, depended on popular acceptance of his material. The blacklisting of writers and the witch hunts of the Dies Committee in the late 1930s and again during the "McCarthy era" had a profound, chilling effect on those whose living depended on their literary efforts.

In the early 1960s, Hughes saw a shift back to what have been called propaganda, or agit-prop, plays. He characterized the shift as "dark" and expressly believed that it could be detected in the poetry and theater of the period. He provides a rationale rarely articulated in academic investigations of leftist literature. From Hughes' perspective, after a long hiatus, writers started to realize the plethora of social problems in need of forceful and strong artistic treatment. He explained the absence of social dramas, noting "social material has not been fashionable since the McCarthy era because it has been dangerous to use it."[18] Political and social didacticism is evident in any of the scripts by Langston Hughes, whether they are the political scripts of his early years or the comedies of the later. When Margaret Larkin called Hughes a "Proletarian Poet," she did not realize that a more fitting title would be "Proletarian Playwright." It is not surprising, given Hughes' associations with the political Left, that his plays of the 1930s fit the mold of experimental political plays from those years.

The influence of the American Communist Party on Langston Hughes and other writers addressing issues of racial oppression and societal injustices during the 1930s cannot be underestimated. In *Renewing the Left: Politics, Imagination, and the New York Intellectuals,* Harvey Teres makes a strong case for party influences in the African American community in New York:

> The Party played a key role in Harlem throughout much of the decade; in the realm of culture alone, it influenced . . . a very high proportion of African American writers, and artists among them Richard Wright, Ralph Ellison, Paul Robeson, Langston Hughes, Sterling Brown, William Attaway, Chester Himes, Countee Cullen, Dorothy West, Arna Bontemps, John Oliver Killens, and Margaret Walker. . . . [T]he Party was active within the larger community on a number of cultural fronts. It was deeply involved in promoting black theater through the Negro People's Theatre and Hughes' "Harlem Suitcase Theatre."[19]

The 1930s offers fascinating artistic examples of how theater was used by the American Communist Party and other groups for propagandistic and political ends. The domestic concerns that preoccupied American artists and critics on the Left throughout the decade are clearly depicted in Hughes' scripts. Leftist groups were most vocal about labor issues; however, their concerns mirrored those held by the American mainstream, including fear of involvement in another European war. In 1932, *Workers Theater,* the official publication of the Communist-supported League of Workers' Theaters, issued a call for more anti-war plays, and an official resolution against fascism appeared on the front page of *Workers Theater* in April 1933. Hughes' anti-fascist parody in *Em-Fuhrer Jones,* produced in 1938, reflects a trend in leftist plays of the late 1930s that satirized the Nazis. One finds similar elements in the International Ladies' Garment Workers' Union production of *Pins and Needles* (1938) and Clare Boothe Luce's *Margin for Error* (1939). Hughes contributed another anti-war propaganda play to the leftist collection with *For This We Fight* in 1943.

Communist *influence* unquestionably permeated leftist plays of this period. As Wendy Smith claims in her noteworthy study of the Group Theatre, "Communism dominated intellectual life on the left to an unprecedented extent in the 1930s." Whether ideological influence or intellectual interest can be construed as political control is a debatable question. Morgan Himmelstein takes an alternate position, claiming that ultimately "the Communists failed to control the new theater movement because they were unable to control either the playwrights or the audience."[20]

The leftist theater groups and plays of the 1920s, 1930s, and 1940s are characterized by their relentless efforts to raise social consciousness on a myriad of issues using a variety of artistic approaches. Hughes employed his own unique approach by using jazz and blues as agents of social propaganda rather than mere social lament. Hughes' musical structure in his labor plays distinguish them from others of this period, yet in the four plays in this study, one discovers many of the same rhetorical strategies. Like other labor plays, Hughes' scripts provide a justification for the militancy of labor and characterize the labor leaders in messianic imagery. Though the areas may differ in labor plays, from New York to North Carolina, the allusions within the plays rely on religious and folk motifs and strong appeals to ethnic pride.

Before embarking on the analysis of the texts presented in this book, one must understand the critical approach taken in their examination. In the preparation of this manuscript, I was strongly encouraged to employ a semiotic approach to Hughes' scripts, basing the analysis of the texts on the interpretive guidelines of Umberto Eco. There is much to be gained from a reading of Eco that could be applied to this study. Whether it is his discussion of "openness" that he applies to the text of Joyce or the elements of "points of tension" found in the plays of Brecht, Eco provides one scholarly approach to the literature for those so inclined to use it. As Eco points out in his introduction to *The Role of the Reader*, "No text is read independently of the reader's experience of other texts." Later in the book, he discusses elements of Brecht's plays that fit well into an analysis of Hughes' labor scripts:

In Brecht's theoretical work on drama, we shall see that dramatic action is conceived as the problematic exposition of specific points of tension. Having presented these tension points (by following the well-known technique of epic recitation, which does not seek to influence the audience, but rather to offer a series of facts to be observed, employing a device of "defamiliarization") Brecht's plays do not, in the strict sense, devise solutions at all. It is left up to the audience to draw its own conclusions from what it has seen on the stage.

Eco concludes this section by noting that the artistic work is "open" in a manner similar to a debate being "open." "A solution is seen as desirable and is actually anticipated, but it must come from the collective enterprise of the audience. In this case the 'openness' is converted into an instrument of revolutionary pedagogics." Additionally, his discussion of the construction of a world of references is pertinent to an analysis of historical scripts.[21] I encourage the reader to apply the same logic in reference to an examination of Hughes' scripts.

But this study does not employ the techniques of a semiotician, nor does it adhere strictly to reader response theories or Kenneth Burke's dramatistic pentad. My approach is to examine Hughes' labor plays from a rhetorical perspective, in the sense that rhetoric is an art of adaptation to a particular audience; it is intended for specific rather than general audiences. Wendy Smith states succinctly, "Any writing worth its salt has a definite point of view; authors (and critics) who pretend not to have one are kidding themselves and their audience."[22] The guiding conviction in the present analysis is that "art argues." *How* it argues and *what* it argues give way to many scholarly approaches and interpretations. In approaching the plays from a rhetorical perspective—one that examines how the work attempts to persuade an audience—one must consider not only the work of art itself but also its intended audience. This marriage of rhetorical and historical analysis spawns yet another theoretical approach labeled "new historicism." It is within this "ism" that my predilections reside.

Rhetoric, for our purposes here, can be defined as written or oral persuasive discourse. Within the categories developed for rhetoric, oratory was divided into three distinctive types, each having a specific purpose: forensic, deliberative, and epideictic oratory. Forensic oratory had as its intent argument supported by hard evidence, as one might find in legal proceedings. According to Aristotle, deliberative oratory was concerned with expediency, with encouragement and dissuasion, and with getting things done for a common good. Political oratory fell into this category. Epideictic oratory is often mislabeled as oratory intended for display or entertainment. Yet under the rubric of epideictic, one finds the Greek funeral orations, eulogies, and speeches honoring institutions, nations, and ideologies. The original intent of the epideictic speech was the articulation of praise and blame. It carried with it the ancillary intent of display and entertainment. Epideictic oratory requires a sympathetic audience for its success because its suasory powers rest on identification of cultural mores and beliefs held by the audience. It has as its intent the strengthening of already-held beliefs rather than the inculcation of new ones.[23] Greek epideictic oratory also served an educative function for the young. Keeping these distinctions in mind, it is easy to see that political theater of the 1920s, 1930s, and 1940s functioned as epideictic oratory. These plays offer both economic and moral instruction to neophyte political audiences, but as with all serious epideictic literature, there is a strong undercurrent of exhortation. What is praised or condemned is also what should be sought or avoided.

Hughes' plays share similarities in approach and theme with other leftist playwrights of the 1930s. Like many of the other writers, Hughes found that the theater served as an ideal forum for reenactment of contemporary labor disputes and the often violent responses to them by vigilante groups. *Harvest* is a documentary drama, and to some extent so is *Scottsboro, Limited,* since it reenacts the details of the young boys' arrest and trial. As documentary or quasi-documentary dramas, they become part of a body of American labor literature as well as theatrical literature intended for use for political ends. The devil identified in these scripts is American capitalism, and salvation from modern social problems comes with the color-blind brotherhood of trade unionism and Communism.

The documentary nature of Hughes' scripts adds to the evidence that there was a whole movement in the American theater of the 1920s and 1930s that was using reportage and documentary detail in the labor plays before the Federal Theater Project ever began producing Living Newspapers.[24] In his 1922 article "Steps Toward the Negro Theatre," Alain Locke commented on innovative dramatic techniques surfacing in university theatrical productions: "[I]n its new affiliation with the drama, the American college under the leadership of Professor Koch . . . now of the University of North Carolina, has become a vital agency in community drama, and has actively promoted the dramatization of local life and tradition. By a threefold sponsorship, then, race drama becomes peculiarly the ward of our colleges, as new drama, as art-drama and as folk-drama."[25] The most identifying feature of these plays, as they were written and produced by Koch's students, was the incorporation of a folk idiom in the dialogue of the characters. In "Langston Hughes: Rhetoric and Protest," Margaret A. Reid credits Hughes as being the "most avant-garde of [the] poetic innovators during the Harlem Renaissance" in the use of the black idiom. Her conclusion asserts, "Langston Hughes was to be the forerunner of the militant poets of the Sixties who poeticized their protests about the moral blemishes that scarred America's sense of justice."[26] Reid, Rampersad, and others comment upon the criticism directed toward Hughes for his use of folk sources and folk idiom, which characterize his plays of this period.

Notably, Hughes lectured at the University of North Carolina at Chapel Hill in the early 1930s at the invitation of North Carolina playwright Paul Green at about the time that *Strike Song,* a play about the Gastonia textile strike of 1929, was being produced by Koch's students. The university received considerable criticism for both the play and Hughes' lecture. Because there had been pressure on the university to cancel his lecture, extra police units were added to ensure Hughes' protection as he spoke in the theater. Ironically, a 17 December 1931 issue of the ultra-conservative *Southern Textile Bulletin* carried its first salvo directed toward the *Strike Song* production right above an article that characterized Hughes' address and reading as "insulting and blasphemous statements [made by] a Negro . . . prior to being honored at the University of North Carolina." *Strike Song,* more than any other labor play of this period, used music and folk, religious, and labor songs to persuade its audience. This technique became a hallmark of Hughes' dramatic works. Hughes met Frederick Koch as well as *Strike Song's* authors, Loretta and James Osler Bailey, close friends of Paul Green's, but whether Hughes knew of their script or saw the production is purely speculative.

Nonetheless, the models for labor scripts, with their use of documentary evidence in dialogue and choral responses, were there for Hughes, whether in the plays of the Carolina Playmakers in North Carolina or in the plays of the League of Workers' Theater in New York. His short stint as a writer for the Federal Writers' Project brought him into contact with individuals penning political plays using a documentary form in the Living Newspaper productions. The documentary nature of the labor scripts was part of an indigenous movement in the American theater of the 1930s, and Hughes' scripts must be examined in that light. Hughes recognized his own affinity for historical detail and commentary. His reflections on the 1931 southern lecture tour included his own assessment of the style employed: "Many of my verses were documentary, journalistic and topical. All across the South that winter I read my poems about the plight of the Scottsboro boys."[27]

The four scripts in this study offer four distinct approaches to leftist and labor issues. *Angelo Herndon Jones* uses the unseen character of Angelo Herndon, a black Communist organizer jailed for leading a march on behalf of the relief of blacks in Georgia, as a foil to discuss Marxist politics and social injustice and to elevate the organizing labor leader to the level of folk hero. The issue of housing for a pregnant black woman, whose child will be called Angelo Herndon Jones, couples religious imagery with the organizing effort to blur the lines between the church and the union.

Harvest offers dramatic documentary evidence of specific abuses involving the cotton workers in the San Joaquin Valley in 1933. It is similar to *Strike Song* and Mary Heaton Vorse's play, *Strike!,* which use woman labor leaders as protagonists. Hughes' female protagonist in *Harvest* is based on Caroline Decker, who organized workers in a California strike that would change agricultural policy in that state. The dialogue of the play is often a verbatim account of answers offered by cross-examined witnesses in the subsequent court trials and of reports found in newspapers of the day.

De Organizer is a gospel play lionizing an unnamed union leader who stands up to the field boss. Hughes uses folkloric allusions combined with blues forms to rally his characters and the audience in song. Hughes' plays are most moving and most persuasive in the use of ritualistic elements such as song, call-response, and choral chants. *De Organizer* and *Scottsboro, Limited* are the most innovative of the scripts in terms of dramatic structure and style.

Scottsboro, Limited employs a traditional agit-prop technique of audience plants and chants to allow the action on stage to spill out into the house, thus establishing the psychological participation of the audience while encouraging their physical participation in songs and chants. *Scottsboro, Limited* is structurally surreal and evokes a nightmarish quality of victimization and group guilt. It calls for recognition of a corrupt justice system that can be eradicated only by an active audience response. The play ends in typical agit-prop style with the audience rising en masse shouting, "Fight! Fight! Fight! Fight!"

MUSICAL STRUCTURE/LITERARY FORM

Hughes' plays bear striking similarities to other labor scripts in their treatment of theme, character, and issues, but in dramatic structure they are markedly different because of the musical form used. Hughes is credited with merging blues and jazz in his poetry in the 1920s. This literary style was innovative, even radical, adapting the musicality of lyric poetry to a completely recognizable musical style, the blues. The music of the blues, jazz, swing, and other popular forms is omnipresent in his lines of poetry and in several of his dramatic works. By using the blues and jazz structure, Hughes established a musicality in his literary lines that reflected a distinct African American ethnicity as well as a distinct African American experience. This innovation seems a conscious break from traditional structural forms of drama for Hughes. His essay "Jazz as Communication" provides a glimpse of his approach in assertively combining lyric with jazz forms:

> You can start anywhere—Jazz as Communication—since it's a circle, and you yourself are the dot in the middle. . . . Jazz seeps into words—spelled out words. Nelson Algren is influenced by jazz. Ralph Ellison is, too. Sartre, too. Jacques Prevert. Most of the best writers today are. Look at the end of the "Ballad of the Sad Café." . . . Some of it came out in poems of mine in *Montage of a Dream Deferred* later. Jazz again putting itself into words. . . . But I wasn't the only one putting jazz into words. Better poets of the heart of jazz beat me to it. . . . [J]azz is only what you yourself get out of it. . . . Jazz is a heartbeat—its heartbeat is yours. You will tell me about its perspectives when you get ready.[28]

Hughes criticizes the "self-styled 'high-class,' Nordicized Negro[es]" who relinquish their cultural identities in emulating the white middle class. He writes disparagingly of their efforts to adopt "Nordic manners, Nordic faces, Nordic hair, Nordic art (if any) and an Episcopal heaven." He preferred instead the influences of "the common people" whom he believed would "give to the world its truly great Negro artist, the one who is not afraid to be himself." Of his own effort to write out of his own experience Hughes, explains: "Most of my own poems are racial in theme and treatment, derived from the life I know. In many of them I try to grasp and hold some of the meanings and rhythms of jazz. . . . [J]azz to me is one of the inherent expressions of Negro life in America: the eternal tom-tom beating in the Negro soul—the tom-tom of revolt against weariness in a white world, a world of subway trains, and work, work, work; the tom-tom of joy and laughter and pain swallowed in a smile."[29]

Hughes was not alone in using music and more abstract artistic forms to assert political positions, nor did his efforts go unrecognized or unattended. Dance of this period was "going through [its] own phase of turning crude agit-prop into new images and forms . . . thought more socially important." The New Dance Group and others like it in the Workers' Dance League employed a number of dramatic and innovative accompaniments in their performances, including jazz, folk music, and the poetry of Langston Hughes. The revolutionary message in the dance performances were reviewed regularly and with greater acceptance in leftist publications like *New Theater,* but critics like Michael Gold in the *Daily Worker* were not as easily won over. Jay Williams, author of *Stage Left,* contends that their aim was to combine revolution and modern dance. However, he maintains, "[T]heir task was complicated by a number of factors, not least of which was the resistance of working class audiences to the curious posturing and symbolic representations of the performers."[30]

Particularly interesting was the dramatic use of Hughes' poetry by performance and dance companies within leftist organizations that were not involved with the staging of plays. Hughes was part of this artistic movement within the larger leftist movement in the United States. The musical quality of his poems also stirred artists in a number of fields. A 1936 letter from Hughes mentions interpretations of his poems by Margaret Bonds, a pianist with the Chicago Symphony, who Hughes indicated "has done some excellent settings for some of my poems. One is of *The Negro Speaks of Rivers,* quite different from the Hayes-Parham setting, but equally as beautiful, I think—which she has submitted to Marion Anderson."[31]

Conspicuous breaks with standard literary forms are not usually met with universal approval. Some critics of Hughes' musical drama found they could not evaluate it using the traditional techniques of literary criticism. Hughes' poems, as well as his dramatic works, enjoin the reader, the critic, and the audience to employ the language and sensitivity of the music critic. A discerning and perceptive ear is required for an appreciation of his works, and the drama resides in the orchestrated rhythms and crescendos of the lines. *De Organizer* offers clear evidence that Hughes intended the play far more as a concert than a dramatic propaganda play. His marginalia contains indications of musical style assigned to lines or sections of dialogue. "Swing," "syncopated," "recitative," and other such notations pointed out rhythmic and aesthetic changes in mood and sound. Reading the lines as simple prose dialogue renders them flat. Reading them as a choral score comes closest to the intent of the author. In 1961, Dudley Fitts went so far as to label Hughes' jazz poems "non-literary," asserting that they could not "be evaluated by any canon dealing with literary right or wrong."[32]

De Organizer is structurally similar to Hughes' blues poems that were initially criticized by some as simply "Jazz" and "doggerel."[33] Because the play uses a different form—a concert form—one needs to approach it with a director's eye for production and the conductor's ear for the power of the music to persuade. Merely looking for rhetorical appeals in individual speeches without consideration of the shifts and builds in rhythms and tones results in an unsatisfactory reading. A clue to how one should read the scripts comes from Hughes himself. Referring to Robert Breen's Shakespeare in Harlem, Hughes calls the production "the theatricalization of [my] poetry."[34] This assessment is one that proves useful in approaching any of Hughes scripts. When reading the scripts printed in the following chapters, work to achieve a "theatricalization of the poetry." When this occurs, the plays come alive.

HUGHES AND THE THEATER AND FILM

Langston Hughes had a lifelong desire to break into the film industry as a screenwriter or to write a play that would be a great success on Broadway. But his forays into screenwriting did not prove successful, and his endeavors in the commercial theater, while more lucrative, never reached the heights for which he hoped. Hughes was a lyricist, a librettist, more than he was a playwright. But lyricists need collaborators, and Hughes had continual problems working with others on dramatic projects. His early battle with Zora Neale Hurston over the authorship of Mule Bone adversely affected subsequent collaborations. He suffered lasting suspicions that manifested themselves in an extremely cautious, almost obsessive, need to have firm contractual delineation of royalties and rights.[35] Had he been able to find a partner with whom he could comfortably collaborate, his reputation in the theater would far exceed what it is today. The closest he came to achieving the collaborative notoriety he sought was his 1947 work with Elmer Rice and Kurt Weill on Street Scene, an operatic adaptation of Rice's play of the same name. There were intriguing earlier collaborations, but these never came to fruition. One, of particular interest, involved his work with Kaj Gynt on a play called

Cock o' de World. According to Hughes, he wrote the lyrics while Duke Ellington supplied the music. Gynt wanted Paul Robeson to play the lead, but Robeson was committed to other projects in London and she was not able to find funding for the production. Though she tried for years, it was never produced.[36] Two of the four plays in this study represent collaborative endeavors. *Harvest,* initially called *Blood on the Fields,* was begun in collaboration with Ella Winter in 1933. Winter and her husband, noted muckraker Lincoln Steffens, took more than a passing interest in the strike activities and union organizing efforts of labor groups in northern California, and their zeal proved infectious to Hughes. Ultimately, the play was completed through the efforts of Hughes, Winter, and Ann Hawkins. *De Organizer* is a musical for which Hughes supplied the poetry and lyrics, with the score completed by James P. Johnson. One problem in approaching the leftist plays written by Hughes stems from the fact that they were rarely, if ever, produced. Of the plays examined here, only *De Organizer* was produced as part of the International Ladies' Garment Workers' Union Convention in 1939.

Hughes continually sought and cultivated professional and personal associations and regularly wrote scripts with an eye to transforming them into screenplays, but his "break" into the film industry never came. Despite the success and prominence achieved during his lifetime, Hughes' inability to find acceptance in films gnawed at him, and comments edged with bitterness surfaced in articles, speeches, and interviews throughout his life. Statements in two speeches provide compelling evidence of the painful discrimination he felt. In an address before the League of American Writers, his condemnation of the system pours forth: "The market for Negro writers is very limited. Jobs as professional writers, editorial assistants, publisher's readers, etc., are almost nonexistent. Hollywood, in so far as Negroes are concerned, might just as well be controlled by Hitler."[37] His 1957 speech before the National Assembly of Authors and Dramatists Symposium offers similar bitter commentary on what he considered Jim Crow policies at work in the entertainment industry of the 1930s and 1940s:

> My chance to be heard, as a Negro writer, is not so great as your chance if you are white. I once approached the Play Service of the Dramatists Guild as to the handling of some of my plays. *No,* was the answer, they would not know where to place plays about Negro life. . . . We Negro writers, just by being black have been on the blacklist all our lives. . . . There are film studios that have never

hired a Negro writer. Censorship for us begins at the color lines. . . . Not once in a blue moon does Hollywood send for a Negro writer, no matter how famous he may be.

Hughes' ended this short speech with a reading of his now-famous "Merry-Go-Round" poem that concludes with the lines:

> But there ain't no back
> to a merry-go-round;
> Where's the horse
> For a kid's that's black?

Hughes' resolve "NOT to die of theateritis—nor even to have a stiff knee!" was borne out despite his disappointment in being unable to break the Jim Crow barriers in Hollywood.[38]

Hughes helped found the Suitcase Theater in Harlem, the Skyloft Players in Chicago, and the Negro Theater in Los Angeles. His association with these three theater groups, as well as with the Karamu Theater in Cleveland, which produced many of his plays, constitutes an area of American theatrical history not fully explored. The Suitcase Theater was founded, by Hughes' account, in 1937 to present his play *Don't You Want to Be Free?*, which he characterized as a play "made from my poems and it was 99 1/2% Negro." This script is not included here because it has more of the characteristics of a protest pageant than a play. Hughes did, however, take pride in the fact that the play ran 135 performances on weekends and had the distinction "of being the longest running play to anyone's knowledge in Harlem." He believed in the cultural significance of his theater company, calling it the "forerunner of the American Negro Theater, and of the various little theater groups that sprang up in Harlem in the late 30's and 40's." The Suitcase Theater provided precisely the kind of opportunities Hughes wanted in the theater: "It certainly had some impact and encouraged a lot of young people to try to write for the theater, and out of it came two or three people who became professional actors."[39] Among the most noted of these actors was Earl Jones.

After returning from Europe, Hughes went to Los Angeles and founded the Negro Theater, again to produce *Don't You Want to be Free?*, the most lucrative of his scripts of the 1930s. The West Coast production was directed by Clarence Muse. In the East, his works were regularly produced by Rowena Jelliffe at the Karamu Settlement in Cleveland, which Hughes attended as a child, participating in writing classes and even taking art classes. His Skyloft Players in Chicago also grew out of a community organization, the Good Shepherd Community House, which reaffirms the contention that Hughes continually envisioned a theater that drew from its community roots. He addressed this issue at the end of his career, lamenting the shift in productions of the Karamu Theater to what he called "rehashes of Broadway stuff."

> I have felt that Karamu was in an enviable position to be the expressive theater of the Negro people in America, particularly since most of the time there has been no other dramatic theater functioning anyway, and Karamu, for a long time, was the theater that presented practically all of the plays that were good about Negroes and by Negroes. . . . Until it became a highly integrated organization and had its new building, it was primarily a Negro theater really. . . . Since there is no place in America where . . . the accent is on the presentation of Negro drama and Negro creativity in the theater, I . . . would have preferred to see Karamu, with its very beautiful plan and its ability to give beautiful expression to the Negro in the theater, I would prefer to see it concentrate entirely on that. . . . Karamu has been a very great influence in the acting end of the theater in relation to the Negroes and many fine actors have come out of Karamu. As a theater school . . . it is, indeed, excellent. . . . I would like to see this theater be what a regional theater might be in Texas or Oklahoma or what Paul's [Green?], or the folk theater was . . . for the Negro playwright, or for people writing plays about Negro life, or the problem of the Negro in relation to American democracy. . . . I simply see no reason why Karamu or any other theater primarily in a Negro neighborhood would do rehashes of Broadway plays. . . . I did not say Broadway trash. . . . I simply said that they were plays that had nothing to do with Negro life. . . . They had nothing to do with the life of this community. . . . [T]here is such a scarcity of theater that concentrate on the subject matter that I . . . am interested, leave those things to the other theaters, let them alone. [Karamu] is doing more good for young Negro playwrights because the white playwright has all the theaters in America in which to attempt to get his material on the stage and it's not easy for anyone. The Negro playwright has a very limited field in which he might even hope to be presented. . . . I think it would be worth Karamu's while to go out of its way and to make a very intensive effort to develop the Negro playwrights. It's been invaluable to me and I think it would be invaluable to others, to those who are young now, who are beginning the theater and who find Broadway almost

insurmountable, and off-Broadway almost insurmountable if it's a play with a largely Negro cast . . . or if it's on a Negro theme. . . . I think it is a cultural shame that a great country like America with 20 million people of color has no primarily serious colored theater. There isn't. Karamu is the very nearest thing to it. The American Negro Theater in New York developed a number of fine actors and one production went to Broadway, *Anna Lucasta,* and became very commercial minded and suddenly everything turned Broadway after that, which is the wrong slant. My feeling is not only should a Negro theater, if we want to use that term, do plays by and about Negroes, but it should do plays slanted toward the community in which it exists. It should be in a primarily Negro community since that is the way our racial life in America is still. I should do material of interest to that community. Which doesn't mean that it should pander to the bad taste of some of the members of the community, or to the narrow-mindedness of them. . . . It should not be a theater that should be afraid to do a Negro folk play about people who are perhaps not very well educated because some of the intellectuals, or "intellectuals" in quotes, are ashamed of such material. They should do the play anyway and the "intellectuals" in quotes, will sometimes be very impressed and come to the viewpoint and see that this is a wonderful and beautiful play even though they may not agree with it when they read it or on first seeing it.[40]

Though none of the plays in this study were ever produced by the Karamu Theater, the Skyloft Players, or even the Suitcase Theater in Harlem, they do demonstrate Hughes' lifelong commitment to developing a theater wherein black playwrights and actors would have equal opportunities to hone their skills.

A unique stylistic element encountered when examining Hughes' plays centers on the interrelatedness of all of his texts. The whole fabric of his writings—poems, autobiographical writings, short stories, and plays—is woven with threads of social consciousness. His approach to social themes, whether in comedy or more serious works, provides the subtle hues that color the vivid theatrics of his work. When questioned about his shift from serious works like *Mulatto* or *Harvest* to lighter comedies such as *Little Ham* or *Simply Heavenly,* Hughes saw no separation. "To me," he said, "most of my plays are similar in intent and purpose although the treatment may be lighter of heavier or melodramatic or comic."[41] Not only are his plays similar in intent; they also often have similar characters. Hughes' works constitute a literary saga in which characters migrate from one genre to another. Sometimes they retain the same name, as do the characters of Jesse B. Simple or Alberta K. Johnson in their permutations from prose to drama. Other times, characters re-emerge as shadows or remnants of characters, encountered in the verse or essays. Hughes' characters move in a gigantic unnamed landscape, generally urban. Occasionally they migrate down rural roads away from the prejudices of the city. Yet, if one reads enough of Hughes, one sees the same people in different stages of life and in different guises.

Hughes also capitalized on transformations of the same story between genres. Several of his plays and operas began as prose and were revised for the stage. *Mother and Child* was taken from a short story in *The Ways of White Folk; The Barrier* is an opera adapted from Hughes' play *Mulatto; Simple Takes a Wife*, an adaptation from Hughes' Chicago newspaper columns, was put to music and transformed into *Simply Heavenly. Soul Gone Home* was both a drama and an opera; and *The Emperor of Haiti* began as a historical drama and ended as *Troubled Island*, a historical opera. Hughes found the raw material for his works in a variety of sources. At times his plays are derivations of his own works in other genres; at times they find their source in works by his associates and friends such as Arna Bontemps or Countee Cullen; still others have their genesis in the political events of the day, as did the scripts of *Scottsboro, Limited; De Organizer; Harvest;* and others.

Two final sources, religion and folklore, provide deep wells from which Hughes drew background and character for his prose, poetry, and drama. The ethnically charged combination of the two often blurs the line between faith and superstition in his works and depends largely on spiritual and folk songs to establish mood and rhythm. The religious/folkloric combinations spawned specific characters as well. Susan L. Blake recognized this in her article "Old John in Harlem: The Urban Folktales of Langston Hughes." Old John, as a folkloric character, evolved from slave narratives where he served the role of community spiritual leader. Old John appears in different permutations in Hughes' prose and drama, including *De Organizer,* in which he is a central character. Dissecting Hughes' works by looking separately at his use of folklore, religion, music, and dialect reduces the whole only to its parts. However, the whole of his dramatic pieces, his prose, his poetry far exceeds the sum of its parts. This is particularly true of his plays, which merit far more attention than this study can provide.

This study intends to extend the scholarship on Hughes by examining those works that have not been examined. In doing so, the politics and private motivations of the man may become more focused for others who embark on similar investigations in the future. Making available texts that have remained hidden in collections and archives should spark new interest in Langston Hughes as a political artist.

Hughes' Move to the Left: *Scottsboro, Limited*

Langston Hughes' embrace of the political Left in the early 1930s coincides with two events, one personal, the other public. First was his very traumatic personal split with Charlotte Mason, his wealthy New York patron, who had supported his writing efforts through a kind of perverse philanthropic bondage. Mason, a prominent New York socialite, took it upon herself to financially support and encourage promising black writers. In return, she assumed the role of artistic mentor and literary agent. In reading accounts of Mason's control of young artists, one is struck by an unsavory, even unhealthy, quality in these professional relationships. Mason's support came with conditions. Hughes was one of the few who sought personal independence in his writing schedule and choice of topics. It cost him dearly both financially and emotionally.

The second event that caused Hughes' embrace of leftist politics and personalities was, according to Arnold Rampersad, "certainly the Scottsboro Controversy."[1] The incarceration of nine black youths charged with raping two white women in a railway car ignited a national outcry. Many artists immortalized the "Scottsboro Boys" in the 1930s. But Hughes' embrace of the political Left was more complex and self-serving than would appear at first glance. Attributing Hughes' political rebirth solely to the Scottsboro incident might move one precariously close to the sort of post hoc fallacy historians and critics are careful to avoid.

The early 1930s, the depression years, were a period in which Hughes needed to find financial as well as artistic moorings. Thrown out of "Godmother" Mason's white bourgeois environment that had served as a safe, even affluent, haven during the first two years of the Great Depression, Hughes sought solace and redirection in a trip to Cuba. The Scottsboro incident occurred prior to Hughes' departure. In the intervening months before his return to the United States, the legal defense for the Scottsboro defendants was supplied by the American Communist Party, which raised the case to national prominence in order to attract new members. Scottsboro became a vehicle to advance leftist political and labor issues. The Scottsboro case allowed the International Labor Defense (ILD), the legal branch of the American Communist Party, to garner national favor with political liberals and minority workers. Rampersad saw this as a direct campaign to enact Stalin's goals to increase "black participation in the party" and to establish "self-determination for Afro-Americans as a commitment of the communist effort in the United States."[2]

Hughes' return to New York came in the midst of the Scottsboro appeal. Feeling the need to reestablish himself professionally, he sought new, independent literary associations. Hughes gravitated towards individuals among the political Left, particularly writers and editors. Fortuitously, the radical writers who formed the membership of the John Reed Club in New York offered friendship as well as literary connections and publication outlets for Hughes. His poems and translations of poems by Frederico Garcia Lorca soon appeared in the pages of *New Masses*. The camaraderie extended by the JRC and the adoption of the Scottsboro case as the American Communist Party's cause célèbre resulted in Hughes immersion in leftist politics and art. Whether this commitment was part of a newfound political activism or a part of a psychological distancing from the controlling wealth of Charlotte Mason is not clear. Nonetheless, Hughes was drawn to the dramatic racial controversy marked by white injustice towards young black men. Consequently, he became actively involved not only in the John Reed Club but also in the American Negro Labor Congress and other groups with leftist leanings.

The whirlwind of labor causes in the early part of the 1930s touched all aspects of society. An artistic development that grew out of leftist activities and the American labor movement was political theater. It emerged strongly in New York and was evident in the South as well. Plays used by leftist and labor groups as political ends for agitation and propaganda surfaced in a variety of forms, ranging from documentaries to strident proselytizing scripts. The style and content of these plays was revolutionary and politically topical. They generated a great deal of attention in the press and attracted theatrical artists such as playwrights Paul Peters, Elia Kazan, Clifford Odets, George Sklar, and John Wexley. Production companies that evolved out of this revolutionary movement include Labor Stage, the Group Theatre, and the Federal Theater Project.

The theater offered a potentially lucrative means to reach a broader audience and brought with it, if not fortune, some fame. Though Hughes' initial foray into commercial theatrical writing with Zora Neale Hurston had been unsatisfactory because of the controversy over authorship, throughout his life he continually eyed the theater and film industry as a potential outlet for his own dramatic writings. His failed collaboration with Hurston colored all of his subsequent cooperative efforts, which were undertaken in a shadow of suspicion. Initially he embarked on the script for *Scottsboro, Limited* with Wallace Thurman, but when Thurman withdrew, Hughes had him attest in writing that the idea had been Hughes'.[3]

SCOTTSBORO, LIMITED

Scottsboro, Limited offers a unique example of Hughes' verse coupled with leftist agit-prop techniques. The mention of "agit-prop" and other forms of didactic drama usually call up images of Bertolt Brecht for most American readers. Yet there was an indigenous political theater in the United States that took root in the late 1920s and early 1930s employing the same techniques as its European counterpart. Traditionally, agitation-propaganda plays were loosely structured presentational plays whose intent was the movement of the audience to some kind of discernible action. This might be an immediate action characterized by audience participation in shouting slogans or calling for strikes. Many of the early agit-prop plays relied on performers planted in the audience to encourage and prod the audience to participate. The action may have been less immediate but equally profound, asking audience members to join unions or demonstrate for worker rights. There was a general call for the audience to recognize that strength in numbers comes through solidarity, whether it is ethnic solidarity or the solidarity of labor. The agit-prop scripts and productions of the 1930s were rallying vehicles produced for union meetings or mounted near factory gates. Because they sought to move the audience to action, they were often bellicose and reactionary and used the productions as a means to shock and affront their audience.[4] In 1930, the Communist Party in the United States established theatrical companies in New York for the sole purpose of producing agit-prop plays: the Proletbuehne, a German speaking troupe; the Workers' Laboratory Theater; and the Theater Collective. Some speculate that the Communist Party began using agit-props as part of their campaign strategy in the elections of the early 1930s.[5] The structure of agit-props influenced the Living Newspaper productions of the Federal Theater Project in the middle of the decade.[6]

Scottsboro, Limited employs all of the traditional early agit-prop techniques to great effect. It has audience plants designated in the text as "Mob Voices," who unexpectedly shout out from the audience in support of a racist white character. These voices are eventually overpowered by "Red Voices," who also rise from the audience. Eventually they join the Scottsboro defendants on stage, clasping hands in a biracial show of support against the injustices of the American system. One of the hallmarks of this kind of agit-prop theater is a conclusion that prompts the audience to rise en masse, shouting slogans or singing songs. Hughes' script does both. *Scottsboro, Limited* ends with stirring intensity as characters inveigh against the color line, hands joined onstage and in the audience, shouting "Fight, Fight, Fight, Fight!" As they sing "The Internationale," a red flag descends above the heads of the workers. The audience is manipulated to respond to the event both physically and emotionally. The group participation strategically called for in these plays imbued the audience with a fervor, enmity, even rivalry, the intensity of which might be compared to that provoked by frenetic sporting events. What might ordinarily be perceived as a mob response becomes transformed and sanctified by song, chants, and participatory zeal. Workers onstage and in the audience raise their voices in a collective hymn against capitalism. The song, the group choral response, and the injustices exposed galvanize a righteous indignation and moral imperative within the audience to "Fight!"

The agit-prop techniques used in *Scottsboro, Limited* reveal unquestioningly that Hughes was familiar with the form. He consciously set about to use all of the propaganda techniques he saw already being staged in New York. In *Scottsboro, Limited,* eight black men are employed to represent the collective protagonist of the Scottsboro Boys. One white actor assumes multiple roles of antagonists: racist audience member, Sheriff, Judge, Prison Guard, and Preacher. Hughes employs this rhetorical tactic masterfully. He maintains the individuality of the Scottsboro defendants with lines revealing their individual ethos. The white actor, on the other hand, comes to represent the entire white race in the United States. Each social and professional persona he assumes in the script espouses a racist and discriminatory position. Hughes' decision to have the white antagonist rise unexpectedly from the audience presses the antagonist's association with them. His emergence from them as an unchosen spokesman poses a dilemma and creates extraordinary tension. The audience must find ways to disembarrass themselves and to show that he does not represent them as a group. This is made more difficult as other audience plants shout racial slurs and seemingly corroborate the racist activity of the trial. As the "Red Voices" bravely assert themselves from the audience toward the end of the play, the "real" audience members readily side with them against the atrocities that they have seen enacted and to which they have been tacitly accused. Hughes employs social psychology so aptly in the script that everyone, actors and audience, will be on their feet shouting, "Fight!" and singing the Communist anthem.

In *Scottsboro, Limited*, as in subsequent scripts, Hughes takes pains to establish the musicality of the lines and to provide indication of how they should be delivered. While some playwrights write with a specific look, feel, or attitude in mind, Hughes consistently wrote with a specific sound for his plays and included musical directions. Essentially, he scored his scripts for the reader so that it would be clear that the tension in certain scenes resided in rhythmic, almost orchestral, builds. An example in this play is found in the stage directions for the court scene. Hughes writes, "The trial is conducted in jazz tempo: the white voices staccato, high and shrill; the black voices deep as the rumble of drums." This scene builds as the two girls sit at the downstage corners with the judge alternately pointing from one girl to the other accusing the defendants, "You raped that girl!" and being answered with a resounding "No!" eight times. This is repeated with the repetition of "You had a gun," again met with negative responses. The rhythm and tension builds until the mob voices in the audience erupt with "Kill the niggers!" Hughes has the defendants rise and circle the judge's chair, dance-like, echoing the slurs of the mob. His juxtaposition of scene and rhythmic shifts is masterful. Reading the script, one feels the tensions build and recede only to flare up again in heated exchanges that culminate in the burning resolve to fight.

The fight to which the audience should commit itself seems purposely ambiguous. The group call for "Fight!" in the closing moments of the play would find some audience members crying to fight racism, while others would be convinced that they were fighting capitalism. The first half of the play stands as a chronicle of racism. The trial scene offers a climactic moment not only in terms of dramatic structure but also in terms of political propaganda. As the defendants await execution, they talk of the Communist lawyer sent to appeal the sentence. The racial issue becomes subordinated to an economic labor issue. The Scottsboro defendants defiantly assert that they will speak for themselves, ultimately conceding to the Red Voices who assure them that "the Red flag, too, will talk for you." The Scottsboro Boys are transformed from maligned individuals suffering the atrocities of a racist society to workers who, like the audience, suffer under a capitalist system. In this script, the identification forged between the Scottsboro Boys and the audience is more economic than racial.

When finally the Red Voices rise as a group, it is in response to mob calls to kill the Scottsboro defendants in the electric chair. They rise from the audience as the eight Scottsboro victims proclaim that "[t]he new Red Negro will come: / That's me!" Their unified front announces, "NO DEATH IN THE CHAIR!" A litany of pain and despair chronicles the suffering of workers, white and black. The promise is held out to the characters and the audience that "the red world" will bring about change. Hughes' characters boldly assert party propaganda in statements about the "Red Negro" and in lines intoning "The voice of the red world *is* you! . . . The hands of the red world *are* you!" Finally, the singing of "The Internationale" and the unfurling of the red flag leave little doubt where the political sentiments of the play and its author rested.

Although Hughes would not renounce his leftist activities until a decade later, he realized that such associations jeopardized his literary career. His business venture with Prentiss Taylor and Carl Van Vecten that resulted in the founding of the Golden Stair Press may have been an attempt to ensure that someone would publish his works. Hughes and Taylor decided that the 1932 publication for their new press would be a small volume of works on the Scottsboro theme incorporating Hughes' *Scottsboro, Limited,* four related poems, and four lithographs of Scottsboro by Taylor. Hughes, however, capitulated, wondering whether the play was "too red to be included."[7]

Despite this instance of private reservation, Hughes remained publicly dedicated to the Scottsboro case through the mid-1930s. He was an active participant in the National Committee for the Defense of Political Prisoners (northern California branch), and his name appears on its letterhead along with other prominent leftist artists and writers. In November 1933, Hughes participated in a letter-writing campaign to American authors soliciting their financial support and statements for publication protesting the incarceration of the Scottsboro Boys. A month later, Noel Sullivan, Hughes' patron in Carmel where he was staying, sent a telegram to the National Committee for the Defense of Political Prisoners in New York. In this correspondence, he requested advice or permission for "a small delegation from [the] national committee here to go now to Decatur. . . . If we could be guaranteed admission to court room during trial . . . or would Scottsboro Committee prefer to receive money we would expend for journey for continuation of defense."[8] Presumably, Hughes planned to participate in this delegation, since he stayed with Sullivan throughout December 1933.

The two organized an auction in January 1934 to raise money for the legal defense fund of the Scottsboro defendants. Their efforts were met with positive responses from several literary figures who sent signed manuscripts and memorabilia to be auctioned. Elmer Rice sent a draft of *Street Scene*, a version of which Hughes would work on years later with Rice and Kurt Weill. While the auction enhanced Hughes' reputation and commitment with the members of the literary Left, it would become a personal and political liability to him and to many of its participants. It haunted actor James Cagney, who served as the auctioneer for the event and who would later need to disassociate himself from all previous leftist affiliations to save his career.[9] Allegations of Communist affiliations surfaced ominously against Hughes in the coming years, and he too would find renunciation of past political associations a personal necessity.

Neither *Scottsboro, Limited* nor the other plays examined in this study nearly ended Hughes' literary career in the late 1930s. However, his political poems written after the plays came back to haunt him. In the 1930s and 1940s, the general public was unaware of Hughes' leftist plays calling for the rise of the "Red Negro." Only years later would Hughes gain public notice as a dramatist. His entrée into the ranks of recognized playwrights came because of his dramatic and humorous treatment of social themes rather than political ones. His early political plays of this study went unnoticed in the controversy concerning his Communist associations that came to a head in 1941. Rampersad explains Hughes' dismissal of the inflammatory poem "Goodbye Christ," written after *Scottsboro, Limited* and his renunciation of his leftist associations, as "a regrettable error of his immature youth, an error that he would not repeat."[10] After 1941, this political shift extended to Hughes' writing dramatic works as well. Though all his plays have a political edge, only scripts in this volume vehemently express the radical political ideology associated with the American Communist Party.

Hughes was not alone in treating the Scottsboro theme dramatically, but unfortunately his script failed to be produced in New York. The most notable New York productions came in the mid-1930s when the Workers' Laboratory Theater presented a production of the play *Scottsboro,* directed by Alfred Saxe in 1934. On 21 February of that same year, John Wexley's *They Shall Not Die,* a Theater Guild production treating the Scottsboro trial, opened. Wexley's production, though it used fictitious names of characters and organizations, incorporated dialogue from the actual court transcript, giving it a documentary element not contained in the other scripts.

The production of Hughes' script in New York may well have been hindered by his departure from the city to embark on a western tour. Hughes left New York in March 1932, arriving in Los Angeles in April where he visited Loren Miller, a black lawyer, active in the local John Reed Club. Hughes' script preceded him. When he arrived in the city, the Los Angeles police had banned the local John Reed Club's production of *Scottsboro, Limited.* The political atmosphere in which Hughes found himself led him to write a poem supporting and lionizing Tom Mooney, a political radical convicted in a 1916 terrorist bombing in San Francisco. Lydia Filatova maintains that Hughes wrote the poem "after an interview with Tom Mooney in St. [sic] Quentin prison."[11] Mooney's conviction earned him martyr status with some elements of the political Left. Hughes' poem, intended as a participatory chant, was performed Sunday, 8 May 1932, and accompanied a production of *Scottsboro, Limited* that finally escaped police censorship.[12] Though relatively short, the poem retains the elements of agit-prop structure in its encouragement of audience participation through unified chanting:

A Chant for Tom Mooney

Tom Mooney!
Tom Mooney!
Tom Mooney!
A man with the title of governor has spoken:
And you do not go free.

A man with the title of governor has spoken:
And the steel bars surround you,
And the prison walls wrap you about,
And you do not go free.
But the man with the title of governor
Does not know
That all over the earth today
The workers speak the name:
Tom Mooney!
Tom Mooney!
Tom Mooney!
And the sound vibrates in waves
From Africa to China,
India to Germany,
Russia to the Argentine,
Shaking the bars,
Shaking the walls,
Shaking the earth
Until the whole world falls into the hands of
The workers.
Of course, the man with the title of governor
Will be forgotten then
On the scrap heap of time—
He won't matter at all.
But remembered forever will be the name:
TOM MOONEY.
Schools will be named:
TOM MOONEY.
Farms will be named:
TOM MOONEY.
Dams will be named:
TOM MOONEY.
Ships will be named:
TOM MOONEY.
Factories will be named:
TOM MOONEY.
And all over the world—
Banner of force and labor, strength and union,
Life forever through the workers' power—

will be the name:
TOM MOONEY.[13]

For Hughes, the political Left of the early 1930s served as a boon to his career rather than the bane it would become years later. As his capital increased with leftist activists, so did the pressure to continue writing in a radical vein. Eugene Gordon singled out Hughes for political praise in his 1933 article "Negro Novelists and the Negro Masses." Noting that Negro writers such as Wallace Thurman, Countee Cullen, Rudolph Fisher, and Langston Hughes all dealt with Negro workers in fiction, "none of them except Hughes has evidently heard of the class struggle." In reference to *Not Without Laughter*, Gordon maintained, "Hughes . . . has written the only novel in which the Negro worker is pictured as seeing the way out through the class struggle." For Gordon, Hughes' subsequent political leanings to the Left "indicated a fulfillment of the promise it contained."[14]

Hughes' political stock was high, and subsequently he received an invitation to address the first American Writers Congress, a gathering of liberal and leftist literati to promote the political efficacy of literature as a means to unite the masses. His address led a series of speakers who chastised the audience for indifference and lack of political involvement. Hughes' speech entitled "To Negro Writers" was a call to action. He exhorted other American Negro writers

> to reveal to the Negro masses . . . our potential power to transform the now ugly face of the southland into a region of peace and plenty . . . reveal to the white masses those Negro qualities which go beyond the mere ability to laugh and sing and dance and make music and which are a part of the useful heritage that we place at the disposal of a future free America . . . expose . . . the sick-sweet smile of organized religion—which lies about what it doesn't know and what it does know . . . expose . . . the false leadership that besets the Negro people—bought and paid for leadership, owned by capital, afraid to open its mouth except in the old conciliatory way so advantageous to the exploiters . . . [and] write about the irony and pathos of the *colored* American Legion.

The conclusion of the speech uses language reminiscent of the final scene of *Scottsboro, Limited.* Clearly Hughes intended a rousing finale to his speech: "We want an America that will be ours, a world that will be ours—we Negro workers and white workers! Black writers and white! We'll make that world!"[15]

Fortuitously for Hughes, Eugene Gordon, who had publicly praised Hughes' political activism, spoke directly after Hughes. Gordon's speech, "Social and Political Problems of the Negro Writer," expressed disappointment with "Negro writers from the middle class." Gordon saw the "Negro writer . . . along with the Negro preacher" as his people's chief propagandist. "It is the writer," he maintained, "more than any other articulate agent of the Negro people, who interprets and pleads for them to the white ruling class." Eugene Clay, who in turn followed Gordon, claimed in his address that "most Negro intellectuals have remained indifferent to the increasing leftward movement in American thought." His address continued as a diatribe against Negro intellectuals who participated in the white discovery and exploitation of the "Harlem tradition." Surprisingly, Hughes, who has come to be known as a leading figure in the Harlem Renaissance, is spared Clay's invective. Clay asserted: "The most notable example of one who has made the decisive step to the Left is Langston Hughes. . . . Hughes has not followed in the retrogressive paths of his 'new Negro' renaissance colleagues. His works from 1926–1931 were links in his evolution, with only occasional retrogressions. . . . There began to appear in his work an anti-bourgeois-intelligentsia outlook. . . . As long as Hughes' technique and purpose seem to be in an ascending scale, we can hope to see his work progress."[16]

This pressure placed on Hughes to carry the party banner as its leading black proponent is discernible throughout the 1930s. The relationship was symbiotic. The Communist Party, hoping to attract more black members, often encouraged and solicited Hughes to speak at John Reed Club meetings on both coasts. Hughes, in turn, found himself "hobnobbing" with some of the most successful leftist writers of the period, who provided him entrée into prominent homes and publishing houses. Mrs. Mason, the domineering patron who had controlled his writing, became a distant memory. He found a willing patron in Noel Sullivan, a liberal San Francisco millionaire who offered Hughes the use of his Carmel retreat. In Carmel, Hughes socialized with muckraking journalist Lincoln Steffens and his wife, Ella Winter, a founder of the John Reed Club in what was then a rural artistic conclave. There, he became involved, at least by association, in yet more leftist activities as Winter and Sullivan visited labor camps and organized meetings. Hughes willingly lent his name to labor causes and rallies, the result of which would be a script done in collaboration with Ella Winter about California's most notorious labor strike.

The International Workers Order chose Hughes as "its first author in a series of literary pamphlets for the people." In 1938, the International Workers Order published a volume of Hughes' poetry entitled *A New Song*. Claiming that "American labor [had] at last entered the field of culture," Michael Gold in his introduction noted that the IWO published ten thousand copies of the first edition of the work, "a rare and startling figure in the American poetry world."[17] Even at fifteen cents per copy, the price listed on the cover of the book, Hughes stood to do well on royalty receipts as well as to increase awareness of his works.

Scottsboro, Limited punctuated a radical period in Hughes' literary endeavors. Coming at the beginning of the decade of the 1930s, it is a part of Hughes' initiation into American leftist politics. Clearly, he wrote it as a signal that he, too, could work and write with the best of the leftist literati. The significance of the leftist political scripts in the body of Hughes' works is equal to his Simple essays, his poems, or even his later plays of social satire, which achieved greater commercial success. The political proselytizing that marks his plays of the 1930s and his commitment to left-wing causes provide evidence that the labor movement in the United States achieved the support of minority writers. His political plays of this decade have not received the attention they merit possibly because they reveal Hughes' very close working relationships with Communist groups and individuals deemed subversive by agencies of the United States government.

Though Rampersad supports Hughes' contention that he was never an actual member of the Communist Party, Hughes' protestation belies the truth. Whether Hughes' activities on behalf of the American Communist Party were those of a member or of an interested nonmember does not matter today. Such political associations do not carry with them the damning exile from American letters they once did. Bringing to light the leftist plays of Langston Hughes will not cause a fall from literary grace or remove him as a figure studied in American schools. It does, however, reveal a new avenue of inquiry in American cultural history, that of the activities and support of black artists for the political Left in the 1930s. The whole idea of the "Red Negro" and "the black masses," as Hughes calls them, a labor group seeking a political franchise within the American system as a political force, is a fascinating area not fully examined by historians or literary critics. Whether Hughes used the party or the party used Hughes is not as significant as the political works written because of that relationship. *Scottsboro, Limited* marks the beginning of Hughes' sojourn into radical politics, a journey he would wish later he had not taken. Bringing these plays to light helps to understand the man as well as the leanings of disenfranchised labor groups in the United States who rejected New Deal altruism in favor of political revolt.

Scottsboro, Limited: A One-Act Play

By Langston Hughes

Characters

8 BLACK BOYS

A WHITE MAN

2 WHITE WOMEN

8 WHITE WORKERS

VOICES IN THE AUDIENCE

Setting

One chair on a raised platform. No curtains or other affects [sic] needed.

THE PLAY OPENS: (The eight BLACK BOYS chained by the right foot, one to the other, walk slowly down the center aisle from the back of the auditorium. As they approach the middle of the house, there is a loud commotion, and the WHITE MAN rises in the audience.)

MAN: *(To BOYS)* What are you doing here?

(The BLACK BOYS continue marching without turning their heads.)

MAN: *(Louder, more sternly)* What are you'all doing in here?

(As the BOYS mount the stage, the MAN rushes up to them threateningly)

MAN: What the hell are you doing in here, I said?

1ST BOY: *(Turning simply)*
              We come in our chains
              To show our pain.

MAN: *(Sneeringly)* Your pain! Stop talking poetry and talk sense.

8TH BOY: *(As they line up on the stage)*
              All right, we will—
              That sense of injustice
              That death can't kill.

MAN: Injustice? What d'yuh mean? Talking about injustice, you coon?

2ND BOY: *(Pointing to comrades)*
              Look at us then:
              Poor, black and ignorant,
              Can't read or write—
              But we come here tonight.

MAN: *(Sitting down jauntily on the edge of stage)* Not supposed to read or write. You work better without it.

1ST BOY: *(Shrugging his shoulders)*
              O. K. Chief,
              We won't argue with you.
              Tonight there's
              Too much to do.

MAN: Now that you got the public eye, you want to show off, heh?

2ND BOY: *(Seriously)*
              Not show off—die!

5TH BOY: *(Earnestly)*
              So the people can see
              What it means to be
              A poor black workman
              In this land of the free.

2ND BOY: *(Harshly)*
              Where every star in the flag
              Is stained with a lie!

MAN: Do you want to get arrested for treason?

8TH BOY: We're already in jail.

	Have you got a darker cell
	Any worse
	Than this-here Southern Hell?
7TH BOY:	Can a man die twice?
MAN:	You-all ain't dead.
8TH BOY:	(Defiantly)
	No, but we will be dead
	If we stay quiet here.
	That's why we come tonight
	To lift our troubles high.
	Like a flag against the sky.
2ND BOY:	To show that we're living—
	Even though we die.
3RD BOY:	To let the world see
	That even in chains
	We *will* be free!
4TH BOY:	Watch this play for our misery:

(*The chains break away and the* BOYS *find themselves on a moving freight train. They sit down in a haphazard line on the stage as though they were seated on the top of boxcars, rocking back and forth as the train moves.*)

6TH BOY:	(Happily)
	Man this train sho is speedin!
	Look a-yonder at de Sunny South.
4TH BOY:	I wish I had some sugar cane in ma mouth.
	I'm hongry!
7TH BOY:	Well it's sho too bad
	How when you ain't got no job
	Things get sad.
5TH BOY:	I ain't got no job.
1ST BOY:	Neither is I, but I wish I had.
2ND BOY:	Looks like white folks is taking all de work.
5TH BOY:	Is niggers got *exclusive* rights on work?
3RD BOY:	Shut up, boy!
4TH BOY:	He ain't joking, Perk.
2ND BOY:	All them little town jobs we used to do
	Looks like white folks is doin' 'em now, too.
1ST BOY:	Just goes to prove there ain't no pure nigger work.
6TH BOY:	(In wonder)

Look a-yonder you'all, at dem fields
Burstin' wid de crops they yields.
Who gets it all?

3RD BOY: White folks.

8TH BOY: You means de rich white folks.

2ND BOY: Yes, 'cause de rich ones owns de land.
And they don't care nothin' 'bout de po' white man.

3RD BOY: You's right. Crackers is just like me—
Po' whites and niggers, ain't neither one free.

8TH BOY: Have to work like a fool to live and then you starve dead.

4TH BOY: Man, this country is sho too bad!

(The train stops and the rocking motion of the BOYS ceases. One or two of them get up and stretch)

3RD BOY: Uh-O! This train done stopped. Where is this?

7TH BOY: Well, wherever it is, I'm gonna take a— *(Turning his back)*

5TH BOY: No, you ain't. Can't yo see this is a town?

MAN: *(As Sheriff, at foot of stage, with a police star and a club)* Come on, you niggers, and get down.

6TH BOY: Uh-ooooo! Yonder stands the sheriff!

2ND BOY: Ha-ha-ha! Uh!

3RD BOY: Fool, this ain't no time to laugh.

SHERIFF: Come on and get down off that train!

6TH BOY: Yes sir, Mister Boss Man!

4TH BOY: Soon's we can. *(The BOYS climb down.)*

SHERIFF: What you-all doin' on that train?

BOYS: Just tryin' to bum our way on through
To Memphis where maybe there's work to do.

SHERIFF: *(Yelling up the line)* Get everybody off this train, deputy. *(To BOYS)* Stand over there, boys. *(Shouting to deputy)* What you say? Some girls getting off dressed in overalls? White girls? *(To himself)* Whee-oooo! *(To BOYS)* What you-all doin' on the same train with them white women there?

BOYS: *(In wonder)*
Where?

SHERIFF: There!

BOYS: Where?

SHERIFF: *(Fiercely)* You'll see where! Get back and let these white ladies by. (*While the succeeding action goes on the* BOYS *get behind the chair, four on each side in a line—convicts already*)

MOB VOICES IN THE AUDIENCE: (*Murmuring and muttering*) Damned niggers . . . white girls and niggers riding together . . . nerve of them niggers . . . had no business in there . . . etc.

SHERIFF: (*As the* TWO WHITE GIRLS *enter left, powdered and painted, but dressed in overalls*) What you doin'? Out for a ride?

GIRLS: Yes sir.

SHERIFF: Where to?

1ST GIRL: Goin' home, I reckon.

SHERIFF: Where?

2ND GIRL: Huntsville.

SHERIFF: And these niggers on the train with you?

1ST GIRL: Ain't seen 'em before.

SHERIFF: Ain't these black brutes been botherin' you?

GIRLS: No, they ain't been near.

SHERIFF: Is that true? (*Sternly*) Ain't they had their hands on you?

GIRLS: (*Wavering*) Well, they . . . er . . .

SHERIFF: (*Positively*) I knew it! Which one of these black apes touched you?

GIRLS: Why . . . er . . .

SHERIFF: We'll have a trial and burn 'em up. And you'll get paid for testifying and your pictures in the paper. Which ones?

1ST GIRL: That two there.

SHERIFF: Two? You sho it wasn't more?

2ND GIRL: No, we ain't sure.

1ST GIRL: It might-a been all right.

SHERIFF: All right? A trial's too good for black bastards like that. (*Pompously*) But we owe it to the state.

(*He parades sternly up to the raised chair. He is the judge now and as he mounts the legal bench, he puts on a black gown that has been lying there.* THE GIRLS *slip off their overalls, displaying cheap, loud dresses underneath and powder their faces tittering. It is the courtroom and the black prisoners come forward before the Judge. The trial is conducted in jazz tempo: the white voices staccato, high and shrill; the black voices deep as the rumble of drums.*)

MOB VOICES IN AUDIENCE: (*Murmuring*) Imagine a trial for niggers . . . a trial for niggers . . . a trial for niggers . . . etc.

JUDGE: The State of Alabama versus Andy Butler, Willie Johnson, Clarence Bates, Olen Jones, Ozie Jenkins, Roy Perkins, Ted Lucas and Haywood Lane. *(The GIRLS sit, one on either side of the stage, grinning and pleased)* You raped that girl? *(Pointing at each boy in turn.)*

1ST BOY: No.

JUDGE: You raped that girl? *(Pointing from one girl to the other in rotation)*

2ND BOY: No.

JUDGE: You raped that girl?

3RD BOY: No.

JUDGE: You raped that girl?

4TH BOY: No.

JUDGE: You raped that girl?

5TH BOY: No.

JUDGE: You raped that girl?

6TH BOY: No.

JUDGE: You raped that girl?

7TH BOY: No.

JUDGE: You raped that girl?

8TH BOY: No.

JUDGE: *(To GIRLS)* How about it girls?

1ST GIRL: They lie!

2ND GIRL: They raped us in a box car underneath the sky.

JUDGE: You niggers lie.

BOYS: We lie . . . White man always says we lie . . . Makes us work and says we lie . . . Takes our money and says we lie.

JUDGE: Shut up. No talking back in the court. *(Pointing at each one in turn)* You had a gun.

1ST BOY: No.

JUDGE: You had a gun.

2ND BOY: No, sir.

JUDGE: You had a gun.

3RD BOY: *(Shaking head)*
                Not one.

JUDGE: You had a gun.

4TH BOY: Not nary one.

JUDGE: You had a gun.

5TH BOY: We didn't have none.

JUDGE: You had a gun.

6TH BOY:	No gun.
JUDGE:	You had a gun!
7TH BOY:	No, sir, none.
JUDGE:	You had a gun.
8TH BOY:	No gun.
JUDGE:	How about it, girls?
1ST GIRL:	They lie.
2ND GIRL:	They all had guns.
JUDGE:	(*To* BOYS) You all had guns. (*To* GIRLS) And they raped you, one by one. (*Girls nod heads*) How long did it take? How long was it?
1ST GIRL:	Why they didn't even let us up to spit!
2ND GIRL:	It was rough!
JUDGE:	To spit what?
GIRLS:	Snuff!
JUDGE:	You hear that, Jury? This court is done.
1ST GIRL:	Convict these brutes. (*Smiling at audience*)
2ND GIRL:	Every black one. (*Also smiles*)
MOB VOICES IN AUDIENCE:	Convict 'em. Ever damn black one!
JUDGE:	Don't worry, folks, 'tis done.
MOB VOICES IN AUDIENCE:	Kill the niggers! Keep 'em in their places! Make an example of 'em for all the black races . . . etc.
BOYS:	(*Rising and circling round and round the chair echoing the angry mob*) Kill the niggers! Keep them in their places! Make an example of 'em for all the black races, for all the black races, for all the black races.
JUDGE:	(*Descending from the bench to audience*) Don't worry, folks, the law will take its course. They'll burn, and soon at that. (*He and* GIRLS *exit, talking and smiling.*)
MOB VOICES IN AUDIENCE:	(*applauding and shouting*) Make it soon. Kill the niggers. Let 'em die.
BOYS:	(*echoing the voices*) Make it soon. Let us die. Make it soon. Soon. Soon.
6TH BOY:	(*Breaking away from the dumb circle*) No! No! No! What do they want to kill us for?
3RD BOY:	I'll break free!

(*The* BOYS *divide up into groups of two's now in a row across the stage, in the cells of the death house, some of them sitting down, some of them weeping, some of them pushing against the bars with their hands.*)

2ND BOY: How you gonna git out o' here
With these iron bars and this stone wall
And the guards outside and the
Guns and all?

8TH BOY: There ain't no way for a nigger to break free,
They got us beaten and that's how we gonna be
Unless we learn to understand—
We gotta fight our way out like a man.

5TH BOY: Not out o' here.

4TH BOY: No, not out o' here,
Unless the ones on the outside
Fight for us, too.
We'll die—and then we'll be through.

MOB VOICES IN AUDIENCE: You oughta be through—
Oughta be through.
In this white man's land
There's no place for you.

MURMER OF RED VOICES IN AUDIENCE: We'll fight for you boys. We'll fight
for you.
The Reds will fight for you.

6TH BOY: We'll die, and then we'll all be through—
Through livin', through lovin', through lookin'
at the sky.
I don't want to die.

8TH BOY: Who does want to die?
That's why all the free black men
Have got to fight,
Or else we'll all die in poverty's night.

3RD BOY: You're right.

RED VOICES: We'll fight! The Communists will fight for you.
Not just black—but black and white.

3RD BOY: Then we'll trust in you.

MAN: (Becomes the PRISON KEEPER now, marching across the front of
the cell-row with a long stick in his hand.)
Shut up in there, with your plots and plans.
Don't you niggers know yet this is a white man's land?
And I'm the keeper, understand.

8TH BOY: We ain't half as low as you!
Paid to kill people, that's what you do.
Not just niggers—but your white brothers too.

RED VOICES: (*Stronger now*)
             That's true! True!
PRISON KEEPER: (*Striking* BOY) Shut up!
8TH BOY: I won't shut up.
             I've nobody to talk for me,
             So I'll talk for myself, see.
RED VOICES: And the Red flag, too, will talk for you.
1ST BOY: Listen boys! That's true—they've sent a lawyer
             to talk for me and you.
6TH BOY: But they told us not to bother with a communist.
8TH BOY: But who else is there will help us out o' this?
3RD BOY: And not just us, but help all the black South
             Hungry for freedom, and bread, and new words in
             their mouths.
MAN: (*Entering this time as a* PREACHER, *sanctified with a Bible in his
             hand.*)
             Ashes to ashes and dust to dust—
             If the law don't kill you then the lynchers must.
             (*Piously*) I've come to say a little prayer
             Before you go away from here.
3RD BOY: (*questioning*)
             A prayer to a white God in a white sky?
             We don't want that kind of prayer to die.
6TH BOY: I want a prayer!
             (*the Death Bell rings*)
             Oh, Lord, I want a prayer.
8TH BOY: No prayer! No prayer!
             Lemme out o' here.
             Take me on to the chair
             With no God damn prayer.
             (*to the Preacher*)
             May they choke in your mouth,
             Every praying white lie!
PREACHER: (*in horror, hurrying out*)
             Let the niggers die!
MOB VOICES IN AUDIENCE: Let 'em die!
8TH BOY: (*Starting on the march to the chair, walking straight across the
             stage to the center, then turning, straight back to the Electric
             Chair where he seats himself, unafraid, slipping his hands into
             the cords that bind him to the arms of the chair.*)

	Because I talked out loud, you kill me first:
	Death in the flesh is the fighters curse.
MOB VOICES:	Yes, you must die! Let the nigger die! Let all of 'em die!
8TH BOY:	Let all of us die:
	That's what the mobs cry.
	All I've ever known:
	Let the niggers die!
	All my life long:
	Let the niggers die!
BOYS:	(helplessly crouching back at the foot of the chair)
	Let us die! Let us die!
MOB VOICES:	Let 'em die!
	Beat 'em! Shoot 'em!
	Hang 'em with a rope,
	Burn 'em in the chair.
	Let 'em choke.
BOYS:	Burn us in the chair!
	The chair! The Chair!
	Burn us in the chair!
8TH BOY:	Burn *me* in the chair?
	NO!
	(He breaks his bonds and rises tall and strong)
	NO! For me not so!
	Let the meek and humble turn the other cheek—
	I am not humble!
	I am not meek!
	From the mouth of the death house
	hear me speak!
RED VOICES:	Hear him speak! Hear him speak!
MOB VOICES:	Shut up, you God-damn nigger!
RED VOICES:	Hear him speak!
BOYS:	Hear us speak!
8TH BOY:	All the world, listen!
	Beneath the wide sky
	In all the black lands
	will echo this cry:
	I will not die!
BOYS:	We will NOT DIE!
MOB VOICES:	(Snarling)

Quick! Quick! Death there!
The chair! The electric chair!

8TH BOY: No chair!
Too long have my hands been idle
Too long have my brains been dumb.
Now out of the darkness
The new Red Negro will come:
That's me!
No death in the chair!

BOYS: *(Rising)*
No death in the chair!

RED VOICES: *(Rising in the audience)*
NO DEATH IN THE CHAIR!

BOYS: NO DEATH IN THE CHAIR!
(They circle platform and lifting the electric chair up, they smash it on the stage)
NO DEATH IN THE CHAIR!

MOB VOICES: *(Roaring helplessly)* Aw-w-w-w-w-ooo-aw!

RED VOICES: No Death in the Chair.
Together, we'll make the world clean and fair.

8TH BOY: Too long have we stood
For the whip and the rope.

RED VOICES: Too long! Too long!

8TH BOY: Too long have we labored
Poor, without hope.

BOYS: Too long!

RED VOICES: Too long!

8TH BOY: Too long have we suffered
alone.

BOYS: Alone!

8TH BOY: But not now!

RED VOICES: No, not now!

8TH BOY: The voice of the red world
Is our voice, too.

RED VOICES: The voice of the red world *is* you!

8TH BOY: The hands of the red world
are our hands, too.

RED VOICES: The hands of the red world *are* you!

8TH BOY: With all of the workers,

	Black or white, We'll go forward Out of the night.
BOYS:	Out of the night.
8TH BOY:	Breaking down bars, Together.
BOYS:	Together.
RED VOICES:	Together. (*The Red Voices of the white workers come forward toward the stage.*)
BOYS:	(*Breaking their bars and coming forward toward the front of the stage to meet their white comrades*) Seeking the stars!
RED VOICES:	Seeking the stars of hope and life.
8TH BOY:	Not afraid of the struggle.
BOYS:	Not afraid of the strife.
RED VOICES:	Not afraid to fight.
8TH BOY:	For new life!
BOYS:	New life!
RED VOICES:	New life!

(*The white workers and black workers meet on the stage*)

BOYS:	Comrades!
RED VOICES:	Comrades!

(*They clasp hands and line up in a row of alternating blacks and whites*)

BOYS:	Joining hands to build the right.
RED VOICES:	White and black!
BOYS:	Black and white!
8TH BOY:	To live, not die!
ALL:	To fight! To fight!
8TH BOY:	In the heart of a fighter, death is a lie! O, my black people, you need not die!
RED VOICES:	All the down trodden—you need not die!
AUDIENCE:	We need not die! We need not die!
8TH BOY:	Black and white together Will fight the great fight To put greed and pain And the color line's blight

Out of the world
Into time's old night.
BOYS AND REDS: All hands together will furnish the might.
AUDIENCE: All hands together will furnish the might.
RED VOICES: Rise from the dead, workers, and fight!
BOYS: All together, black and white;
Up from the darkness into the light.
ALL: Rise, workers, and fight!
AUDIENCE: Fight! Fight! Fight! Fight!

(Here the "Internationale" may be sung and the red flag raised above the heads of the black and white workers together.)

The End

An American Documentary Play: *Harvest*

In 1933, Langston Hughes returned from his trip to Russia, Korea, China, and Japan, not realizing fully the controversy it had caused, nor that the FBI had taken a particular interest in his activities. The results of their international surveillance became an official federal file labeled "The Communist Activities of Langston Hughes," which was added to throughout the thirties. Hughes' return to American soil brought him to San Francisco where he was met by Noel Sullivan, with whom Hughes had arranged to stay. Hughes had visited Sullivan previously in 1931 at the completion of a speaking tour of California and stops at the John Reed Club in Los Angeles.

Sullivan was an independently wealthy member of the San Francisco art community. His father, John, was founder and first president of the Hibernia Bank; his uncle James D. Phelan was a state senator and former mayor of San Francisco whose will established cash awards to develop talent in California in literature and art. Sullivan carried on his family's patronage of the arts. He was a trustee of the Phelan Awards and became in 1930 the director of the San Francisco Art Association.[1] In Sullivan, Hughes found a replacement for Charlotte Mason, whose patronage had sustained him when he lived in New York. Sullivan allowed the writer far greater independence than had Mason, and their association remained a long and cordial one. Before leaving Moscow in January 1933, Hughes wrote Sullivan: "I will be accepting your generous invitation, if it still holds, for a corner of your cottage where one might set a typewriter, and be quiet for awhile. My last two years have been continual movement: Haiti, then those 37,000 miles of lectures, and now all over the Soviet Union. I want to rest and create again."[2] Sullivan provided financial support without interference or personal control of Hughes' artistic endeavors. He offered Hughes a year at his home in Carmel, a kind of literary refuge, in which Hughes might "consolidate his career as a professional writer."[3]

As a professional writer, Hughes gravitated to those individuals who might provide opportunities for publication of his works. Carmel's literary opportunities were distinctly tied to leftist, "progressive" politics. Lincoln Steffens and Robinson Jeffers, both longtime residents of Carmel, regularly contributed articles to leftist publications such as *New Masses*. Hughes was soon a routine visitor to the homes of both Steffens and Jeffers and just as quickly became an active participant in the local John Reed Club, which served as the political and social gathering place of local literati and artists.

Liberal and leftist writers were involved in the formation of the John Reed Clubs nationally. It was, in fact, the editorial board of *New Masses* in New York that formed the first John Reed Club. At its inception as a left-wing journal, *New Masses* was thoroughly committed to a philosophy appropriate to a proletarian labor publication. Ironically, the fledging journal faced the hard reality of a capitalist system—insolvency. Initially, the ideological commitments of the editors led them to ignore the pecuniary reward of publishing established writers. They opted instead to publish lesser-known writers sympathetic to the board's political and economic positions. In 1929, the editorial board formed the John Reed Club to relieve itself of publishing commercially questionable, little-known, or even unknown writers yet still provide a supportive network for young authors interested in developing works on political themes. According to Eric Homberger, who has written extensively on American writers and radical politics, the formation of the John Reed Club in New York was an important moment in the history of the Left in American literature. "What the club represented is best understood through its slogan 'Art is a Class Weapon.'"[4]

Writers and artists were targeted for membership in the JRC and actively solicited. Minority writers had particular appeal because of their affiliation with politically disenfranchised groups who suffered most under capitalism. The *New Masses* editorial board recruited and employed Richard Wright to establish a John Reed Club in Chicago; other clubs soon sprang up around the country. The formation of the clubs was an inspired move on the part of the editorial board and one that proved a great success. The attraction of the John Reed Clubs to young writers, artists of all colors, and those looking to find outlets for their polemical works was unprecedented. Various clubs published their own literary magazines that, in turn, received national attention; they included *The Red* (Cleveland), *Left Front* (Chicago), *Leftward* (Boston), *Revolt* (Paterson, New Jersey), *John Reed Review* (Washington, D.C.), *The Partisan* (Hollywood and Carmel), and the most prestigious of all the JRC journals, the *Partisan Review,* published by Phillip Rahv and "Wallace Phelps" (William Phillips) in New York.[5]

The John Reed Club in Carmel, headed by Ella Winter, wife of Lincoln Steffens, held the same political proclivities as did other clubs, but it differed in two respects: it was very small, and its membership had a distinct makeup. The Carmel JRC counted among its members a remarkable list of artists who participated by virtue of their residences in the area. Carmel-by-the-Sea had long been considered an enclave of artists, free thinkers, and wealthy Californians who enthusiastically took up the gauntlet for unusual, though not always liberal, causes. In the early days of its formation, a degree of uncertainty surfaced as to how the organization would proceed and what it would support. In a letter to Joseph Freeman in 1932, Ella Winter asked if it would be "all right" for the JRC to sponsor a meeting at which Martin Flavin would speak against movies produced under capitalism, on the condition that members would "get up afterwards and tell them [others in attendance] exactly what communism offers." She complained that the members had not received rules, regulations, or a constitution "telling what the JR clubs are meant to do. . . . We don't even know what people must subscribe to to be allowed to join, and so at present are keeping everybody out who isn't a communist in feeling." The group, though small, initially generated local interest and support. In 1932, though the club had but nine official members, an audience of 120 attended a lecture by Lincoln Steffens entitled "Why Communists Have to Be Blankety-Blanks."[6]

In the beginning, responses to the JRC were cordial to cool, but at times they were comical. Possibly, the low membership figures in the JRC moved its leaders to initiate a clever recruiting plan, but more likely it was just an honest misunderstanding that led to a story that appeared in the *Carmel Pine Cone* in 1932. Under the headline "Residents Blush on Realizing They Are of Communist Party," the article reports a significant increase in party members in Carmel. The incident in question occurred in June 1932, when prominent residents of Carmel found they had signed a petition circulated by John Reed Club members "on the understanding that the signatures were merely to put the Communist Party on the presidential election ballot." However, the signatories did not read the fine print on the petition and the next day found themselves bona fide members of the Communist Party. The *Pine Cone* reporter did not miss the humor in the situation: "As a result, long hairs of the John Reed club were frantically pulling at their manes. John Catlin found himself the only communist mayor in the country; Frank Sheridan, chairman of the county democratic committee, may lose his political standing; sons and fathers, brothers and sisters, were not on speaking terms; several local stores were being boycotted." The report continues to explain how residents had filed suit in the superior court in Salinas to have their names "deleted, expunged and removed" when the county clerk had refused to comply with their request. Their contention, as put forth in the lawsuit, maintained that "unless due relief is granted, the signatures will forever remain an incorrect and misleading public record of the state of California . . . and that the continued retention of names and signatures upon election petitions will result to each of us a substantial inconvenience and hardship and grave and irreparable injury and damage." The *Carmel Pine Cone* article concluded by indicating that the members of the John Reed Club would be called to testify in the hearing. The final jibe: "Again, it will be another *Red* Letter day for Carmel!"[7]

This brief article may well shed light on the discrepancy about Hughes' membership in the Communist Party. If, in fact, the Carmel residents who signed the petition became party members, then Langston Hughes would have been among them. Though Hughes' biographers, Arnold Rampersad and Faith Berry, insist that he never "officially" joined the Communist Party, he may well have joined inadvertently, as did other Carmelites. Berry states unequivocally that while in Carmel, Hughes "signed his name to a petition supporting the Communist Party's 1932 presidential Candidates, William Z. Foster and James W. Ford."[8]

The Carmel chapter of the JRC found their proletarian cause in the agricultural strikes and union organizing efforts in California in the early thirties. Hughes returned to Carmel in early October 1933, a year characterized by labor historians as one unmatched in the history of labor relations in the United States for sheer commotion and friction.[9] The

Carmel Pine Cone noted his arrival in the local gossip column: "Langston Hughes, famous American Negro poet and writer, is spending a few months in Noel Sullivan's cottage on Carmelo. He has just returned from Russia where he has been collecting material for his new book, which he is writing now." A week later, a short article announced that Hughes was scheduled to speak on "Soviet-Asia" and address, among other issues, lifestyles in Russia, racial problems, and how the New Russia affected the lives of its citizens. The John Reed Club sponsored the lecture and Lincoln Steffens introduced Hughes that evening. A curious article the following week reported that the fire marshal padlocked the building in which the John Reed Club held its meetings because the "barn loft meeting place of the JRC" lacked egress. This was only the beginning of a series of harassing incidents that would unfold through the following year.[10]

The *Carmel Pine Cone* lists Hughes as one of the attendees at a November John Reed Club meeting held in the home of Steffens. This meeting allowed Caroline Decker, identified as the "strike organizer in the San Joaquin cotton picker troubles," to address a crowd of sixty people. After Decker's account of the organizing tribulations of the strike, the actress Helen Ware read Marie Welch's verse "Harvest" and Noel Sullivan spoke on the National Committee for the Defense of Political Prisoners, of which he was a member. Rising Hollywood actor James Cagney also attended that evening. Hughes later enlisted Cagney to help with other political defense projects. A collection at the end of the affair netted $118, intended as a contribution towards the bail of strike organizers jailed on charges of criminal syndicalism.[11]

Ella Winter was most involved in the strike activities. She met Caroline Decker at the San Jose home of Alice Parks, an ex-suffragette active in support of union organizing efforts in the Santa Clara Valley. Caroline Decker, holding court amid the assembled clergymen, liberal middle-aged women, and newspaper reporters, clearly impressed Winter. Winter recounted the incident in her autobiography: "I noticed a small blond-haired, delicately boned girl on a footstool, who dropped a quiet remark, or gave some needed information. . . . She had pink and white skin and very fair straight hair that fell to her shoulders, and tiny white hands that she used as she talked. She looked like a dancer, but she talked like an economics instructor as she told what the workers earned, the market price for cherries, the relations of the banks to big and little ranchers and how agriculture was financed."[12] Decker became a frequent visitor to the Steffens home, and her comings and goings on the streets of the small village were dutifully recorded in the pages of the *Carmel Pine Cone.*[13]

Winter served as the chief activist and advocate for the strike in Carmel. As both a financial and sympathetic supporter of the cause, she worked to enlist similar support from her friends. Counted among them was Langston Hughes:

> In Carmel, they listened to my accounts with excited interest. Strikes were something most people knew very little about, something connected with railroads, steel mills, coal mines—damp, dark dreary factories or places underground—not with sun and scented trees and bright fields. But because of our fragrant valleys, the human element in our stories of these strikes, and all the talk there had been about them, there gradually grew up a small nucleus of public-spirited Californians who became increasingly anxious to help in the struggle of the underprivileged workers in the California fields; Noel Sullivan, a gentle, courteous millionaire with a Catholic conscience: Langston Hughes, the Negro poet, Francis, the blacksmith; Dan, from Yale, and others who had sympathy and understanding. A few joined us from San Francisco, including Marie de. L. Welch, my poet friend, and Emily Joseph, the shrewd, hard-hitting wife of a wealthy businessman who happened to have a "social conscious [sic]." . . . We could not stay in Carmel and merely read about it. Our little bunch gathered one early dawn and traveled to the valley in three automobiles, led by Noel Sullivan in his Cadillac. In Tulare, the heart of the strike area, we met a small worried relief worker, Miss Throckmorton, who was glad to be able at last to talk to her own kind. . . . I saw Noel write something and hand it to Caroline. "For the pipes." He hesitated. "I hope that will be enough." It was a check, and it was enough.[14]

The visit to the strike encampment occurred within a few weeks of Hughes' arrival in Carmel. Following this visit, which he found very moving, he began work with Ella Winter on a play that had as its title *Blood on the Cotton.* This would later be revised to *Blood on the Field,* the title by which the play is referred to in most studies of Hughes. Only later would the title be changed to *Harvest.* Clearly, Winter intended the play to be documentary in nature. Hughes' and Winter's prefatory notes to the play indicate that she had maintained a large clipping collection on the strike from which she had drawn the details of the plot and the dialogue. Hughes and Winter made it plain that they wanted the director of any production to use this collection of material for both historical and visual effect.

Their intent was to write a documentary play about the strike, disguising slightly the primary participants through name changes. The real-life counterparts of the characters are readily recognized, however, and the dialogue is taken from court transcripts and newspaper reports. There is evidence to suggest that some of the dialogue was culled by Winter and Hughes from their firsthand interviews with strikers and strike leaders. One need only read the newspaper accounts of the strike in the *San Francisco Chronicle* or *Examiner, Fresno Bee, Times-Delta, Californian,* or the smaller newspapers from Corcoran or Pixley to recognize each character and incident dramatized in the script.[15]

Rampersad maintains that Hughes drew "on the drama techniques he had seen in Moscow," a reference to the agit-prop plays produced by radical workers' groups there. These plays did use documentary detail. A more compelling case can be made that the inspiration for the documentary structure of the script came from sources closer to home. Hughes had, in fact, seen the same documentary techniques used in the United States in North Carolina and in Provincetown, Massachusetts. As mentioned earlier, Hughes would have had opportunity to see *Strike Song* while on his southern speaking tour in Chapel Hill, and his visits to Provincetown seem to coincide with the production of Mary Heaton Vorse's labor play, *Strike!* In theme, tone, and tenor, *Strike!, Strike Song,* and *Harvest* bear notable similarities: they have a female protagonist as the strike leader, they use primary documents as sources of dialogue, and they celebrate the unionizing efforts of labor against a diabolical capitalistic system. A letter from Hughes to his literary agent, Maxim Lieber, and Michael Blanfort of the Theater Union confirms the idea that the script for *Harvest* was intended to be documentary and would follow incidents of the cotton workers strike "almost exactly."[16]

Hughes and Winter worked on the script throughout the fall of 1933 and the winter and spring of 1934. Their collaborative efforts blossomed and seemed to flourish in a whirlwind of public political activities. Hughes became an even more prominent addition to the John Reed Club and other leftist rallies. Rampersad refers to him as "the most obvious symbol of the Left in Carmel," a distinction that brought with it notoriety that Hughes would come to rue. In December, he sat atop an ersatz float at an anti-war rally "under a ghastly skull and thumped a big drum."[17] The following day, he spoke at the Peninsula-American League Against War and Fascism. Within weeks, Hughes accompanied Winter and Marie Short to San Jose to speak at an anti-lynching rally. Hughes, with Winter, Steffens, Short, and occasionally Sullivan, fraternized with union and cannery workers, championing their causes with speeches and public displays of support. An article in the 25 October 1933 edition of the *San Francisco News* carried word of Sullivan's involvement. "Declaring 12,000 school children are being worked to break the cotton pickers' strike in San Joaquin Valley, Lincoln Steffens and his wife Ella Winter, authors, and Noel Sullivan, San Francisco capitalist, appealed to President Roosevelt today against this use of child labor."[18]

Hughes and Winter became the targets of criticism and threats in Carmel. Winter's involvement in leftist activities was well known, but her association with a Negro leftist writer caused the community to become restive. Hughes, for his part, appeared to revel in the California literary opportunities and seemed equally unaware of the political and personal repercussions his actions engendered. A prominent figure in the activities of the John Reed Club in Carmel, Hughes also gained public attention because of his trips to San Francisco, where he organized a Scottsboro Defense Fund Exhibit and auction. He actively supported Sullivan's involvement with the League to Defend Political Prisoners, and his appearances on behalf of the organization increased public awareness of his political leanings. Additionally, Hughes was very public in his support of Jacques Roumain, who founded the Communist Party in Haiti. Ultimately, the speeches, rallies, petitions, and sheer notoriety associated with leftist labor and politics were more than even the liberal residents of Carmel could abide.

The critical rebukes appeared first in the local Carmel and Monterey newspapers. Editorials and snide commentary moved away from the John Reed Club as a whole to target Winter and Hughes personally. Hughes either chose to ignore or failed to heed the festering resentment directed towards him. He continued work on his script with Winter. In July 1934, Hughes wrote to Sullivan: "Ella and I are panting over the last lap of the second act. Determined to finish it this week."[19] All the while, rumors circulated in the community that Hughes was having an affair with Winter, and he was implicated falsely with other white women of the area. Each public appearance by Hughes or Winter, each statement of political support for leftist causes, exacerbated a situation already tense because of the labor protests of cannery workers in Monterey and farm workers in the Santa Clara, Salinas, and San Joaquin Valleys and the general economic suspicions and uncertainties of the depression. The violence directed towards strikers by vigilante ranchers in Hughes' and

Winter's play began to show itself in communities painfully close to Carmel and Monterey. Radical conservative groups engaged in Klan-like cross burnings and rallies. Hughes and Winter were singled out by these jingoist groups as objects of a slanderous campaign, which moved from malicious gossip to physical threats. Winter's account of the violence was published in Berry's biography of Hughes:

> The "Vigilantes"—whom Ella and Langston cited and equated in their play as "Ku Klux"—were hardly fictional. . . . Some local people referred to them as legionnaires, others as terrorist strike-breakers, who cooperated with police, "Red Squads," or wealthy landowners bent on keeping agricultural workers' wages at twenty cents an hour. . . . Although *Blood on the Fields* was neither pub-lished nor produced, word of it seems to have gone around and that, added to the general knowledge of Hughes' "radical" poems and some of the stories of *The Ways of White Folks,* and his membership in the local John Reed Club made him a target for the Vigilantes. . . . They accused Hughes of having an affair with Ella. . . . [T]hey men-aced her ten-year-old son and Steffens, his father. Years later, Ella Winter remembered that the Vigilantes went down to Hughes' "little cottage and danced their filthy devil's dances and shouted God knows what obscenities." It was a summer's night no one in Carmel's John Reed Club ever forgot. [Winter, Steffens, and their son] were among the last to see him before he escaped the Vigilan-tes, who came knocking at his door in the dead of night, in late July 1934. Fearing damage to Sullivan's Carmel property if he stayed, Hughes fled to Sullivan's house in San Francisco.[20]

Because of this incident, Sullivan sold his Carmel home, called Ennes-free, and bought Hollow Hills Farm in Carmel Valley where, according to the *Monterey Herald,* "his guests of all races and political persuasions could visit unmolested."[21]

Hughes' escape from Carmel came on 24 July 1934. Berry's chap-ter on this period of Hughes' life concludes with the statement that his having "been pushed to the wall by right-wing mob violence broke his heart."[22] But Hughes rebounded with a vengeance. He related his account of the incident in "The Vigilantes Come Knocking at My Door" and spoke with Ella Winter about the continuation of their project at the April 1935 First Pacific Coast Congress Against War and Fascism.[23] Winter seem-ingly relinquished the project to Hughes. Collaborative work on *Blood on the Fields* had already come to a halt in July when, fearing threats against herself and her son, Winter instructed Hughes to remove her name from the script.

Hughes persevered and, safe within the refuge of Sullivan's San Francisco home, continued work on *Blood on the Fields*. By August he was ready to send the script to Maxim Lieber. His letter includes his account of Winter's reluctance to have her name appear on the script, a commentary on the unpleasantness directed towards him in Carmel, and suggestions about sending the script to the Theater Union. Details of the letter belie the fact that Hughes was "heartbroken" or that Winter had permanently extricated herself from the project. Its contents provide evidence of Winter's continued interest in the project once things had settled down and her desire to be present at any rehearsals of East Coast productions. Its conclusion suggests again Hughes' concern for entering into collaborative theatrical endeavors without signed contracts:

> Our play is finished and a copy went off to you this morning. Its title at present is BLOOD ON THE FIELDS, although I am sending a list of other suggestions as to its name. . . . Ella Winter, when I last saw her ten days ago in Carmel, did not want her name used on the script—although it is copyrighted in our joint names. The Red Scare in Carmel and the vicious rumors put out concerning my associations with whites there and the fact that the Steffens home was branded as a nest of Reds and a meeting place for Negroes and Whites, etc. etc. prompted this move on her part. After all she does have to live there and send her kid to a school headed by a Legionnaire and get her milk from a dairyman who declared he was just waiting for the day when he could get behind a machine gun and drag all the members of the JRC out in Ocean Ave. and shoot 'em. And lots of good citizens visiting the City Council and urging them to do something about the Steffens. And one Jo Mora, a sculptor, (And a banker's son-in-law) heading a Committee of 110 to do active duty against the 24 members of the JRC. And not a hall to meet in any more as the landlords are all threatened with destruction of property if they rent to us. And a great frothing at the mouth of the New Dealers when Steffy issued from his sickbed a statement to the press, saying among other things, "Let them come and get me. Let them send me to jail. I'd rather go there than to the White House. It's more honorable!" . . . A good time was had by all. And if Ella Winter changes her mind about her name on the play, I'll let you know. Meanwhile, she has no objection to having the Theater Union know she is a co-author, and we are to share equally in any proceeds. She will probably come East for any rehearsals should any-

body decide to do the play. . . . At the moment I cannot locate the Theater Union's address. But please go ahead and submit the play to them, saying that we realize it is probably too long, and that we are perfectly amenable to suggestions as to cutting and revisions, etc. . . . If the Theater Union or anyone else does the play, we have a huge scrap book of newspaper pictures and clippings covering the whole strike in the San Joaquin Valley last October, as well as many photographs and handbills, etc. that will be of use to the producer, and which we will send on when needed. Jennie, the heroine of the play, is, of course, Caroline Decker—and most of the happenings and situations in the play come directly from the things we ourselves saw in the Valley last fall, or from what the participants, both growers and strikers, told us. The play follows the strike almost exactly. We hope it is dramatic as well as historical and true. Having worked so intensely on it the last few weeks, I am too close to it to read it critically now. Let's hear what you think of it. And the Union . . . [a]s to details, had Ella Winter and I better draw up a legal agreement out here on our half-and-half share in royalties? And should she join the Dramatist Guild, etc.?[24]

By September, the play received its first rejection from the Theater Union, a company founded in 1933 to provide a more professional outlet for proletarian plays. According to Rampersad, "Paul Peters [leftist playwright] and Margaret Larkin [leftist producer] . . . found 'Blood on the Field' grandiose and lacking in cohesion."[25] Rejected by their most promising theatrical outlet, Hughes and Winter sought the assistance of Ann Hawkins, a director and sometime leftist writer. The final collaboration resulted in the script renamed *Harvest*. The revised title came from one of Marie Welch's poems, "Harvest," which Winter especially liked.[26] The Theater Union, fraught with internal strife and financial problems, never saw the revised version. The producing organization closed the following year.

Two details of the collaboration remain uncertain: one pertains to the final version of the script, the other to Winter's final assessment of the project. The script published here comes from the Langston Hughes Papers held in the Beinecke Library at Yale. It is labeled "final draft," but it might not have been the last draft the three authors—Hughes, Winter, and Hawkins—intended to write. In the Hughes Papers are notes and remnants of multiple drafts, including a working draft written with Ella Winter that bears the title *Blood on the Cotton* as well as the canceled title, *Blood on the Fields;* this typescript version is 163 pages in length. Additionally, there is another script labeled "final draft" that bears the names of all three authors; this is the *Harvest* script published here. This script, which archival records list as being 128 typescript pages in length, posed its own problems. As organized in the Hughes Papers, one easily ascertains that this version is a composite script, put together from earlier drafts. Though listed as 128 pages, in reality it was far shorter: after extricating duplicate scenes, the final draft numbered only 114 pages. The script published here has been carefully reconstructed so that the order of scenes follow the strike.

The final ambiguity surrounding the play entails Winter's retrospective comments about Hughes and this period of their association. Citing a letter from Ella Winter, Berry characterizes Winter as recalling sadly: "Langston came out of the migratory workers strikes the only black there. We thought he would go on with this kind of 'revolutionary' activity, but he didn't, he went up the Valley and lived with Noel Sullivan, the non-active Catholic, gentle, gentleman. . . . I decided I had asked too much of a lonely black in our funny village."[27] Certainly, Hughes' renunciation of his leftist leanings and associations years later would have been a blow to Winter, but this statement implies contemporaneous recognition on Winter's part that Hughes was only a superficial participant in the ideological Left. Though their association remained cordial, Hughes did not seek out new collaborations with Winter after the death of Lincoln Steffens.

Harvest remains an atypical, anachronistic piece in the canon of works by Hughes. Examined within the context of leftist plays written during the 1930s, it fits well within a recognizable political literary schema found in other plays by other authors. Taken in isolation, the script does not fit particularly well with Hughes' style or treatment of leftist themes. Though one finds documentary allusions and topical references in Hughes' poems and prose, this appears to be his only play written as a documentary. The emphasis on documentary detail can most probably be credited to Winter's influence. Yet taken together with *Scottsboro, Limited* and *Angelo Herndon Jones,* one gains greater insight into Hughes' experimentation with various dramatic forms. One also begins to understand Hughes' vision of the theater as a means to a political end.

HARVEST

The stage directions at the beginning of the script make plain that any production was to use various agit-prop techniques similar to those

Hughes employed in *Scottsboro, Limited*. Again, cast members were placed in the audience to establish a psychological association with the audience. Interestingly, one technique used in *Harvest* is very reminiscent of Living Newspaper productions of the Federal Theater Project. The stage directions actually call for a "newspaper curtain" on which contemporary published reports of the strike and inflammatory literature associated with it would be projected onto a scrim or screen for dramatic effect. The play identifies the salient strike issues in the first few pages: pay, child labor, lack of food, unsanitary water and camp facilities, the mix of ethnic groups in the diverse migrant work population in California, and the like. The response by the characters to these issues follows closely the accounts of the strike and contributes to the accurate documentary quality of the script.

Black and white cotton pickers use racial epithets to refer to each other as well as to the Mexican migrant workers. Surprisingly, only the Mexican family in the play escapes the racist label. Though the script is peppered with disparaging comments made against Mexicans, the Mexican characters are portrayed as simple and well intentioned who bear none of the spitefulness of their co-workers. While all laborers are portrayed as victims in this play, the Mexican migrant worker is characterized as the most pathetic, the most victimized by the capitalistic system. The white family with the Southern accents—Aunt Marty, Adam, Shorty, and Luther, who will betray the strikers—refer repeatedly to "niggers," "greasers," and "wops." They represent the migration of uneducated white laborers from the southwestern dust bowl into California in the early 1930s. Adam's resentment of Mexican labor is borne out in lines like, "Damned Mexicans! Tha's why a white man ain't got no work here now." Later in the first act, Marty reprimands Shorty for talking while picking cotton, chiding him: "Standin' there a-jawin, that's why we can't get ahead o' the darkies."

The first scene establishes the antipathy towards "foreigners," which feeds the hate-mongering of the ranchers in the later scenes. Ironically, the foreign-born national, an Irishman, Mack Saunders, first calls the workers "comrades." As the union organizer out in the fields, he is the first to point to the potential for disease in the worker camps because of polluted water and unsanitary conditions. Mack identifies the source of the labor problems in the play and, by extension, in the state. The problem lies not with blacks or Mexicans who take jobs away from whites but with the "big ranchers" who lobbied against limits on immigration so they could retain cheap labor and who failed to honor promises of schools and acceptable wages. Mack persuades others to strike: "Mexicans ain't terrible, Mrs. Dobbs. We ought to get together. You heard about the Gallus Peach Ranch. The pickers there struck for more money—and got it."

The script makes every effort to keep the focus on ideological issues rather than racial ones. One must remember that Ella Winter, more than Langston Hughes, had been active in Communist causes for years. Many of the arguments in this script echo standard leftist accusations against American capitalism. Leftist political rhetoric surfaces in several statements made by poor ranchers as well as poor workers, who reveal their beliefs that only the rich have rights in America and the rights of the poor are trampled by the system. Their low station in life and wariness of "making waves" in a capitalistic system are conveyed subtly in lines spoken by characters like Ada: "You reckon de Lawd ever meant for po' folks to go around kickin up trouble sich as this, Mis' Dobbs? I declare to Jesus, I don't believe He did." In a later scene, Jose describes Mexico to Shorty, who asks him what it is like there: "Pretty, kind o' like California. All over mountains and deserts, and moon like this. But plenty poor people, they don't get along so good. We make plenty revolution once. My papa fight with Zapata, try to get land and work. But the generals win—and they kill us. Always, they kill us poor peoples." Every opportunity is taken to rhetorically reinforce the idea that unionization works only with all races represented. Towards the end of the first act, Dan states boldly, "We'll make a union," and the field hands stop to listen. Buster, a Negro picker, queries: "You gonna let colored in it?" When Adam hesitates, Mack cuts him off with a clear affirmation that all groups would be represented. Buster responds slowly, "Then that's a good union."

Not all of the workers, whose distrust of each other was something exploited by ranchers to prevent workers from organizing, share Buster's position. When Buster comments that Mack, the Irish organizer, is "a right nice guy," Ada responds: "I don't know. I ain't never seed no white folks I thought was right nice. All they wants you in de union for is to strike and git yo' haid broke, and then they'll put you out."

An element addressed in East Coast union plays during the thirties was the employers' complete control of worker disposable income and the workers' enslavement to the company store. This is particularly evident in plays about the steel industry, but this issue reemerges in the dramatic depictions of the company town in plays treating the textile industry as well. It is unique in American dramatic literature to find an example of the western equivalent of the company store. The "company store" and "company currency" in eastern mill towns were standard issues of organizers and the press of the period. In the western equivalent of the company store owned and operated by ranchers, workers were coerced to buy necessary supplies and food from them at exorbitant prices. Much of the pay migrant workers received was returned to their employer through the company stores. The ranch in the *Harvest* script becomes an analogous social environment to the company town. This play offers an incident where the ranchers attempt to control the would-be strikers by closing the commissary, thereby cutting off not only their supplies for work but also food for their families and children. Ironically, the characters of children are given lines that most closely espouse the philosophy of the labor movement and that are some of the most compelling rhetorical arguments in the play. The character Bud repeatedly asks his father if he is against the strike. To his father's evasive answers, he counters: "I heard Mack askin about you. And he said if you was against the strike, you was just going aginst yourself."

Initially, *Harvest's* depiction of the ranchers is equivocal; the audience is given both negative and sympathetic portrayals of them. A scene towards the end of act 1 introduces the ranchers at a luncheon meeting at which poor farmers articulate their worries about their inability to pay water bills and the necessity of taking promissory notes to operate their farms. The audience identifies with them as small businessmen struggling to keep their heads above water. Simultaneously, the audience sees the corrupting power of wealth in the characters of the large ranchers, who control not only the meetings but also the financial success or failure of smaller ranchers, designating, for example, which farmers they buy cotton from for their gins. Interesting topical commentary reflective of issues of the day surfaces in their conversations about the National Relief Administration. The wealthy ranchers know how to play the system that allows them to sign federal contracts whereby they are paid not to raise hogs when they had no intention of raising hogs. The political ignorance of the smaller farmers is contrasted with some poignancy, though they are not portrayed completely as sympathetic characters. Rhetorically, the script indicts the wealthy most harshly for their exploitation of migrant labor and also for their manipulation of governmental assistance programs aimed at providing relief for struggling farmers. The authors clearly intimate that blame for the strikes that beset America's agricultural centers should be placed on the rich ranchers.

The lines given Tilden, owner of the largest ranch, seem written with a biting irony. He intones about the need for ranchers to receive a fair profit; he blames the National Relief Administration for price hikes; he takes part in the disparaging laughter that erupts with his mention of the Cannery and Agricultural Workers Industrial Union. What becomes clear in his suggestion to raise the picking rate from forty cents to sixty cents per hundred pounds is that it is a measure that only the wealthy can afford to absorb. The script's negative comments directed towards the NRA expand to include the Roosevelt Administration, which is blamed for making the White House "socialistic." Government functionaries in the characters of Miss Prather, the administrator charged with gathering information about the migrant families in the tent camps, and the Mexican Consul, seen as an agent of the American government rather than a defender of Mexican labor, work to strengthen the arguments for a labor revolution. The personal assessments of Hughes and Winter seem embedded in the negative descriptions of ranchers and particularly in the negative representation of the Mexican Consul. As stage directions and commentary on characters, these statements would not have been available to audiences; their intended audience obviously was the actors cast to play certain roles. Yet the descriptions seem more a reflection of the attitudes of the authors towards the individuals rather than mere suggestions for interpretation of character.

The dialogue of the script consistently identifies union and union organizers as Communists, foreigners, and Reds who receive their financial support from Moscow. Both sides, ranchers and union organizers, refer disparagingly to the International Workers of the World, commonly called the Wobblies. This labor organization was responsible for earlier strikes in the agricultural regions of California. Mack condemns them for their violence and dissociates his union from them, instructing his followers: "[W]e ain't annarkists an' we don't believe in violence. No weapons, no force used unless you are attacked." The ranchers inveigh against the Wobblies in various references, ending with their resolve to meet their organizing efforts with violence.

The play's use of documentary detail is striking, particularly in its depiction of the problems in the tent city in Culver, the script name for the actual camp at Corcoran that held over four thousand migrant workers. While most of the incidents of the strike and the ensuing violence would be easily recognized by anyone familiar with California agricultural history, there are other allusions to incidents that touched the authors of the plays. One such reference comes during the discussion about forming groups to deal with the problem of migrant workers and

Communist agitators. At one point in act 1, scene 3, Lowe suggests to the group of prosperous farmers, "Why don't you boys get a Legion Post started?" This seemingly innocuous line alludes to the formation of the American Legion post in Carmel and its members' threats towards Langston Hughes and Ella Winter. The suggestion to form a Legion Post is followed immediately by another suggestion tying the group to Klan activities. Burtle says: "Bet a fiery cross'd work wonders," to which Floors responds: "Yes, they walked out on me once just when I had my hops ready to pick. After that, no more quarter for any striking bastards. I joined the Klan." The authors thus link the political conservatism of the American Legion with the prejudicial attitudes of the Ku Klux Klan.

This is even more pronounced in act 3 when the meeting of the Farmers' Protective Association is depicted in jingoist terms. The set displays the American flag prominently between portraits of George Washington and Abraham Lincoln. The stage directions have Bud Peterson, a grower, take over the platform "in the midst of a fiery and demagogic speech" to deliver his own form of patriotic invective:

> [I]n all the years I lived in this state, men, I ain't never seen the time before when a dirty bunch of Mexicans would rare [sic] up on their hind legs and defy a white man. That's what they're doing today in the richest cotton county of this state, gathered out yonder in their Culver Camp, four thousand strong, in league with alien agitators, plotting and planning to tear down our government and that flag up there. . . . Why? Because a lot of foreign agitators have come down to this valley and got our pickers stirred up. I say, fellow Americans, any self-respecting man would run 'em out of here. . . . How're we going to get this viper out of here? Democracy is our watchword. I say we take off our hats to the *flag* for a change, and not stand here and pay tribute to traitors who'd step on that flag and tear it limb for limb. How's for our gettin up fer once and saluting our flag, and telling it: Our Country, we are here! And to the racketeers who stir up strikes and destroy the principles of Liberty and Justice on which our country was founded, let's say to them: You shall not pass.

The early intimations of the ranchers that they would form a vigilante committee come to fruition in the closing moments of the play. In its similarity to other strike plays, the vigilante committee here is referred to as the Committee of 110 while in the contemporaneous plays treating the textile strikes it was called the Committee of 100.

Harvest offers yet another example of an American labor script that features the female labor leader as the protagonist. Jennie Martin of this script is the fictitious equivalent of Caroline Decker, the actual organizer sanctified by California laborers as "the maid of Tulare." Mack Saunders, the union organizer in the script, is a thinly veiled characterization of Pat Chambers, the leader in the 1933 strike. All the other individuals— dignitaries, bureaucrats, reporters, as well as migrant workers—who featured prominently in the activities at the Corcoran Camp are represented in some form in the play. The Mexican Consul is Enrique Bravo. The character of Professor Bankley in the script is a composite of students from the University of California, Berkeley, who studied the strike at its location. Miss Prather, the government functionary, is undoubtedly Miss Throckmorton of the NRA.

The final scene contains the most overtly agit-prop dramatic techniques. In this scene, Luther, the betrayer of the strikers, moves from the stage setting into the audience and leans against the wall. His new physical position as part of the audience perpetuates an uncomfortable guilt by association. He becomes one of them, and they must find a way to disassociate themselves from him. Additionally, the props used in the form of banners and placards are standard in agit–prop drama. In the closing moments, as Jennie holds the dead Jose in her arms, Shorty picks up a fallen banner that reads boldly BLACK AND WHITE UNITE TO FIGHT and displays it to the audience. In addition to being a call to arms, it also provides the opportunity by which the audience can separate itself from the presence of Luther. *Harvest* employs the common agit-prop technique of getting the audience to its feet, shouting slogans in the final moments of the play.

Even as a collaborative effort, *Harvest* provides insights into a turbulent period of Hughes' career. It offers a glimpse of the racism institutionalized in the migrant worker camps of the period, and when one knows the personal accounts of Hughes life in Carmel, the play carries echoes of the discrimination and racism directed toward him as well.

Harvest

By Langston Hughes, Ella Winter, and Ann Hawkins

[The original typed copy of this script, held in the Beinecke Library, is fraught with inconsistencies in spelling, punctuation, and capitalization and contains no diacritical marks for Spanish words. The script is reprinted here with the inconsistencies of the original and without the diacritical notations.]

This play should give the effect of a mass play. It is suggested that the audience as well as the stage be used, that runaways be employed, and that the old frame of the proscenium be broken. . . . .Between scenes, a "newspaper" curtain might be used, reproducing actual portions of the reporting of the strike. Bits from the strikers' handbills, or from the Vigilantes' and growers' advertisements could be flashed on the screen. (Such as the enclosed "Notice to the Citizens of Tulare.")

If possible, one or two Filipinos might be included among the strikers, to add to the melting pot of races that is California's low-paid agricultural reserve.

In the possession of the author is a huge album of pictures, clippings, leaflets, handbills, etc., of the strike. This material is at the disposal of the producer.

ACT 1

Scene 1

(A California road. Night. Sound in distance of a noisy rattle-trap approaching. Sputtering, it slows almost to a stop, its weak headlights pale on the road. A lantern for a tail light. Sound of gears and brakes, and a sputter of curses in Spanish as the old Ford jerks to a dead stop. In the darkness Mexican voices are heard within the stalled car.)

JOSE: Cabron!

DOMINGO: *(In a weary quaver)* What's the matter?

ROSITA: *(Sleepily)* Porque no anda? Why we stop?

(In the darkness a young man gets out, goes round to the back of the car and detaches the lantern hanging there. He approaches the hood and raises it up. Curses in Spanish and tinkers with the engine.)

JOSE: Car's broken down.

(Tall old man climbs over the side of the old car, knocking into the road a big bundle of bedding. Domingo stands holding the lantern while Jose inspects the engine.)

MILLIE: *(Whimpering)* 'S matter, mama? Why we stop here?

ROSITA: *(Crossly)* We no stop here. Car stop here.

JOSE: *(Bending over car)* Jesus, no gas!

DOMINGO: No gas! *(Comes with lantern)* Jose, look in can.

JOSE: *(Picking up a can tied to running board and shaking it)* Empty.

(For a moment there is a dead silence. Then Rosita begins to mutter in Spanish inside car. Suddenly a baby begins to cry.)

ROSITA: Ay, Maria! *(She rises and climbs from the car, reaches inside and picks up the baby. As the men talk, she sits down on the running board and suckles the child. The older children with American names, a boy, Roy, and a little girl, Millie, pile out of the car. They stand shivering in the road. The old man puts down the lantern.)*

DOMINGO: *(To Jose)* Where's nearest gas station?

JOSE: Bakersfield, I guess.

ROSITA: What for you talk gas? Who got money? Got one quarter left, buy can beans, buy milk for ninos. These child no milk today, yesterday . . .

DOMINGO: Tienes razon. No money. *(Pleadingly to wife)* Rosita, maybe buy one gallon gas?

JOSE: *(Matter of fact)* No get there on one gallon gas. Tilden ranch thirty, forty miles.

ROSITA: *(Positively)* No buy gallon gas! *(Angrily to Jose)* Why you no say ranch so far? Ay! Que cosa!

MILLIE: *(Shivering)* Mama, put mattress down for me to sleep.

ROY: Mama, I'm tired.

ROSITA: Sleep, heh? Tomorrow's work day, we lost eighty cents if we stop here sleep. Then you get no beans, no tortillas. *(Wrapping her baby, to the neglect of the other children)*

JOSE: Maybe 'nother car come by. *(He rolls and lights a cigarette from the lantern flame)*

ROSITA: Why we leave Oxnard? Beets good. We pick beets we live. . . .

DOMINGO: What you mean good? Pay no good. Sixty cents day. Contractor take some, commissary take some, you take some. What I got?

JOSE: Yah, better go pick cotton.

DOMINGO: *(Pointing at his children)* Kids can help pick cotton.

ROSITA: (*To Roy. She pulls the skinny boy to her side on running board and puts a part of her ragged coat about him*) Come here.

MILLIE: (*Envying her brother wrapped in mother's coat*) Me cold, too, mama.

ROSITA: (*Sharply*) Get back in Ford, go to sleep.

(*Millie begins to cry. The woman rises to push her into car. The baby begins to cry too. The old man curses in Spanish. Jose stands forlornly with the lantern, when the sound of a motor is heard. Pale headlights flood the road—picking out the broken down Ford and the miserable Mexicans standing there. Jose begins excitedly to swing his lantern. Rosita grabs their bundle from the road and throws it in the car.*)

DOMINGO: (*Crossing himself*) Audame, Jesus querida, audame.

JOSE: (*Standing squarely in the road swinging the lantern*) Get out way!

(*The old Mexican, the woman, and the children scatter to side behind the Ford. Sputtering and rattling, the approaching car is forced to come to a noisy stop.*)

ADAM: (*The high thin voice of a Southern white in the car*) Don't get funny, greaser,—standing there in the road. What do you mean? What you want?

JOSE: Gas.

ADAM: This ain't no travellin' gas station.

JOSE: We got no gas.

LUTHER: (*Voice in car*) Goddam. . . . Go on. . . . What the hell? Stoppin' like that, wakin' everybody up.

DOMINGO: You give us ten cents gas. My boy he suck it out tank.

ADAM: Ain't got enough for myself.

MARTY: *(A woman's voice in car)* Give 'em a little gas, Adam. Look like they mighty nigh po' as we air.

ADAM: Let 'em buy it, like us. Damned Mexicans! Tha's why a white man ain't got no work here now.

SHORTY: Reckon won't hurt to give 'em enough to get to Bakersfield, pa. *(To Jose)* Whar you-all goin', boy?

JOSE: Tilden Ranch. *(There is a burst of voices in the white folks' car)*

SHORTY: That's where we goin.

MARTY: You-all goin' to pick?

ADAM: *(Climbing out of his car)* What they payin' up there for a-pullin bolls? You heard?

JOSE: Maybe .40¢ hundred.

ADAM: .40¢! A human can't live on that!

MARTY: Give 'em some gas, honey, and let's go on.

LUTHER: *(Gets out of car, morosely)* Why let 'em take the bread out o' our mouths? Greasers.

(Jose and the old Mexican are already busy getting a hose and can. A short stocky young white fellow, Shorty, gets out of the second car and glares at Luther.)

SHORTY: What's that to you? And you payin' no fare? *(To Jose at gas tank)* Take wot you need, but remember we ain't the Standard Oil.

MARTY: *(To Mexicans)* You-all got children with you, ain't you?

ROSITA: Si, lady.

MARTY: It's hard enough trapsin' over the country lookin' for work youself, let alone with young ones.

ROSITA: We no can pay, lady.

LUTHER: That's how they all are—steal, but no pay! No honesty in these wops.

MARTY: (*Gently to Rosita*) I ain't askin' you 'bout payin'.

SHORTY: Aw, Dad, let 'em have it. It won't kill us.

ADAM: They said ten cents worth.

ROSITA: (*Pleading*) No can pay. We got one quarter, no eat all day.

MARTY: (*Calling*) Let 'em have it, Adam. This is my car. I reckon I got some say-so.

LUTHER: Generosity's cheap, Aunt Marty.

ADAM: (*To Mexicans*) Alright, go ahead. (*To woman*) You mighty worried about a car load o' greasers tryin' to beat us to the Tilden Ranch to take the bread out o' our mouths.

(*Jose begins to suck out some gas. There is a flood of light on the road and the sound of a popping motor.*)

SHORTY: One eyed car coming. We gotta move. (*Jose picks up gas can. Shorty calls to the driver.*) Pull aside, pa, somethin' comin'.

(*A motorcycle cop pulls up before the white family can clear the road.*)

COP: What the hell are you doin, blocking the highway?

JOSE: No gas, Mister.

COP: Where are you going?

SHORTY: (*Under his breath*) What's that to you, General Perishing?

COP: What's your name? (*Flashes light on license plates*)

DOMINGO: We go pick cotton, Mister.

COP: Where you come from? (*To the whites*) Where's your home?

SHORTY: Home? Ha! Ha!

MARTY: Home's in Arkansas. Little Rock, Arkansas.

COP: (*To Mexicans*) Where'd you come from?

JOSE: Mexico.

COP: I mean now?

DOMINGO: Come from Oxnard now.

COP: (*Suspiciously*) Oxnard, heh? You had trouble down there, didn't you?

DOMINGO: No, senor, no trouble.

COP: You come up here to pick cotton, heh?

JOSE: Yes.

COP: (*To whites*) Where're you goin? (*His flashlight plays on the white family's car.*)

MARTY: (*Sharply*) We goin' where there's a few bolls to pull.

COP: The whole lot of you cotton pickers, heh? Did you pick cotton here last year, any of you?

ADAM: No.

COP: (*To Jose*) Where was you last year?

JOSE: Pick melons, El Centro.

COP: (*To Domingo*) And you?

DOMINGO: I pick oranges, Riverside.

SHORTY: I was lappin' up that lousy soup from Pasadena relief.

COP: Lousy, heh? What you do to earn it?

SHORTY: I hope you have to drink it once, big boy.

COP: That's enough out of you. *(To both groups)* You can't bum around here. This Valley's overrun with tramps now. Get your gas and keep moving. Keep on going.

JOSE: We pick cotton.

SHORTY: *(To cop)* That's more'n you do!

COP: *(To Shorty)* I got a good mind to pick you up. *(Angrily)* Where's your driver's license?

(The Mexicans begin to back away. Shorty stands his ground)

SHORTY: My old man's drivin, not me.

ADAM: *(To his wife)* Marty, look in the car pocket for my license.

COP: *(Takes the license from Adam and notes down its number. To the Mexicans)* Let's see your license.

(Domingo searches in his pockets for his license)

COP: Hurry up! I haven't got all night.

DOMINGO: Yes, sir.

COP: *(Glaring)* Lousy foreigners.

LUTHER: You made a mistake, brother. We ain't foreigners.

COP: Well, I'm keepin' track of you, too. You look to me like one of those goddam trouble-makers.

LUTHER: Oh no. But I can tell you who is. (*Looks significantly at Shorty*)

SHORTY: You sonofabitch! So that's your gratitude for us bringin' you out. (*Socks him*)

COP: (*Making a grab for Shorty*) Startin' a riot—afore you even get to the cotton fields! (*Shorty dodges*)

MARTY: (*Screams*) O-ooo-oo!

SHORTY: And you look out too, you big bully!

COP: (*Lifts his night stick*) I'll get you yet, you . . .

(*Cop looks the two families up and down, his motorcycle sputters and pops, then he drives away*)

SHORTY: Bastard!

JOSE: Why he so angry? What we do?

ADAM: (*Mildly*) Nothin! But Shorty's too quick tempered. (*To Luther*) And as for you . . .

LUTHER: (*Sulky*) Aw, pipe down, I just wanted to git the cop out o' the road.

MARTY: (*To her family*) If you want to be in them fields tomorrow, let's git goin'. Adam, come on.

MEXICANS: Vamanos! Andale! Ya nos vamos.

(*The whites pile in and drive away. The Mexicans climb into their car, too. Rattle! Bang! Pop, pop, pop, pop! The road is clear as the curtain falls*)

Scene 2

(*A cotton field on the Tilden Ranch. Mid-morning. Blazing sun. Many men, women, and children, whites, Mexicans, and a few Negroes are working in the field, dragging cotton sacks behind them. The men wear overalls with leather* knee pads. *Some of the women also have on overalls, others ragged dresses. During the action there is a constant slow movement of pickers up and down the rows.)*

SHORTY: *(To a Negro carrying two full cotton sacks on his back across the field)* Heavy, bo?

BUSTER: *(Drawling)* It ain't light. I'm carryin mine an' ma girl's too.

SHORTY: *(Joking)* Who collects the cash?

BUSTER: I collects—but she takes it away from me.

FRANKIE MAE: *(Straightening up to fix her hair)* She's got the right idea.

SHORTY: How do you know, baby?

MARTY: *(Sharply to Shorty)* Standin' there a-jawin, that's why we can't get ahead o' the darkies. Old as I am, I picked more cotton 'n you did yestiday.

BUSTER: How much?

MARTY: *(Proudly)* Nigh 130.

BUSTER: Sho is good.

MARTY: *(Sees Roy going towards stream)* Boy, don't you go a-drinkin that gulley water. *(To the others)* I found a calf's foot in our bucket this mawnin!

FRANKIE MAE: You have to boil it first.

BUSTER: We ain't got nothin to boil it in yit.

MARTY: Why don't you buy something?

BUSTER: Bucket cost 95 cents in that there Ranch commissary.

(JOSE enters with an old bag)

BUSTER: (*To Jose*) We put in a whole day a-ready.

JOSE: Car break down four times. Had to push it.

SHORTY: (*Stopping to play, mimicking accent*) Strong man, him push-a da car! (*He gives a punch at Jose across the cotton row.*)

ADAM: We gonna be pushing that rattle trap o' ours if we don't make some money here to buy a new set o' plugs.

LUTHER: (*Lazily*) Well, I don't see how you gonna do it. They don't pay but .50¢ a hundred on this damn ranch.

ADAM: If you work, it's a'right. You never did care much for work, did you, Luther?

LUTHER: My back is weak.

SHORTY: You sure it ain't your head?

MACK SAUNDERS: We need some solid food, comrades, that's what's the matter. Eating this commissary canned stuff—and not enough o' that.

MARTY: An' they make a lot of profit on it too, don't they?

ROY: (*barefooted*) I'm tired.

MARTY: Well, set down and rest. Pore as a Mexican chile, havin' to pick.

LUTHER: (*Squatting on the ground rolling a cigarette.*) I never seed such shift-lessness.

MACK: We ought to have more for breakfast, that's the truth. We can't eat decent, on this pay.

LUTHER: (*Righteous*) I can eat on it.

ADAM: I sho can't.

FRANKIE MAE: It gives me a rash.

(*Buster returns dragging his empty sack through the rows*)

SHORTY: How much'd you weigh in?

BUSTER: 'Bout enough to pay for the string on this sack.

JOSE: How much sack cost?

SHORTY: (*Mimicking*) Sack him cost-a more you make-a one day.

ADAM: (*Sarcastic*) Stop makin fun o' that greaser, Shorty. They're human, ain't they? First thing you know he'll slice you.

JOSE: I no slice nobody, mister. I wanta know how much new bag cost this year.

BUSTER: Dollar forty cents, pal. That's what they cost.

JOSE: Last year bag cost eighty-seven cents.

MACK: Sure, everything gone up.

BUSTER: Last year they ain't paid but forty cents around here.

MACK: Yes, but eats has gone up a hell of a lot more. Your fifty cents is worth around twenty-five now.

MARTY: Any ranches around here got better water, Mister?

MACK: No, and most got worse toilets.

BUSTER: I wuz wo'kin on the W'ite place afore I cum here and their water was about two miles from camp. Had to carry it in buckets all the way.

MARTY: No better 'n it was down Cal'patria all I kin hear.

MACK: (*Interested*) You bin down there?

MARTY: Sho have.

MACK: Well, I'm afraid there's going to be sickness in all these camps. Ditch water, and holes in the ground for toilets all over this area.

MARTY: That ain't sanitary!

FRANKIE MAE: It's no life for a lady.

SHORTY: Wot you want? Runnin hot and cold pianos in marble-tiled bathrooms?

LUTHER: (*Agreeing*) That's what I say! (*To Shorty*) Not often we agree, eh, pal?

(*As they are picking down the rows they catch up with some Mexicans, including the Rodriguez*)

SHORTY: Hi, greasers, yo'all workin hard? Goin to put by yer savin's fer a Rolls Royce? I heard yer Ford's none too good—but I see you a-pickin quite well.

DOMINGO: Before, I never pick cotton.

ADA: (*A Negro girl wearing ten-cent pieces in her ears*) Yo gits pretty expert at it aftah a time. I kin pick two hundred a day when I'm well, can't I, Buster?

BUSTER: Uh-hum.

MARTY: (*Enviously*) Yo' can? (*Aside to Adam*) Them Niggers'll be stealin the bread out uv our children's mouths.

MACK: That's a funny thing to say, Mrs., er—Mrs.—

SHORTY: Dobbs, me lad. Dobbs, rimes wi' sobs and mobs and robs and a hell of a lot other thing we might be doin before long.

MARTY: Shut up, Shorty. (*To Mack*) What do you mean—funny?

MACK: I mean the white folks out here, big ranchers, is to blame, Mis' Dobbs, not the Mexicans or the Negroes. When the growers wanted cheap hands for this valley, they sent agents to Washington askin 'em not to limit immigration so they could get plenty Mexicans and Filipino boys to pick cotton and grapes and lettuce. They offered train fare and promised good wages and schools for their children. Then when they got all the help they needed, the growers started payin' the starvation wages we're gettin' now.

MARTY: I ain't blamin them pickers. I'd as soon blame them farmers livin in big houses and eatin the fat o' the land and me out here breakin my back in the sun.

(*A loud cry is heard and a pretty young Mexican girl comes running by sobbing and screaming, followed by Pancho.*)

JUANITA: Madre mia! Oh, save me! Don't let him hit me. Help, help!!

PANCHO: (*An elderly Mexican*) Cabron de diablo! I'll show you! no daughter o' mine, you! (*He rushes toward her, brandishing knife. Shorty and Mack hold him.*)

FRANKIE MAE: (*excitedly*) Help! Aw-oo-o!

MACK: Quiet, quiet, what d' you want, the cops on top of us?

PANCHO: (*Cursing and half sobbing*) Cops, yes, polzia! Let 'em come, take her jail. No daughter o' mine.

(*Everyone in the field has stopped picking, turning around to listen, putting their hands in the bend of the back where it hurts as they straighten.*)

BUSTER: (*To Pancho*) Keep yo' shirt on, bo. Why, she's on'y a little girl.

PANCHO: Little girl? Madre de dios! Yes, little, an' already bad . . . I kill 'er. (*Struggles to get loose*)

JUANITA: (*Crying with fright*) Oh, help me! help me!

(*People edge in slowly from all parts of the field to hear the excitement.*)

LUTHER: Damn fool Mexicans!

MARTY: (*Stepping up angrily*) Here! here! When I'm a-pullin boles I don't want no trouble. What's the matter with you?

PANCHO: Senora, she make me disgrace. She—she—gonna have baby!

SHORTY: Is that all? (*There is a murmur of relief and amusement in the crowd*)

MARTY: Well, she ain't the first woman what's had a baby. You put that knife down.

ADA: You gonna kill her fer that?

PANCHO: Si! Si! Baby without padre.

(*Smiles and some laughter*)

SHORTY: It's gettin' better and better.

PANCHO: (*furious*) She make me disgrace.

ADA: (*Placidly*) You can't tell. It might be a sweet child. (*To Juanita*) Who's its father?

SHORTY: (*Singing line from Casey Jones*) She's got a lovin' papa on the Salt Lake Line.

BUSTER: Po' chile.

MARTY: (*To Juanita*) Hush yore cryin, now. He ain't gonna hurt you.

JUANITA: (*sobbing*) Yes, he will, he wants to kill me. Night time, he kill me.

LUTHER: You can stay with me, baby, in the night time.

MARTY: (*sharply*) You Luther! (*To Juanita, putting her arm around the girl*) Come here, child. Where is yore baby's father?

JUANITA: Maybe he El Centro, I don't know.

BUSTER: A no-good son of a gun!

JUANITA: (*Defensively*) He good boy. I love him. He want marry me, but we got no money. No can marry, no can love. (*sobbing*) I want die! I want die!

FRANKIE MAE: (*dabbing her eyes*) Ain't it sad?

ADA: It's sho a hell of a life, honey. You right about that.

MACK: She's right. This ain't no way to live, the way we have to. (*Passionately*) Never makin enough to settle down, sleepin in tents and shacks, no decent place to lay your head at night. This girl is sure right. It's a hell of a life! And we got to do something about it. (*The workers have gradually gathered around Mack. Juanita's sobs are less violent. From the crowd there are mostly dumb stares, but some grunts and nods of agreement as Mack continues*) We got at least make enough to buy food and live like humans in shacks. We ain't fools, are we?

JOSE: (*listens to Mack intently*) No.

PICKERS: Sho ain't! No, sir! Verdad que no. I ain't!

MACK: (*Pointing around him*) Look at this Ranch—this here cotton. We pick it, the growers sell it. They get thousands of dollars. We get nothing. They said they would give us cabins, wood and water! And what happens? Nothing.

LUTHER: (*spitting tobacco*) Who's he, shootin' his mouth off?

SHORTY: Shut up, and listen.

(*LUTHER exits*)

MARTY: These here Mexicans is terrible, workin for nothin.

MACK: Mexicans ain't terrible, Mrs. Dobbs. We ought to get together. You heard about the Gallus Peach Ranch. The pickers there struck for more money—and got it.

DOMINGO: Not always get more in strike, Mister.

MACK: No, but you stay broke if you don't try.

ADAM: Well, talkin 'bout gettin together, what should we do?

MACK: There's to be a little meetin Saturday. Come down there and talk to the other fellows.

(*Mack returns to his row. The others slowly begin to scatter. While some are still standing talking, the ranch foreman comes striding into their midst. Behind him straggles Luther, who left as Mack was talking*)

FOREMAN: What the hell is this? Who's standin gabbin here? (*To the Mexicans*) You greasers're on this ranch to pick cotton, not to stand around and yabber. (*To Shorty, standing defiantly upright*) What are you up to?

SHORTY: (*sweetly*) Lookin' at the moon.

FOREMAN: Be careful who you're talkin' to. Are you the fellow come in here with that bunch last Monday?

SHORTY: Oh, no, I was born on this ranch. (*lights a cigarette*)

FOREMAN: (*Hot, sweating, and mad*) Are you trying to start something?

SHORTY: Start what?

FOREMAN: You better weigh in your bag and get on off.

MARTY: He don't mean nothing, mister.

FOREMAN: Who're you?

MARTY: His mother.

FOREMAN: Well, what was goin on here when I come up? What're you talkin so loud about?

LUTHER: Talkin about strikes.

SHORTY: You dirty son of a bitch!

FOREMAN: *(To Luther)* Go call a deputy. I knowed there was agitators in this field. *(Luther exits)*

FOREMAN: *(To Shorty, who stares at him belligerently)* Get to work.

SHORTY: I'm gettin paid by the pound, not by the minute.

FOREMAN: You'll get out of here.

ADAM: *(Comes up)* What's the matter?

FOREMAN: I'll tell you what! We don't intend to have no trouble here this summer cause of a lot o' agitators, and I'm warning you the Tilden Ranch don't put up with trouble makers.

DEPUTY: *(entering)* What's the matter here, Bill?

FOREMAN: Half a field had stopped working when I came by. *(To Luther)* Who was makin' that speech?

LUTHER: *(Frightened at the stares of the workers and the clenched fists)* I-I-I-don't know who . . .

DEPUTY: I thought you knew.

SHORTY: He's too short to see over the crowd, that runt.

FOREMAN: *(Pointing to Shorty)* I don't trust him. He's too smart.

MACK: Nobody has to be smart to see what a sweat shop this ranch is.

FOREMAN: You!

DEPUTY: That's an agitator?

SHORTY: Who's agitatin? You gettin all agitated.

FOREMAN: *(Angrily)* I'll have you locked up so tight it'll be winter when you get out. *(To Sam and Buster)* As for you two, one more cackle and I'll pay you off.

DEPUTY: *(Going toward Shorty)* This the trouble maker?

MARTY: My son ain't done a thing!

SHORTY: They just scared o' me. *(Glares at deputy)*

MACK: *(Starts to speak to deputy)* Say, this man . . .

DEPUTY: *(To Shorty)* Come on.

SHORTY: *(Jocularly)* Have I got to walk?

(As the deputy and the foreman exit left with Shorty between them, Marty and Mack stand looking after them)

MARTY: *(Fiercely)* If you put him in jail, I'll call a strike meself.

(There is a low murmur of approval from the field. Someone spots Luther, the informer, bending over a row. Dan gives him a quick jerk of the collar and points after the deputy. Luther sneaks fearfully away.)

ADAM: We must get Shorty out.

DAN: We'll make a union. *(The field stops to listen)*

BUSTER: You gonna let colored in it?

ADAM: *(Hesitates)* Well . . .

MACK: Sure!

BUSTER: *(Slowly)* Than that's a good union.

ADAM: *(To his wife)* Marty, you hear that? *(Marty only nods)*

MACK: (*To Jose*) You pass the word around to all the Mexicans. Tonight let's hold a meetin. Right tonight. Everybody come.

JOSE: I tell everybody. (*He begins to pass the word among the Mexicans*)

(*The curtain falls*)

Scene 3

(*Conference room: a table at one end. Rows of men talking to each other, smoking, laughing, some standing. A few in conference. A good deal of the conversation is about superficial matters but there is tension and a sense of strain and uneasiness underneath. Obviously, it is not just one more luncheon meeting. Gradually, groups move toward the front of the room. At the table is a man with a gavel, the ranch owner and bank agent, Harry Tilden. Also at the table are Bud Peterson, Ed Lowe, the small-town capitalist, and a woman stenographer taking down the proceedings in short hand*)

LOWE: (*In high thin voice*) Higby says the World's Fair's a sight to see. I ought to go to Chicago.

TILDEN: (*Across the table*) I'd like to see that fan dancer.

VOICE: Why don't they get going, boy. I'm anxious for a foursome.

SETH FLOORS: (*Looking out the window*) You sure won't be stopped by rain today.

MARTIN BURTLE: A little rain wouldn't hurt.

FLOORS: Well, you won't get none for a month yet.

BURTLE: No?

FLOORS: No. My crops OK. I'm glad I put in them extra acres this year. When you going to start pickin?

BURTLE: When the bolls open, when'd you think? I'm at the end of the irrigation line, and that bastard Johnson took all the water for ten days, and I had to wait.

ROY WILLIAMSON: (*A poor farmer*) Paid your water bill yet? I'm having a hell of a time payin mine.

LITTLE: No. I signed a I.O.U.

BURTLE: Yep, the bank's goin to take it.

LITTLE: I thought they had the whole valley already.

WILLIAMSON: I thought under the N.R.A. they give you a two year moratorium so's they couldn't take farms away?

BURTLE: That only applies to houses.

PETERSON: (*yelling across room*) Who won between Delano and Taft, Tim?

BURTLE: (*from his seat*) I lost my five bucks. Delano beat the hell out of 'em—four touchdowns.

FLOORS: Not like it was when we all-stars ran the team!

BURTLE: Nothing's what it used to be.

LITTLE: That government check I get for not planting wheat, that's how I paid for my seeds this year. Just came in right.

LOWE: (*Who has crossed the room*) Did you sign up not to plant?

BURTLE: I certainly did. That's how I got my seed planted this year.

LOWE: That's how I got my land planted. Wouldn't had a row o' cotton otherwise.

PETERSON: (*A big, fat fellow*) That's how Milt got his water assessment paid, only he ain't lettin on. Nothin's ever right for Milt.

BURTLE: I just found out I could sign up a contract not to raise any hogs this year, and I got ninety dollars for it. (*Laughs*) And I wasn't gonna raise hogs!

PETERSON: Pigs will be pigs.

BURTLE: George Caldwell said he wouldn't sign up. The government wasn't gonna tell him how many sows to foal.

LITTLE: It'll cost him five cents a pound to raise and he'll get four.

(The group of poorer farmers have been listening in to the more prosperous ones)

WILLIAMSON: I certainly wish I knew what all this is about—getting money for what you don't do.

LITTLE: I read in the papers that when in history they cut down on crops there's always a famine afterwards.

PETERSON: Well, we haven't got to a drought yet. How many hampers to an acre do you figure, Martin?

BURTLE: Oh, I'll be all right if they don't pull any monkey stuff on us.

PETERSON: *(Aggressively)* What do you mean, strikes? Not a chance. Tilden'll show 'em. He's a smart guy. *(Assuredly)* You can't fool these big fellers. They know just how to do it.

LITTLE: Well, what do you think we gotta pay them pickers?

PETERSON: That's what we come to hear, ain't it?

BURTLE: There ain't gonna be no use in askin me to pay no more than I been payin. *(Positively)* I can shut up shop.

TILDEN: *(Bangs on table)* The meeting will come to order, gentlemen. Well, *(hesitating momentarily)* gentlemen, last year we got our cotton picked without any trouble. Because we paid a fair wage. And we intend always to pay a fair wage. But we must keep the return to labor in harmony with a fair return to the grower. *(General nods of assent)* This year, basic prices of commodities have gone up because of the NRA; the things we farmers have to buy have gone up a lot more than what we farmers have to sell;

and if we pay labor a wage that won't leave us a fair profit on our invest-
ment, you and I can't stay in business. We have to steer a fair and square
middle course. *(Emphatically)* We aren't going to get along paying fifty
cents. There's been trouble other places in the state; in Pascano they set
the same wage as last year, and that gave the agitators their excuse to
come in, and the growers lost money and had a lot of trouble. Now I have
a report that this Cannery and Agricultural Workers Industrial Union
(Laughter) say they're going to make trouble for us, they say we've got
to pay a dollar a hundred. *(laughter)* Now, we won't want trouble. And
prices have been going up, I guess a can of beans costs a Mexican a little
more this year than it did last. That's about all a Mexican buys, a can of
beans a day and he's fixed; and I guess I ought to know, our company
store hardly makes any more profit than it takes to be worth while. Well,
we want to be fair to labor, and *(significantly)* we don't want any trouble.
So we have decided that the picking rate this fall be raised to sixty cents
a hundred.

*(This announcement causes general commotion and a murmur of resentment
rises.)*

VOICES: Good God! I can't make a damn thing on that! Why the hell
sixty? Never paid that in my life, and I won't. Say, they must be in league
with the agitators!

FLOORS: I'm payin forty. That's enough!

LITTLE: I might as well give up right now. Can't even get to first base at
sixty.

WILLIAMSON: Well, the price has gone up this year. It's ten cents a pound.

BURTLE: Cotton ought to be twelve or fourteen cents before a man can
make anything on it.

FLOORS: Mexicans can live on forty cents. Why pay more?

BURTLE: And let 'em make a fuss. They ain't got the guts to carry it
through.

TILDEN: Gentlemen: let us hear your opinions.

(There is silence and hesitation, but general mumbling)

WILLIAMSON: *(Calling out from his seat)* What good is this holding up cotton planting, and plowing-under, going to do to the price of cotton?

TILDEN: There'll be a better price this year, gentlemen. The Chicago market assures us of that.

LITTLE: *(Turning toward a prosperous group)* You're a fine bunch to be talking about prices. You didn't even buy our cotton at your gins last fall for enough cash for us to get seeds this year.

PETERSON: *(A big gin owner)* Can't you fellows see that all that gin owners can pay is what cotton's worth on the market? They don't make much.

LITTLE: Well, who did make the money then?

(There is a knock at the door.)

TILDEN: Come in. *(A bell-boy walks in with a note. Tilden reads it, turns to the others at the table and confers with them in a worried manner. Lowe frowns. Tilden speaks soothingly, then addresses the crowd.)* Friends, a delegation from the pickers. *(To bell-boy)* Tell them to . . .

LOWE: *(plucks at Tilden's sleeve, who bends to listen. Lowe speaks in low voice)* Harry! One's enough.

TILDEN: *(To bell-boy)* Tell one to come in. *(To the gathering)* The pickers have sent a delegation; I propose we hear their views.

LOWE: *(Calling bell-boy as he turns to leave)* Boy! Bring me the evening paper as soon as it comes out.

BELL-BOY: Yes sir. *(exits)*

PETERSON: The pickers are damn restless this year, Harry. There's agitators come in here.

LOWE: No wonder, with the White House gone socialistic!

(Enter Mack. There is a stony silence)

TILDEN: What have you to say?

MACK SAUNDERS: *(A little overwhelmed at first. He speaks in a low voice that takes on strength as he talks—as he is made more certain by his words that they are justified)* This meeting has been called to decide on the price to be paid for picking cotton this year, so I understand. I come from the Field Pickers' Union of the San Vincenze Valley with the demands of my union. *(Reading)* "In view of the rise in the cost of living and the considerable unemployment of cotton pickers last year, our union has unanimously decided to demand a wage of one dollar a hundred for picking cotton this year, clean drinking water, and recognition of our union."

FLOORS: *(snarls)* Well!

TILDEN: *(interrupting)* Thank you.

MACK: I should like to address your meeting a few minutes. I . . .

TILDEN: We have heard your demands, thank you. *(waits)*

MACK: I . . .

(Lowe whispers impatiently to Tilden. There is a sullen murmur in the room.)

TILDEN: This meeting has heard you. Good afternoon.

(Mack looks uncertainly around at the hostile faced farmers, then goes out.)

FARMERS: Demands! For Christ's sake! Goin to dictate to us! Did you hear that? A dollar a hundred! They're crazy!

PETERSON: Can you imagine those guys comin' here and demandin' from us.

BURTLE: They think they own everything. The brass of the bastards!

FLOORS: That's what you can expect from a union—a gang of agitators!

BURTLE: *(Stands)* Mr. Chairman, you never should have raised them from 20 to 40 last year. There was plenty of labor at 20 cents. I told you then, Harry, if we gave in, we'd be in for trouble.

LITTLE: Sure, that comes from going soft and giving in to 'em. Here we are, trying to make a living—and they asking for a dollar a hundred.

WILLIAMSON: What the hell are we going to do, if we have a strike here?

PETERSON: Well, you fellows will have to get together and be deputies again this year. I'm ready.

BURTLE: All you have to do is to stick together and knock the hell out of those rats. There are plenty of people who want work.

FLOORS: *(darkly)* They oughta be lynched, them reds.

PETERSON: If the sheriff can't take care of them, we can.

WILLIAMSON: *(to Milt Little)* Doan' know as I particularly relish going around knocking pickers on the head.

LITTLE: Say, you got too much sympathy. Don't you know where they get their money—what's that furrin town in Russia?

FLOORS: If we have a real sheriff here we'll have no trouble about 40 cents.

LOWE: *(rising)* What business has that Red coming here today talking for Mexicans and niggers. I've always got along with my labor. I never had trouble and don't need outsiders telling me my business.

PETERSON: That's right. Who the hell told Mexicans about running water?

FLOORS: And their rights! *(general laughter)*

BURTLE: They want a privy and there's ten thousand acres of land!

LITTLE: If we did put in a tap the Mexicans'd let it run all day.

BURTLE: They're all communists.

FLOORS: I hear we got a fine new order o' tear gas that oughta fix 'em up. You ought to see 'em run in Lodi.

PETERSON: Yeah, I was there then. You'd have laughed yer head off if ye'd seen 'em coughing and spitting and running like scared hens.

LOWE: (*To the bunch of prosperous farmers*) Why don't you boys get a Legion Post started?

BURTLE: Bet a fiery cross'd work wonders.

FLOORS: (*darkly*) Yes, they walked out on me once just when I had my hops ready to pick. After that, no more quarter for any striking bastards. I joined the Klan.

TILDEN: (*Who has been whispering to Lowe*) Gentlemen: I do not think we have to fear anything from a strike in this valley, especially since we're proposing to pay them more than last year. Sixty cents a hundred will net some of these pickers over two dollars a day. Mexican labor is completely satisfied. We might have to deal with a few alien agitators, but our police know how to meet them quite adequately. We are aware that many of us could not earn fair profits at a higher rate. We therefore propose that sixty cents be the basic wage for this year's crop. Any dissension? (*There is no sound*) Then the meeting is closed. We will hold our next meeting . . . (*Bell-boy enters and lays the afternoon papers on the conference table. Lowe bends over to glance at the headlines. His eyes bulge, his hands grip the table, he is obviously agitated.*) . . . at that meeting we will take up . . .

LOWE: (*shouting*) A strike has been called. It says here . . .

(*The men at the conference table rise excitedly, reach for the papers, and lean over Lowe's shoulder to read the news.*)

VOICES: What? What are you talking about? Strike?

LOWE: Where at? (*holding up paper and reading*) Five thousand cotton pickers have voted to walk out next Monday unless . . .

(The room is in an uproar as men rise, gesticulate. Suddenly the gavel sounds on the table)

TILDEN: *(Rising, the center of tense attention as he speaks slowly and with sinister determination.)* There will be no strike, gentlemen.

(A murmur of approval as the curtain falls)

Scene 4

(A meeting of the Central Strike Committee in an empty barn. The members of the Committee sit on boxes on the floor.)

BUSTER: What if we lose the strike, Miss?

JENNIE: We don't lose strikes, comrade. If we don't win all our demands, we win some. And we will have shown our strength to the bosses and we'll have taught organization to many thousands. That's the big lesson they have to learn.

FRANK: The men are kind of scared, Miss, specially the Yankees. One guy come to me and says "My boss is a pretty good guy, he give me a bottle of wine one day . . . "

JOHN VIZA: Many say, their bosses not so bad.

JENNIE: Yes, there are guys who'll hand out a piece of wood or an extra blanket once in a while. Or likker. But we aren't asking for charity, to let them square themselves with their conscience. We're asking for our rights.

BUSTER: But farmers do get mad. I dowanna get my curls ironed out.

JOHN: They put out extry tear gas and riot bombs in our county. The Council voted for 'em last week.

BUSTER: Dat tear gas burn your eyes, fo' sure. And s'pose they stop relief, Miss, and we don't get any food at all? Guys ask, what they'll live on during the strike?

JENNIE: Of course. Relief is the backbone of a strike. We should get relief trucks out collecting food at once. Who'll volunteer?

VOICES: We will.

JENNIE: Good. Who else? (*silence*) What about the new comrade from the Tilden Ranch?

JOSE: I will do for you what you say, senorita.

JENNIE: (*not noticing his warm voice, businesslike*) That's good, comrade. Mack here will show you the ropes. Go to the small farmers and shop keepers and ask them to contribute to strikers' relief. If the pickers make higher wages, it will be good for them.

JASPER: How do we explain that, ma'am?

JENNIE: Because the extra wages the pickers earn are spent here. Our pickers don't go to Monte Carlo like Mr. Tilden.

(*Loud knock on the door. They all huddle together*)

SHORTY: (*in a loud whisper at the door*) Mack Saunders here? It's alright, you guys. It's me, Shorty—Shorty Dobbs. I jest escaped from the lousy jail.

(*Someone strikes a match*)

MACK: Shorty? (*lets him in the barn*)

SHORTY: Yeh. I jes' escaped. They're after me, but I threw 'em off. I went by Tilden's and ma told me you was meetin here.

MACK: Did anyone see you?

SHORTY: No, I gave 'em the slip. The cops in Purtley they had a load o' greasers they was razzin' and in the mixup I skipped out the open door.

MACK: They'll be after you!

SHORTY: Un-un. I got out afore they got me fingerprinted and mugged.

BUSTER: What's a jail look like?

JASPER: You should not have fled, brother. The Lord will comfort those who in His infinite wisdom he had run into jail.

SHORTY: (*sits*) Oh, yeah!

JENNIE: Report from Buttonwillow?

FRANK: (*Reeling it off as if he'd learned it by heart, or had said it several times at meetings already*) We don't have no fresh water. A pair of overalls that was eighty-six cents is one ninety-three now. We never gets firewood. No 'lectric lights. Kids go barefoot. We know we . . .

(*The CURTAIN SLOWLY DROPS during this speech. When the CURTAIN RISES AGAIN there are faint streaks of dawn. Men are yawning, their faces are whiter, their shirts open. Smoke lies heavy over everything. One man is asleep. Their hair is rumpled, beard grown heavier overnight. Their fingers are stained with tobacco. They yawn, stretch, cross and uncross their legs. Dark rings under their eyes. Two candles are guttering.*)

JENNIE: Does anyone want to ask any questions?

MOSCARO: What if they deport us to Mexico?

JENNIE: Comrades, you must all get in your heads that we have to stick together, be solid, fight side by side like members of one big family in spite of all.

BUSTER: Couldn't we leave dat fighting to dem greasers?

JOHN: (*Angry*) Greasers!

HACK: Buster! Leave that word to the bosses.

JENNIE: Comrades! Is it clear to you all now? Can you go back to your locals and get the men all out?

SHORTY: Greasers never understand anything but women and craps.

JENNIE: (*To Shorty, reprovingly*) Many of the workers don't understand. We are trying to help them learn. They have been sold out and betrayed by corrupt unions so often.

JASPER: I remember the time the Wobblies . . .

MACK: Wobblies!

JASPER: (*Hurt*) You said one big union!

MACK: Yes, one big union . . . but we ain't annarkists an' we don't believe in violence. No weapons, no force used unless you are attacked.

MASCARO: Isn't 60 cents enough? My wife, she say we can live on tortillas.

JENNIE: (*Losing her temper*) Really, comrades, here we are trying to bake a Rev——— . . . (*Corrects herself*) call a strike to better conditions for you and after four and one half hours of planning you still ask . . .

JOSE: (*Gently*) Senorita, Mexicans have big familias. Worry, worry all the time.

JENNIE: (*quickly contrite*) You're right. (*Jose glows, gratified, looks at her for some personal recognition, but Jennie goes on.*) We mustn't be impatient. But this strike must be fought, uncompromisingly, to show the bosses we won't stand for slavery. The picket line is what wins a strike. (*her fire mounts*) They'll come to us with arbitration and sell out proposals, they'll hire thugs and gangsters and try terror and intimidation— but our answer is the picket line. Who'll undertake to captain picket trucks?

SHORTY: You bet me! I'm spoilin' to get at the throat of some o' them goddam cops.

WORKERS: And me. Me too! You bet yer. Si.

BUSTER: Sure, boy, we'll get the bastards out o' them scab fields.

JENNIE: The strike is on. Tomorrow, why no . . . (*Seeing the gray dawn creeping up*) This morning, picket trucks will leave to pull out the ranches that are still at work. Every cotton field must be emptied. From today on there mustn't be an ounce of cotton picked until we have won our strike.

(*Meeting breaks up. Workers get up, shuffle, stretch, yawn, put on shoes, straighten shirts, collect in groups, begin to go to door*)

MACK: Let's go, Jose. We got a long walk. Shorty, you goin' back to Tilden's to sleep?

SHORTY: Sure. I ain't scared.

JOSE: (*Goes up to Jennie shyly*) I like you say goodnight to me, Senorita! (*He gazes at her as the curtain falls*)

Scene 6

[Scene 5 was not included in the script held in the Langston Hughes Papers.]

(*The cabins of the cotton pickers on the Tilden Ranch. Sunrise. Several frail and dilapidated huts built like sheds, of plain boards, some with only wooden flaps for window openings, shingles coming off, doors hanging on one hinge, steps broken down. No porches, no paint, no beauty. A dusty yard way in which may be seen a broken down car or two, one with a canvas flap sheltering a man and wife. Back of the huts a small tent or two may be seen, and a make-shift hovel of sacking and boards, from which a sleeping man's feet protrude. Beyond are the cotton fields, with the bolls bursting white in the morning sun. The stage is empty but from one of the cabins, Charlie's Negro voice is heard singing.*)

BUSTER: (*In slow syncopation*)
> I'm writin you this letter, babe,
> Three days sence I et.
> The stamp on de envelope's
> Gwine to put me in debt.

> I was just about to swallow
> A good meal yestiday

When de garbage man come and
Took de can away.

ADA: (*Cross and sleepy, within cabin.*) Buster what you doin makin all that racket so early this mornin and you know I'm sick?

BUSTER: Woman, I'm hongry. (*He opens the door and stands stretching in the rising sunlight.*)

ADA: You know we' ain't got nary scrap in de pot.

BUSTER: (*Joking*) Damn? That ain't no way for a Christian woman to talk. Wasn't you prayin last night fo' the Lawd to send some manna down?

ADA: Don't you make fun o' me, man! De Lawd will send somethin down if he intend for us to win this strike. Uh, I sho' feels bad.

(*Buster picks up a cook pot and starts off left. He stops before the next cabin door and knocks on it with the cook pot.*)

SHORTY: (*From within cabin*) What the hell you want?

BUSTER: (*Cracking open the door and peeping in*) Looky yonder! All you single-men's bachelors ain't up yet? Shorty, throw me out a cigarette.

SHORTY: (*Throwing a cigarette through the door*) Here, mug.

MACK: (*Inside cabin*) What time is it, Shorty?

BUSTER: Time you was workin, if you wasn't strikin. How was de meetin last night?

MACK: Swell, it lasted all night.

BUSTER: Um-m-huh! (*He starts off left, lighting the cigarette with his head down. He bumps into Frankie Mae, who enters carrying a blanket.*) 'Cuse me!

FRANKIE MAE: (*slightly embarrassed*) O, goodmornin, Mis' Dobbs.

MARTY: (*Chewing on her snuff stick*) Sleepin out?

FRANKIE MAE: I just can't stand them crowded cabins, Mis' Dobbs.

MARTY: (*sarcastically*) So you picks up your bed and walks.

FRANKIE MAE: (*Coyly*) I'm a outdoor girl, Mis' Dobbs.

(*Sam comes in, left after Frankie Mae, and starts to enter the cabin occupied by Mack and Shorty. He sees Marty and looks guilty.*)

MARTY: I reckon Sam's a outdoor boy, too. (*She splits, and passes on. Exit Frankie Mae as Sam goes into the cabin. By now several doors have opened and people are stirring in the dusty yard. A man passes with an armful of brushwood. Another goes toward the field with a piece of newspaper. The feet under the hovel of sacking and boards stir. Somewhere a baby cries. A boy whistles. Inside the curtained Ford, Dan and Ella begin to take down the canvas that has sheltered them for the night.*)

MARTY: (*Continuing her walk, speaks to Ada who is standing in the door-way pulling a comb through her hair.*) Howdy.

ADA: Right po'ly, Mis' Dobbs. How're you?

MARTY: I would feel better if I knowed how this strike was gonna turn out.

ADA: So would I. You reckon de Lawd ever meant for po' folks to go around kickin up trouble sich as this, Mis' Dobbs? I declare to Jesus, I don't believe He did.

MARTY: Now, talkin 'bout the Lord, I ain't bringin Him into this a-tall, 'cause I don't believe He's got nothin to do with raisin wages and buildin out-houses. That's man's business.

ADA: Well, He's carried me through to where I am today, bless Gawd!

MARTY: (*calmly*) But where is you? (*She passes on*)

ROSITA: (*Waddling in from the left with her Millie and Roy across the stage. At right another Mexican worker, Manuel, enters.*) Buenos Dias, senor.

(Meanwhile Marty has approached the cabin occupied by Mack, Shorty, and Sam)

MARTY: You Mack, when you gonna start the picket line. Why don't you'all get up from there and put on you' pants. Shorty, too.

MACK: Yes, Mrs. Dobbs. Comin' out. We just got an hour's sleep.

(Charlie returns with the water and enters his cabin)

MARTY: *(Mounting the steps of Mack's cabin)* You know you the head o' this here ranch local. And if I'm gonna follow you, I want you to act like you the head and get things started to goin. *(She stands in door of cabin. With sudden belligerence she addresses her nephew within.)* You Sam, look at me, sir! Layin out all night with hussies! You a grown man with a half-grown child. You ought to be shame o' yoreself. *(She stares at him fiercely)* Don't say nary word to me. Shorty and Mack, you-all come and get you' breakfast. I reckon I can feed you both today, cause I don't want no hongry organizers.

SAM: *(Meekly)* I'm comin', too. Aunt Marty.

MARTY: *(Leaving the cabin)* You can got eat with Frankie Mae. *(muttering)* if she's got any victuals. *(Bud returns carrying an empty water bucket. He calls to his Aunt who is still talking with Juanita.)*

BUD: Aunt Marty! Hey, Aunt Marty!

MARTY: Stop that yellin at me way cross the yard.

BUD: They wouldn't let me have no water at the pump. The foreman says when we go back to work, we get pump water. When we don't work to hell with us.

(Mack and Shorty have emerged from their cabin. Shorty is tucking his shirt tail in.)

MARTY: Lord-a-mercy me!

MACK: So they're pullin' that on us, heh?

SHORTY: Damn 'em, I'll go up there and take the pump. *(Several others gather around to hear about the denial of the water)*

BUD: Not a drap. They was lots o' men up yonder round the pump, and more of 'em on up by the ranch house. Looked like cops to me. And I was scared, too.

SHORTY: *(Kidding Bud)* Could they chew nails?

MARTY: *(shortly)* No, and neither can you drink plain coffee beans. You and Bud go and git a bucket full o' that ditch water then, an hurry up so's the mud can settle, cause I ain't fitten to fight cops nor nobody else till I get some coffee in me this mornin.

FRANKIE MAE: You sure are right, Mis' Dobbs. A body don't feel good in the mornings till they had their java.

MARTY: *(sharply)* You was up so early, you should-a had yours.

(Sam has emerged from cabin and sits drooping on the steps. Frankie Mae strolls over to him. Rosita and her children return carrying twigs and bits of firewood they have gathered. The little girl looks ill and is holding her stomach.)

ROSITA: *(In friendly manner)* Buenos Dias, Buenos Dias.

MACK: Say, Mrs. Rodriguez, where's Jose?

ROSITA: He be here soon. I send him commissary buy ten cents corn meal. Make plenty all-day tortillas.

MACK: You tell him and Domingo, by and by me go out picket line.

ROSITA: Pick 'em time? What time?

MACK: No, pick-et line. You know, keep scabs out of fields. You tell him, PICKET LINE. He understands.

ROY: I know, mama.

ROSITA: Pickum line. OK, I tell him.

ROY: (*Correcting his mother in good English*) Picket line.

(*Rosita, Roy and Millie exit. Shorty and Bud come back with the bucket of muddy water and cross the stage.*)

MACK: (*To one of the men standing near him.*) Say, Shag, you go around and see how many's got gas, and how many they can carry in their cars out to the picket line, will you? We gotta circle all the ranches in this region. Ten, fifteen miles, maybe. And if they ain't walked out over at Peterson's or Wardman's we gotta go pull 'em out. We gotta persuade 'em.

SAM: (*Rising and leaving Frankie Mae*) I'm gonna try.

(*Millie is seen running through the cabins toward the fields whimpering with a piece of newspaper in her hand*)

FRANKIE MAE: That child's got the "trots."

MACK: Dysentery?

FRANKIE MAE: Something like that. Cholera, or something.

MACK: There's four or five kids sick here. Can't help but be, drinkin muddy water and using open privies and eatin with the flies for company.

FRANKIE MAE: Quit your kidding, Shag! Mack, honey, can I ride in the Buick?

MACK: (*absent minded*) I guess so. Come on, Sam, lets eat. (*exits*)

ADA: (*Looking after Frankie Mae*) She sho is a red hot mama, but Mis' Dobbs got her water on.

BUSTER: That Mack's a right nice guy, though, ain't he?

ADA: I don't know. I ain't never seed no white folks I thought was right nice. All they wants you in de union for is to strike and git yo' haid broke, and then they'll put you out.

BUSTER: Aw, Ada, you don't know . . .

(A loud burst of Mexican voices at right behind the cabins. Charlie and Ada rush out.)

VOICES: Que tu dices, hombre? You no voy niguna parte. Donde esta mi machete? Ay, dice! Qu cabronazo!

(Followed by men, women, and children, Jose enters, right, from behind the cabins and goes toward the hut in which Mack and Shorty slept.)

JOSE: (calling) Mack! Hey, Mack!

BUSTER: What's the matter now?

(From tents and cars the men and women tumble out)

JOSE: (excitedly) Mr. Tilden gonna put everybody off ranch right now.

BUSTER: Huh?

JOSE: (Seeing the door open and the cabin empty) Where's Mack?

MACK: (voice some distance away, right) Yal?

WOMAN: I told you they would put us out o' their damn cabins.

MAN: Well, they can't put me out 'cause I'm sleepin on the ground as it is.

CHARLIE: They can sho move you off the ground though.

JOSE: Plenty deputies, plenty foremen all around cross-roads.

(Mack and Shorty enter on the run, followed later by Sam, Marty, Frankie Mae, Adam, and Bud. There is general confusion and talking)

MACK: What's up, kid?

JOSE: (breathless) I go down commissary. Commissary closed up. Cops all around. One man say to me, work. I say, no, strike. He say, shut up your mouth or I take you off to jail. He give me one push with gun and say, get your traps out o' them cabins. I say, where am I gonna sleep? He say, I'm coming up there and clear everybody out in a minute.

JUANITA: *(crying)* Av, Jesus mio!

SHORTY: So that's their game!

MANUEL: I got one good gun.

PANCHO: I got a plenty sharp corn knife.

MACK: Shut up and listen. Our strike committee's made plans for an emergency like this. What we gonna do is go into a camp of our own. But I gotta find out where. Jennie and Joe Richards suggested trying to get that big strip of empty land near Culver that belongs to Roy Williamson. I'll find out today if we got it.

MARTY: Somebody find out now.

MACK: I mean now, right away. I'll go. Jose, you help get the picket line off. *(To the crowd)* Now, listen, you know the orders. No weapons. Understand? We don't want nobody locked up. Sure, the ranchers got guns. But that's different. They'll be looking for chances to arrest us, don't give 'em that chance. I'll be back. Come on, Manuel. *(He and young Mexican exit through the crowd.)*

ADAM: I heard they gonna bring scabs in from Texas.

SHORTY: We ought to keep scabs out.

JOSE: You right, Shorty.

ROSITA: *(Sitting on the ground holding Millie and the baby.)* This child so sick.

ADA: Me, too.

MARTY: Maybe you both needs a good dose o' castor oil.

ROSITA: Yes, ma'm.

MARTY: (*Garrulously*) But now you take little Bud, he's a right delicate child. His pa don't take no care o' him. Sam's too damn lazy to take care o' his self.

BUSTER: Do he belong to our union, Mis' Dobbs?

MARTY: No, Sam don't belong to nothin but the Sons o' Rest.

BUD: (*Running into Marty and Adam*) Aunt Marty, the men's done come and start to throwin your bed clothes out o' the house.

ADAM: Well, goddamn!

ADA: (*Coming out in the middle of the yard with her poker and pointing toward the disturbance off stage.*) Buster, you see that? (*Standing staunchly with the poker*) Lawd, and me sick!

(*By now a number of persons have come into center of yard and are looking toward the racket off stage that is becoming louder and louder. The voices of the deputies commanding the cotton pickets to vacate can be clearly heard.*)

VOICES: (*Deputies, off stage*) Orders're orders. Move on, and move quick. Work or get out. You dumb greasers. Three days notice? Ha, ha, ha, haw! Take that tent.

ADA: Lawd! Lawd! Lawd!

(*Entering right, a rancher deputy walks towards the cabins.*)

DEPUTY: You pickers get out. Come on, get a move on.

BUSTER: What's the big idea?

(*Those evicted farther down begin to move across the stage toward the roadway. Several deputies and the ranch foreman now come onto the scene. Marty, Ada, Shorty, and Bud carrying various belongings move into sight.*)

FOREMAN: Orders are everybody clear out. (*As nobody says anything*) Clear out! Understand?

MEXICAN: *(stolidly)* But we on strike.

FOREMAN: *(As the deputies laugh)* Strike! You can't strike. You can quit, but you can't strike.

SHORTY: *(Putting down his bundle of bedding.)* Is that so?

MARTY: *(Standing beside her bundles, to Bud.)* Where is Sam, that good for nothing pappy o' your'n?

BUD: *(Half-crying)* I don't know.

DEPUTY: Folks, get a move on. Vamanos. Scat. *(He begins to move among the crowd with a club which he carries.)*

FOREMAN: And you who go, don't need to come back to this ranch any more.

BUSTER: Who gonna pick yo' cotton?

FOREMAN: Don't you worry. You just take your black bottom on down the road.

(Some folks have begun to pack up and move. A pregnant woman wanders about calling Manuel. From now on until the end of the scene, there is a constant stream of people leaving the grounds, crossing the stage right to left with their few belongings, some with babies in arms, some with a lean dog or a kitten, a child with a baseball bat, a Mexican with a guitar, etc. Through all this Rosita sits calmly on the ground holding Millie and the baby, and Roy leans at her side.)

FRANKIE MAE: *(Strolling by in a red dress and a wide floppy white hat, and carrying a worn beauty case.)* Who's got room in their car for a lady?

JOSE: *(Entering left, out of breath, calling)* Mama, mamacita! Where is mama? *(He sees her sitting in the dust with the children)*

ROSITA: Aqui estamos.

JOSE: *(Running to his mother and embracing her. Helping her to rise, speaking in a flood of Spanish)* Mama, tenemos que ir. Donde esta papa?

ROSITA: (*calmly*) You make pickum lime? (*Millie begins to cry*)

JOSE: You go to car, mama. I find papacito. (*He exits right asking everyone*) Where is Domingo? Domingo esta Domingo? (*Rosita and the children exit left, Millie clinging to her mother and sobbing.*)

DEPUTY: Come on, what's holding you? Pick up. Gwan.

FOREMAN: (*To a Mexican who is arguing heatedly with him*) Now you boys don't start trouble.

SHAG: The laws says three days notice.

DEPUTY: (*Approaching belligerently with gun bared*) Get on!

(*Shorty enters left. Calls to Marty*)

SHORTY: Come on, ma. (*He is helping her with their bundles when there is a great commotion in the doorway of Charlie's cabin. A deputy is attempting to put them out. Ada and the deputy struggle through the door and down the steps, Ada fighting like a fiend. Suddenly she breaks away and stands in the center of the stage holding her poker aloft.*)

ADA: (*To the sweating deputy*) Don't you tech me, white man! Don't you lay your hands on me!

DEPUTY: (*making a lunge for the enraged woman*) I told you to get out. (*The deputy attempts to grab Ada and receives a sound wack on the head with the poker*) Aw-oooo!!!!!

ADA: I told you not to fool with me!

FOREMAN: (*Coming to aid of the deputy*) I'll attend to you. (*He grabs Ada from behind, but Shorty comes to the rescue even before Charlie*)

SHORTY: (*Flinging back the Foreman*) You keep your hands off.

ADA: (*Spitting like a cat*) You . . . ! You . . . ! You . . . !

(*There is a protective murmur from the crowd as the deputy and the foreman withdraw thwarted.*)

MARTY: You Shorty! Come on here. I'll pick you up dead yet, stopping to fight over niggers.

SHORTY: They belong to the union, ma.

BUSTER: *(To Ada)* You see, I tole you, Ada, some white folks's alright. *(Ada still glares about her with poker raised)* Now you put that poker up and come on let's leave here.

(Buster picks up their suit case from the cabin door and they start out right. As she exits, Ada flings back a last word at the Deputy. The deputy glares after them as they exit. In the doorway of one cabin several Mexicans laugh loudly at the scene. The deputy and the foreman turn on them from the house.)

DEPUTY: You greasers make yourselves scarce quick. Gwan, Git.

FOREMAN: If you want these lousy clothes *(throwing a bundle into the yard)* pick 'em up and beat it.

DEPUTY: You black Indian-looking bastards. Get out. Get. *(He pushes them and their belongings from the yard. They struggle. Someone throws a heavy tin can. General pandemonium breaks out. There is cursing and struggling all over the stage. General cries)*

VOICES: Get the hell out. Help! Help! Swat him on, Ken! Move, you bastards. Don't hit that woman. O-ooo-ooo-oo-o?! Hit him, Bill. Stop! Stop!

·*(Pancho, under arrest, enters right with two deputies, his head bloody. He has apparently been fighting with them, refusing to be evicted. Juanita rushes at the deputies, crying. She is flung back hard against the wall of a cabin, and stands there faint, her hands over her pregnant belly.)*

JUANITA: *(As the deputies continue across stage with her father)* O, my baby! *(She falls to the ground, weeping hysterically, but in a few moments, rises and rushes after her father and the deputies who exit left, crying)* Adone va con mi papa? *(Exits.)*

(At right, Mr. Tilden, the ranch owner, enters in a business suit and a wide Stetson hat.)

TILDEN: Say! Say! (*Loud voice*) What's the matter here? Can't you men handle things any better than this? All this commotion to evict a few strikers? (*There is silence. The remaining persons exit or step aside revealing to Mr. Tilden the old Ford in which Dan and his wife live, and before which they are standing now, in an attitude of defiance.*)

FOREMAN: Mr. Tilden, this man won't move this car off your property.

TILDEN: (*without ceremony*) Turn the car over boys, if they don't want to move it.

FOREMAN: That got 'em, Mr. Tilden.

TILDEN: I've dealt with 'em before in the I.W.W. days. They ain't got nothing. Just a lot of goddam tramps, that's all. Day after tomorrow, they'll be back here, or a hundred more just like 'em, ready and willing to work for what I want to pay. (*He mops his brow and looks about. The whole place is cleared of people, save one man, Luther sitting barefooted in front of his lean-to of boards and sacking*)

TILDEN: (*To deputies*) Who's that?

FOREMAN: He's alright. He'll work.

LUTHER: (*rising meekly*) You know me, Mr. Tilden.

TILDEN: (*Recognizing an old scab*) Oh! (*Turns his back on Luther and walks away, but stops suddenly and calls to him*) Say, come here. Listen! You go on strike, too, see? Get with the rest of them-------. Hang around that union office of theirs in Purtley, go to the meetings, and come back here every night and tell me what's going on. I'll pay you as usual.

LUTHER: (*Grinning obsequiously*) Yes, sir, Mr. Tilden. I sure will. (*He returns to his lean-to and puts on his shoes, sitting on the ground*)

FOREMAN: We threw 'em out on their cans, alright. (*As they walk toward the right, he picks up a baby's cap that has been lost in the exodus. He stops and looks around*) Well, here's plenty of empty cabins now, a lot o' cotton—and one goddamn scab! (*He handles the baby cap, holding it up ap-*

praisingly) Say, maybe my kid could wear this. (*They exit right as the curtain falls*)

ACT 2

(*Camp Culver. Late afternoon. This scene has the most elaborate setting. A barbed wire fence runs across the front, at the proscenium line. Tents, lean-to shelters, etc., on lower and upper levels. Camp kitchen, long table of two-by-fours resting on a clothes horse and some boxes, with bench above it and upended boxes below it, to sit on. A typewriter and some papers at the upper end. Cook, John Viza, Shorty, and Jasper at lower end, idling. Marty and Miss Prather visible in Domingo's tent, with the sick Rosita.*)

COOK: You fellers don't need to come here lookin for no breakfast tomorrow cause there ain't gonna be none—less they bring some relief or other in here soon.

JASPER: Just you keep the fires burning, Cook. The Lord will provide for his lambs. (*Cut the Cook's next line, as Jasper's gets a laugh, and the Cook's is not strong enough to force a second laugh*)

(*Marty comes out of the tent, crosses to the table*)

MARTY: Can I have some hot water, Cookie? (*He gets it*) It's a shame we got no permit yit to get Rosita in a hospital.

SHORTY: Just cause she's a striker! How is she, Marty?

MARTY: Worse. (*Takes water, returns to tent*)

(*Enter Rollins—reporter—R*)

JASPER: (*Primping*) You come to take our pictures?

COOK: What's goin on down yonder at the gate? Who're they keepin out now?

ROLLINS: The guys standing guard say they got orders from Jennie to let in the arbitrators. And the health officials have just started around inspecting.

SHORTY: (*Grinning*) You better clean up this joint, Cookie.

COOK: I ain't got nothin to clean up. These pots been licked clean long ago.

SHORTY: Inspectors never come around inspectin any growers' camps I ever worked in. They want to close us up, that's all.

ROLLINS: Tilden's got 25 scabs pickin on his ranch. Got them off the bread line in Los Angeles.

COOK: Hell, city stiffs can't pick cotton. Get all the bread lines and put them in the fields, if they ain't used to pickin cotton they can't pick it.

(*Enter Health Officer Meyers, and King, R., with Mack.*)

MEYERS: There have been many complaints that your sewage system is unsatisfactory. The piping is insufficient, and the dirty water is spilled out on the ground.

MACK: No, there isn't much piping. We've been doing just about like the pickers are used to in the growers' camps.

MEYERS: We are here to determine whether the camp constitutes a public nuisance. (*Meyers speaks to the cook, inspects the kitchen arrangements meticulously, tut-tutting at the makeshifts*)

(*ENTER Jennie and Professor Bankley, L*)

MACK: (*To King, whom he otherwise almost ignores; jerking his head*) Union secretary. You wanted to see her? (*Remains near table, watching Meyers.*)

KING: (*Crossing to Jennie*) Well, well, and so this is the little lady I have been hearing so much about? I am so very glad to meet you in person, my dear little Miss Martin! My name is King; I have flown out from Washington to act as Arbitrator in—

JENNIE: Good afternoon. (*She refuses to shake hands*) I am sorry. We know your record in the East.

MACK: *(Under his breath)* Strikebreaker!

JENNIE: We should like you to know, Mr. King, before you start your investigating, that our men are sore. Police and thugs are persecuting us at every turn. They have arrested hundreds of strikers. And now the health department is looking for a chance to break up our camp—and we have nowhere else to go.

KING: That does sound like a list of calamities, doesn't it? We shall have to look into them all. I want you to know that we are here to help you, to listen to you. It is to all our interest to settle the difficulty in this valley. We will give both sides a fair hearing—there is right and wrong on both sides. This strike will end in peace.

BANKLEY: How do you do, Mr. King? I am Professor Bankley, of State University. I have been trying to tell this fiery little lady myself that there are two sides to every question.

KING: Glad to meet you, Professor.

JENNIE: Isn't your first suggestion going to be for the men to go back to work, pending arbitration? To break the strike first, and then arbitrate in the growers' favor.

(King says something superior and pacific, insists upon going through the camp without a striker guide, and joins the health officer, who is ready to go on.)

SHORTY: Just a minute, Doctor. You see this fellow's head here? He couldn't get treated at Purtley Hospital. Nor that woman in there *(indicates tent)* couldn't. They won't take strikers.

MEYERS: Why the hospital's pretty well taxed, I believe. It's small—it's run for the benefit of residents of the country. Outsiders pay. *(This line is given to a cop, as written; but a cop would not be admitted to the camp, surely?)*

JOHN VIZA: They told me if I went back to work, they fix me up.

MEYERS: Then you'd be able to pay, wouldn't you?

(Exit Meyers, King, L. Shorty spits contemptuously)

MACK: Shorty, how come you aren't out hustlin some relief food from the farmers?

SHORTY: Out o' gas.

(Mack leans against the table, depressed. He rarely sits down)

BANKLEY: But I did want to ask you this, Miss Martin. Do you think—was this exactly a wise time to strike? Can the farmers pay higher wages? They have so many costs to meet, which are constantly going up—and they have rent, mortgages—so many costs to meet, which are constantly going up—.

JENNIE: They must strike too, against the banks and the power companies. A lot of farmers are organizing. We're helping all the small farmers in this valley to form a union too.

(ROLLINS strolls across to them)

ROLLINS: 'Morning, Jennie. What's the latest on the strike front?

JENNIE: Oh, what's the use of giving you anything? You don't put it in the paper as we give it to you. Last Thursday in that story of the evictions you wrote it as if the strikers started the rioting.

(Bankley occupies himself with a child who is curious)

ROLLINS: I give you my word, Miss Jennie, I wrote it as Mack told me. But the city desk changed it. They always do. Standing orders.

JENNIE: Then why don't you give up working for a lousy sheet like the Herald? You ought to be ashamed of yourself.

ROLLINS: Would you give me a job here at twenty a week? I'd work for you, kid.

JENNIE: You'd want your twenty bucks. No one here has had a cent in wages since the strike began. We can't collect enough for the picket lines.

Five picket trucks didn't go out this morning—they can't go out because they haven't any gas and oil. Why don't you go down and hustle us some?

ROLLINS: OK, kid. Will you have supper with me tonight?

JENNIE: If you'll drive me to Buttonwillow afterward. I have a meeting there tonight. (*He asks her about posing some pictures; children for choice, and the office wants more of her because of her looks; disgusted, she expresses herself briefly on the subject of singling out individuals. Rollins retires to the background. He does not exit. All the opponent forces gradually collect from this point on*)

(*Enter Jose in a hurry*)

JOSE: Mack—they take my truck!

JENNIE: What—!

MACK: The relief truck?

STRIKERS: Jesus Maria! What a dirty trick! How we gonna eat now?

JOSE: (*ashamed*) I tell the cops they cannot take food, it is relief for our companeros. I stay in my truck . . . (*Pauses. Jennie and Bankley cross to the table*) They pull me out my seat. (*To Jennie*) Companera, they say we use the truck for picketing. They pull me out.

JENNIE: And the food?

JOSE: They throw it all in road. Spill sacks of flour and sugar all over. (*He adds news of arrests, which Rollins supplements by bail figures*)

BANKLEY: I am convinced, Miss Martin, from what I have seen here, that the ranchers are adding gunpowder to the situation. And the police seem to encourage them. I understand now what you mean by your phrase, "lawless law." The official brutality against your pickets is outrageous, for picketing is not a crime. I shall try to make that clear to my students.

JENNIE: You will send a protest to the governor?

BANKLEY: My connections with the state university—it's a little difficult—

MACK: Well, will you help us raise bail?

BANKLEY: I wish I could do something. Think of putting a little Mexican boy under ten thousand dollars bail. It's outrageous. I will impress upon my students how our courts abuse the rights of citizens.

MACK: Of workers, Mr. Bankley. This is a class war.

BANKLEY: I would hardly say that. Can't we all solve it together? We should work toward cooperation, don't you think? It must not be a war, must it?

JENNIE: They make it a war, not we. We aren't armed.

(ENTER Miss Prather, L.)

PRATHER: Oh, good morning, Miss Martin. What good luck to find you. I want to speak to you about the relief situation. I am giving relief to families now, but we have some trouble.

JENNIE: Yes? Our people haven't been getting much government relief.

PRATHER: That's just it. We have to have certain information and your families seem suspicious of giving it. But there is nothing to it at all. We always ask for the license numbers of automobiles, and we have to have the nationality of the recipient, of course, just as we have to have their birth and marriage certificates, name of their father and mother's father and last address.

JENNIE: We gave orders that the strikers should not give their license numbers or nationality.

PRATHER: But why? We are here to help you, we are here to bring government relief to your families.

JENNIE: We know just how the information you get is used. The car numbers are a black-list. If the owners are Mexicans you deport them.

PRATHER: But we take no part in political questions, no sides—

JENNIE: If the state authorities ask for your lists you give them to them.

PRATHER: Would you have us hinder the Administration?

JENNIE: I'm afraid I'm very busy this afternoon. I'd appreciate it if you'd take this up with one of the boys.

PRATHER: Really! When all one wants to do is to help—

MACK: Well, Miss, our people haven't been getting relief.,

PRATHER: Do you expect us to get around quicker than we do in this heat? I am worked off my feet as it is—but one can't expect gratitude.

ROLLINS: How many relief workers are there?

PRATHER: Two, and we work all day.

MACK: Two relief workers for fourteen thousand strikers and their families—on a strike front of two hundred miles! And your paper says Federal relief is being distributed to all the strikers—and kicks about it.

(Re-enter Meyers and King, trailed by a group of curious strikers, including Frankie Mae)

MEYERS: Miss Martin, we have completed our tour, and I can certify this camp is not at present a danger to health. Of course, at any moment matters may come to a head—that is conditions may alter. (Earnestly) I do advise you to tell these women not to empty their dish water on the ground.

PRATHER: Oh, how do you do, Mr. King? May I have a few words with you? I have a most regrettable situation to discuss. I must tell you about the relief situation—

KING: Isn't that Mr. Hopkinson's province?

PRATHER: These people simply will not take our milk—we have hundreds of gallons here spoiling—good milk from the United States government and they won't take it! You know how misled and ignorant these people are—Well, they are afraid if they take government milk they will have to go back to work. They are quite misinformed—

KING: Who told them that?

PRATHER: Oh, I assure you, Mr. King, no one, they are just naturally suspicious, they don't understand the laws of this country. I've explained to them so patiently—

KING: Have you explained to Miss Martin?

PRATHER: We are told to keep government relief quite separate from the relief being collected by these people—there's quite a good deal of complaint from the farmers that we're feeding them at all—and then of course, as you know, we do not mix in controversial questions—

MACK: No milk at all at Delano. Babies drinkin coffee and tea.

PRATHER: Oh, oh, I don't mean they didn't want the milk. It was a sight, those poor babies standing around with crying babies, and this beautiful rich milk provided by the Government of the United States specially—

SHORTY: Specially laid by Uncle Sam's cows.

PRATHER: They have some idea—some misconception—

MACK: The government relief workers demand that we sign a paper to go back pending arbitration, if we are to have the milk. That's why we don't take it. (Mack walks away. Enter Sheriff, Williamson, and Mexican Consul, R.)

JENNIE: Hello, Mr. Williamson.

WILLIAMSON: Miss, could I speak to you a moment?

JENNIE: Why yes. (To Mexican Consul) You were refused entrance. How did you get in?

CONSUL: With the sheriff. I come to speak to my fellow Mexicans, why not?

JENNIE: You have been trying to separate the white and the Mexican comrades. You urge the Mexicans to go back to work and break the strike.

CONSUL: I do only what my government demands me to. I tell the Mexicans . . .

SHERIFF: *(To Mack)* You-all have to leave here. *(Hands him paper)*

MACK: *(Reading aloud slowly)* It says this camp is a menace to the health of the community and must be evacuated by nightfall tomorrow. Signed, Board of Supervisors, Culver County.

JENNIE: The Health Officer has just pronounced the camp healthy.

WILLIAMSON: But that paper says I am personally responsible for maintaining a public nuisance. It's addressed to me as owner of the land. I don't want you to have to leave, but—

JENNIE: Well, Mr. Health Officer?

MEYERS: I was merely expressing my private opinion. Sanitary arrangements are in a very bad condition. The sewage system is inadequate. Yes, it will be a public safeguard to have the camp evacuated. *(General stir)*

BANKLEY: But, Dr. Meyers, you just said—

SHORTY: The dirty sons!

JENNIE: Comrades; we must get into action. Protest delegation to the Board of supervisors—a mass delegation. Redouble picketing. *(The crowd is growing. The light is dimming—it is after sunset)*

SHERIFF: Anybody starts a riot'll be run in. Get back! Move on, now, move on.

(Luther is visible on the outskirts of the crowd, DC. He runs off R.—throwing a brick just as he disappears. The sheriff blows his whistle. Two policemen rush in.)

SHERIFF: *(Pointing at Shorty.)* I know you—jailbreaker! Arrest that man.

SHORTY: Hey, comrades, don't let them arrest us.

MACK: Defense squad, forward! *(The strikers make a wall around Shorty; he disappears in their midst. The visitors back downstage and stand against the barbed wire, back to audience.)*

SHERIFF: Well—I guess we scared 'em. Come on, boys. *(Sheriff offers protection to the visitors, who leave with him. Frankie Mae has been making up to the Consul, and makes a date with him; he is thus the last to go)*

MACK: *(mutters)* Diseased offshoots of capitalism . . . tolerance—*(to Frankie Mae)* but there are limits. That consul's a class enemy.

FRANKIE MAE: Boring from within, comrade! *(She goes upstage)* That means five bucks worth of gas for the picket trucks.

(Mack, Jennie, Shorty, Jose, John, Marty gather at the table to plan the strikers' resistance to eviction.)

FRANKIE MAE: *(reads paper)* "What has she got that I ain't got?"

MACK: We ain't goin. We can't go, we got nowhere to go to. So we've gotta figure how we can stay here.

(They plan a mass meeting in Purtley; they set guards. Jose begins to patrol the barbed wire fence. Jennie has a fit of tears, from exhaustion; the rest hearten her roughly, and the comfort of having them there dries her eyes. On the way out she asks after Rosita. Marty goes into the tent. The others go. The cook lies down in an improvised bunk.)

BUSTER: *(In tent at edge of upper level)* Baby, take them dimes out o' your ears and buy some beans.

ADA: I sho' won't. My first husband give me these dimes and I'm gonna wear 'em.

BUSTER: Aw, hell, I'm hongry.

ADA: Stop cussin' or you'll be burnin in hell, an I'll be settin on the front tiers of unclouded glory!

BUSTER: You'll be settin in de po' house, if we don't win dis strike.

(Roy, Millie and Bud wander in at left)

JOSE: Go home, kids. Go to sleep. Andale.

MILLIE: Where's mama?

JOSE: She sick. You go my tent and sleep. *(He leads Roy and Millie off; enter Sam, and Bud runs to him)*

BUD: Pop, where you goin?

SAM: Purtley. *(He reaches into his pocket for a dime.)* Here, buy yourself some bananas.

BUD: Thanks, pop. I'm gonna give it to Aunt Marty.

SAM: Na you don't, I ain't helpin to take care of Shorty and Mack and all these guys. Let em feed themselves.

BUD: Where'd you get so much money, Pop?

SAM: That's all right where I got it.

(Re-enter Jose, patrolling. Sam starts back between the tents for a moment.)

BUD: *(Low voice)* Pop. You ain't against the strike, are you, pop?

SAM: Where'd you get that idea?

BUD: I heard Mack askin about you. And he said if you was against the strike, you was just going against yourself.

SAM: Strikes ain't doin me no good, boy.

BUD: You ain't against the strike, are you, pop?

SAM: *(Savagely)* Shut up, you little bastard. *(He strikes Bud. The boy begins to cry)*

BUD: Pop, you ain't against the strike?

(Exit Sam past Jose. The child disappears in the shadows upstage. A moment's silence, in which Rosita is heard moaning. Jose hears it and shakes his head. Shorty comes in L and lights his cigarette at the stove. He sits down at the cook table.)

SHORTY: How's your ma?

JOSE: She going to die.

SHORTY: Too bad.

JOSE: She think the strike kill her. She was sick before strike—it's work-time, not strike-time, kill her.

SHORTY: Your kid brother's in jail . . . and Shag . . . and Steve. I hope they don't get Jennie or Mack.

JOSE: What for they lock up Jennie? They mustn't.

SHORTY: They'd like to lock us all up. *(Jose paces the length of the wire. Shorty stretches himself on the table)* Pretty old moon, isn't it?

JOSE: Like Mexican moon.

SHORTY: Mexico? What's it like down there?

JOSE: Pretty, kind o' like California. All over mountains and deserts, and moon like this. But plenty poor people, they don't get along so good. We make plenty revolution once. My papa fight with Zapata, try to get land and work. But the generals win—and they kill us. Always, they kill us poor peoples.

SHORTY: It's hell, ain't it? *(A low scream is heard from the tent)*

JOSE: Plenty poor people sleep on ground in Mexico, go hungry, starve. Like here. They fight. They always get beat down.

SHORTY: Hell, ain't it?

JOSE: But someday, maybe we no beat down. Someday, maybe we win.

SHORTY: Yeah. (*Pause*) It's sure tough about your mom.

JOSE: Si. But just as good to die striking as starving.

SHORTY: Yeah. Just as good to die fighting as starving.

(*Curtain*)

ACT 3

Scene 1

(*A lodge room in Purtley. Same night. The Farmers' Protective Association is meeting. There is a raised platform with a rostrum behind which, on the wall, hangs a flag and on either side of it portraits of George Washington and Abraham Lincoln. Benches and cuspidors. In the chairman's chair sits Ed Lowe, a tight-lipped, dried up little man, cruel and powerful in a subtle provocative way. Harry Tilden is also on the platform with a notebook. Several of the growers we have seen before. In the back, a silent observer sits, Sprague, the district attorney. Near him are Tom Rollins and Clem Hogan taking notes for their papers. During the meeting a petition circulates among the crowd. Most of the men sign it readily. As the curtain rises, the grower, Bud Peterson, usurps the platform in the midst of a fiery and demagogic speech. he lifts his arms, bellows. His fat paunch with its gold chain and lodge emblem bounces up and down. His jowls jiggle*)

PETERSON: . . . and in all the years I lived in this state, men, I ain't never seen the time before when a dirty bunch of Mexicans would rare up on their hind legs and defy a white man. (*Wiping the sweat from his face and continuing loudly and hoarsely*) That's what they're doing today in the richest cotton county of this state, gathered out yonder in their Culver Camp, four thousand strong, in league with alien agitators, plotting and planning to tear down our government and that flag up there, (*points behind him*) to ruin our crop, and reduce the good farmers and honest business men of this state to nothing! That's their game! They talk about wanting higher wages! Why, everybody knows a Mexican can live on a dime's worth of beans a day. They talk about wanting their union recognized—(*scornfully*) union—gather in all the greasers and niggers and shiftless bums the alien agitators can collect a nickel from and calling it a union. Recognize, hell! Men, what are we going to do about it? Are we Americans—or not?

VOICES: Yes! Hell, yes. Nobody'll dictate to us. Down with foreign interference. Deport the lot of 'em. Run 'em out.

PETERSON: They talk about suffering. We're the ones that suffer. Look at our cotton busting open, standing unpicked, and who knows when rain will come? Can't get it picked, can't get it ginned. Why? Because a lot of foreign agitators have come down to this valley and got our pickers stirred up. I say, fellow Americans, any self-respecting man would run 'em out of here. (*Again he stops to wipe his brow and catch his breath*)

LOWE: (*Rising*) I think you have well-expressed the sentiment of this meeting, Mr. Peterson. (*Peterson, very pleased with himself, steps down from the platform and stands at the edge of the crowd.*) And don't forget, fellow citizens, we've already voluntarily raised their wages fifty percent over last year! We can't give those people enough, it seems. You see how they abuse any concessions you make. Sixty cents a hundred now. The more rope you give them, the more they take. Wages isn't what they want.

BURTLE: (*interrupting*) Castor oil's what they need. Something to start 'em running.

PETERSON: (*Shows his gun*) This'll start 'em.

FLOORS: What're we waiting for? Why don't we run 'em out of town.

TILDEN: What's the matter with the sheriff?

LOWE: The sheriff has been unable to keep the trucks off the road.

FLOORS: Three of my picking gangs walked off yesterday, scared.

PETERSON: What are we paying taxes for, if that bunch in politics can't even protect our property and keep law and order?

BURTLE: I'm a red-blooded American citizen! My gall rises at the thought of Americans knuckling under to a gang of aliens who should never have come into this country.

HOGAN: Why don't you guys give 'em the bum's rush?

LOWE: Why doesn't the sheriff put them in a bull pen?

LITTLE: Tar and feather's that's better. Why don't we call out the troops?

BURTLE: Hell, we don't need no troops. Ain't we got guns?

FLOORS: Seems to me we left things to officials too long.

WARDMAN: (*rising on the platform*) Look at this sheet I picked up today. (*shows leaflet and reads from it*) It says, "Comrades, force the bosses to give you a living wage. Smash the ginning companies' reign of terror. Defend your rights!"

PETERSON: Who owns this country, yellow livered greasers or us red-blooded Americans?

TILDEN: The agitators don't want higher wages. They're communist. I know it. I went to one of their meetings at Buttonwillow last night, and I heard that Mack Sanders say, "We workers have got to fight our battle united on the whole world front until everything belongs to us."

FLOORS: Lynch the bastards!

PETERSON: Lynchings too good for them. Communists!

LITTLE: Who gives 'em their money?

PETERSON: Moscow!

LOWE: (*using the gavel*) If they win this strike, it means we will have to pay out. Can you afford it? How many of you are behind on your loans now?

LITTLE: I thought we was goin to get lower interest rates this year.

TILDEN: (*suavely*) Certainly, men, the banks could have granted them if there hadn't been this strike.

FLOORS: Them goddamn agitators!

TILDEN: Why should the bankers make all the sacrifices? Has Germany paid us back?

LITTLE: After we fought their war!

BURTLE: Aliens are all the same, fattening off the American farmers. We're just suckers.

FLOORS: (*threatening*) Not I!

OTHERS: Nor I! Me neither! Not me!!

PETERSON: (*At edge of platform*) All right fellows. How're we going to get this viper out of here? Democracy is our watchword. I say we take off our hats to the *flag* for a change, and not stand here and pay tribute to traitors who'd step on that flag and tear it limb for limb. How's for our gettin up fer once and saluting our flag, and telling it: Our Country, we are here! And to the racketeers who stir up strikes and destroy the principles of Liberty and Justice on which our country was founded, let's say to them: You shall not pass. (*wild applause*)

SIMMONS: Why, I'd let my cotton rot in the ground before I'd bow down to them striking bastards.

TILDEN: (*insinuatingly*) Do we want drastic action?

PETERSON: A ten million dollar crop going to waste!

FLOORS: Break that damn strike!

BURTLE: Why don't we stop the picket line from going out?

FLOORS: We should clean out their hall.

LOWE: (*using gavel*) And our government pampering them with tons of food; They're living better than you or me. Have you gentlemen seen the truck-loads of delicacies that come to them and that Jennie Martin, she sweethearts with the whole bunch, greasers and all. That's how she gets her hold on them! Our daughters have to live in the same town with that—, It's time we got our country cleaned up.

BURTLE: That little—!

LOWE: Gentlemen, is the petition fully signed? Is so, pass it up front.

LITTLE: (*Rising slowly holding the petition.*) It says here, "eliminate the leaders." Ain't that word kinder strong?

PETERSON: (*snorting*) Huh!

FLOORS: What do you want? Take 'em out on velvet carpets?

LOWE: We mean to get rid of them, Milt.

LITTLE: But couldn't they be locked up? Bloodshed never gits you nowhere.

BURTLE: (*Pointing at Turner*) Put that bastard out if he don't want to act like an American!

LITTLE: I'm as American as any here, gentlemen. Our government wasn't founded on force and bloodshed, and violence don't get you nowhere.

(*He is howled down. Lowe pounds with gavel. Wardman rises*)

TILDEN: You needn't sign it, Milt.

FARMER: Maybe there's something to what Milt says. (*Again howls of protest*)

PETERSON: (*booming*) Let's have that petition! Who else here wants to side with agitators? (*Silence*) Nobody? Well, then . . . (*He hands the petition to Lowe*) We'll handle this uprising from now on.

VOICES: Yes, sir! You tell 'em Bud!

(*The Sheriff enters followed by Luther who remains at the back of the room*)

BURTLE: Well, look who's here!

TILDEN: Come up front, Sheriff and tell how you're handling things.

SHERIFF: I haven't got a one of them ring-leaders yet. Can't get my hands on 'em.

FLOORS: You should of had 'em long ago.

SHERIFF: But I've asked the City Council for two hundred more riot guns.

BURTLE: Asked for 'em! Why ain't you got 'em?

SHERIFF: The Supervisors have ordered the camp closed by Monday.

FLOORS: Who's gonna close it?

PETERSON: We'll run 'em out, boys.

SHERIFF: I'd rather you'd let the police handle it. (*General mocking laughter*)

BURTLE: You haven't done it.

PETERSON: Suppose we took on the job, Sheriff? (*Sees Sprague*) There's the District Attorney back there. How about it, Sprague?

SPRAGUE: (*A good politician*) Well, we wouldn't have to see you.

VOICES: That's the spirit! Smart man! It's OK now.

SHERIFF: I'd like to say, if you gentlemen will let me, I think it's better to do it legally.

VOICES: Ah you! You let em get away with murder! You never arrested a mouse yet! You can't get yer cops to pinch a cow!

SHERIFF: I arrested every man that broke the law! The jail is full!

BURTLE: They need more'n arresting.

PETERSON: What's the law for? To protect us and our property, or any alien radical that chooses to come in here?

TILDEN: Why don't you arrest that tin Madonna Jennie Martin?

VOICES: Vote him out! Get rid of him! You'll never get re-elected!

FLOORS: We're running our own business from now on.

SHERIFF: *(Very pale)* All right, gentlemen. You do it your way. I'll say nothing. You are all citizens and voters. Certainly, that's what I'm here for—to do what you want done—if I can.

SPRAGUE: Most of you men are deputized. Those responsible ranchers who are not, see me tomorrow and I'll swear you in.

PETERSON: That's the spirit, boys! *(Loud approval from the assembly)*

LOWE: *(Using gavel)* Let us bring matters to a close. The statement has been signed by all here but one or two. They don't matter. *(Reading)* "We agree, we farmers met here tonight in the duly organized Farmers' Protective Association, to take the law into our own hands and eliminate the agitators from our fields and from the entire San Vincenze Valley." *(Puts paper down)*

BURTLE: Deputized or not, we're going to uphold the law, and put a little patriotism and loyalty into this community. *(Loud applause.)*

Scene 2

(Street and sidewalk of the Union Headquarters at Purtley. Saturday afternoon. On the windows of the old store front that serves as Jennie's office are several strike notices and placards. On the door a dirty piece of cardboard: STRIKE HEADQUARTERS (with the S back to front) and below the same in Spanish: OFFICINA DE LA HUELGA. Over the door there is an American flag. The office is in the middle of the block, and on either side may be seen the windows of a cheap hot dog stand and a grain and feed store. During the action a few passers-by, pass on the sidewalk. Two housewives pass with their marketing.)

1ST HOUSEWIFE: Those Reds, at it again.

2ND HOUSEWIFE: *(looking back)* But he don't look like no red.

1ST HOUSEWIFE: He's in disguise.

JENNIE: *(Calling as she picks up some scraps of paper from front of sidewalk.)* Juanita, bring out the broom and sweep up the front of this place.

JUANITA: *(Within)* Si, senorita. *(Exit Jennie into headquarters. Juanita emerges and begins to sweep off the sidewalk.)*

ADA: *(entering slowly)* Lawd, chile, I's so sick!

JUANITA: Buenos tarde.

ADA: Wonder is Jennie got any aspirins here. I sho feels bad.

JUANITA: What senora?

ADA: You don't understand American, does you? Un-huh! I's so sick!

JENNIE: *(Coming to door)* Anybody around could mail a letter for me? Oh, hello, Mrs. Walker.

ADA: Goodmornin, Mis' Jen. *(Brightly)* Is you seen Buster?

JENNIE: Not this morning. Guess he's on the picket line. You know we're massing everyone today.

COLLINS: Have you noticed anything funny this afternoon?

JENNIE: No.

COLLINS: Well, I've noticed that the cops are scarce. You don't see 'em about town, do you?

JENNIE: They're probably somewhere drinking.

COLLINS: Well, up at the hall they're saying that the police left town purposely, so the vigilantes can clean up.

JENNIE: (*A little pale*) The cops have never helped us, have they? Don't worry, if anything happens, they'll be right here to throw their tear gas. (*As she speaks, several strikers enter and go into the headquarters.*)

COLLINS: I'm not so sure. A lot of kids and drug-store cowboys walking around today with arms.

A MOTHER: (*Entering with a switch, driving a barefoot boy before her*) I told you not to stay away all day. All them reds in town this afternoon. You stay home.

BOY: (*Whimpering*) Aw, ma, all the other kids is out.

MOTHER: (*Switching his legs*) You listen to me, young man! . . . (*They exit, the boy crying. Off stage, the sound of a guitar is heard*)

ADA: (*Coming to the door and moving her hips to the distant music.*) They comin, Jennie. But, Lawd, I wish they'd let Buster play that guitar! (*pausing*) Say, they gettin out o' the trucks way up the street. Why for?

JENNIE: (*within*) Police orders—no trucks in this block, Ada.

ADA: Um-m! Listen to that music. (*The sound of the guitar and of many voices grow louder. As the Mexicans enter, left, laughing and singing, the stool-pigeon, Luther, shaven and in Sunday clothes, enters at right and stands before the hot-dog stand a half-amused look on his face, later he goes down a runway into audience, and leans against the left wall. The Mexicans stand speaking in Spanish, others go inside the headquarters*)

MEXICANS: Viva la Secretaria! Buenos Tardas, companero! Viva la huelga!

PANCHO: (*To ADA*) You seen my girl?

ADA: She's around. Where's Buster?

PANCHO: (*Going in*) He come.

(*Enter Jasper Waters, Adam, Marty, Shorty, Buster, Rosita, the children and others. Buster carries a placard on a pole reading BLACK AND WHITE UNITE TO FIGHT*)

ADA: Hy, you-all

MARTY: Tired out. I picketed thirty miles today.

BUSTER: *(Picking up one foot after another and holding it.)* The truck did, you mean.

(Enter Manuel)

VOICES: Hello, Manuel! Hello, papa. How's the proud father today.

ADA: Manuel, your wife sho bored you a sweet chile.

MANUEL: Fine baby, heh? I go inside, tell Jennie about him. *(Goes in.)*

(Enter Ella, the cook, and "Doc" Lee)

COOK: All set? Gee, we hurried! Busted my last tire.

PAT: Say, did you hear them Vigilantes was planning to come after us?

BUSTER: What's vigilantes, Ku Klux?

PAT: Same thing.

STEVE: I heard all the legionnaires was getting deppetized.

PAT: Jim Morales said he met two new ones with guns.

STRIKER: What if we do get killed? It's a dog's life, anyway.

SHORTY: Aw, they're all too yellow-bellied to do anything, the cowards.

JASPER: You all is somewhat wrong. My boy Ezekiel, he met Mrs. Jason's hired girl in the drugstore and she heard Mart Burtle say they were going to end this strike today!

SHORTY: *(laughs)* Or they'd know the reason why, eh? They always add that!

COOK: No, they'd teach us a lesson.

JASPER: Maybe some of us'll have to learn things we don't know yet. Dark things are being said hereabouts and I'm prayin.

(Manuel emerges with a box which he sets on the sidewalk in front of the right window.)

SHORTY: Say, pal, that box ain't big enough! Go get a big one, *(spreads his hands apart)* so we can put a chair on it. *(He and Manuel exit within. Enter John Viza)*

JOHN: *(Goes up to Jack)* Comrade, there was a drunken spree at that hotel last night after the farmer's meetin, and Lupe tell me they said they would bust up this meeting here today. Better tell Jennie.

COOK: *(seriously)* Who was there?

JOHN: Lupe said the highway police and Cop Toad Barker and that bunch of growers that hang out round the poolroom here. I hate to worry Jennie, but . . .

SHORTY: Let's get the Defense Corps ready.

JOHN: These men have guns.

DOC LEE: Don't frighten people, Comrade.

(More and more the stage is filling with picketers carrying banners and placards. They examine each other's posters and comment on them. Among them Dan, Frankie Mae, Domingo, Jose, and others. The banners read: DON'T SCAB! SOLIDARITY WINS! NOT AN OUNCE OF COTTON FOR LESS THAN A DOLLAR A HUNDRED! UNITE & FIGHT! ONE BIG UNION!!

BUSTER: *(shouting)* Ada, I thought you was sick?

ADA: You ain't thought I was gonna miss this meetin, did you? Gimme a flag. *(She takes a placard from someone)*

(*Shorty and Manuel emerge carrying the box and a chair which they put in place. Others come out with leaflets and begin distributing them. Strikers keep arriving. Jasper Water mounts the soap box and stands beside the chair.*)

JASPER: Now, folks, we're about to start. If you are not all here, you should-a-been. Time nor tide . . .

COOK: There he goes! Talking again.

JASPER: Now, Miss Jennie'll be out here directly. Meantime, I'll keep yo' spirits movin. Now, this strike has done something for all of us, folks. It's brought us together. And like Daniel was delivered from the lion's den of iniquity, so this strike's due to deliver us from the sinful wiles of them gin-owners, cause by the help of God and mass picket lines, we'll win. But, brothers, and sisters . . .

(*Just then Jennie emerges from Headquarters. A cheer goes up from the crowd which prevents Jasper saying anymore. He dismounts. Jose helps her up on the chair. Jasper tries to get to her to whisper something but too many Mexicans get in between and he is pushed off the box. The strikers are shouting and cheering.*)

STRIKERS: Viva la Secretaria! Viva la Huelga! Hurah! Hurah! Viva la Companero! (*Clapping and shouts. Jennie holds up her hand*)

JENNIE: Comrades and fellow workers . . .

(*Suddenly a brick comes whizzing through the air, thrown by Luther from the audience where the vigilantes are crouched in the aisles. Everybody turns, shouts, curses, and screams. It is the beginning of panic.*)

SHORTY: (*Shouting across the footlights*) The bastards!

(*Another missile follows. The defenseless workers make a dash down the streets in all directions, some into headquarters—others look around for missiles. Someone pulls Jennie down. Dan grabs the chair to use as a weapon. Others begin to rip the box apart and throw the pieces in the direction from which the rocks come. There is short exchange of missiles. And Dan advances toward the approaching vigilantes with the chair upraised. Suddenly there is*) *a shot. Dan grabs his arm. The chair falls. Another shot, and Dan drops mortally wounded. Women scream. Confusion and panic. Satiric laughter from the wings. Gun-fire. The strikers draw together in a surging mass, but now from every direction the guns of the vigilantes bark. The workers try to crowd into union headquarters. Some tumble from the steps. The windows shatter. Ada grabs her shoulder where a bullet has penetrated. Max, holding a piece of box in one hand and leaflets in another, falls scattering the leaflets over the sidewalk. Blood flows)*

ADA: *(shrieking)* Buster, Buster! *(She collapses)*

(Several strikers fall wounded, their banners falling with them. Some attempt to crawl to the door. By now the street is pretty well cleared. A hysterical child runs through the melee. Buster tumbles into the dust holding a placard, the blood streaming down his face and remains motionless. He is dead. Jose runs across the stage)

JOSE: Jennie, Jennie! *(He sees her standing against the brick wall between the headquarters and the shop, a perfect target. He flings himself in front of her. Again shots ring out and Jose falls. Jennie shrieks, falls to her knees, and spreads out her arms in front of Jose. In one second everyone has vanished. Shouts and firing have stopped.)*

JENNIE: Jose! Jose! *(She lifts his head)*

JOSE: *(Dying)* You here, senorita? Listen, listen to me. You hear me? I want tell you—I love you. I love you, Comrade Jennie—like I love the revolution. You understan?

JENNIE: Jose! *(She is crying)* You one of—our best—our best comrade! Jose! You hear me?

JOSE: *(Pleading)* I love you senorita . . . and . . .

JENNIE: We were comrades, Jose. Companeros. That is the greatest love.

JOSE: *(Holding her hand very tightly, suffering death)* Yes! Comrades! You . . . loved . . . me . . . a little.

JENNIE: (*With great gentleness takes the dying boy's head in her arms. He loses consciousness. A police whistle is heard far down the street. Shorty rushes in with a bruised and bloody face, and torn clothes*)

SHORTY: The bulls are coming, Jennie.

(*Jennie shakes her head, motioning him to be quiet. Tears stream down her face.*)

SHORTY: (*In horror and grief*) Oh! Christ Jose?

(*Jennie nods, unable to shake. Shorty looks down, his face contorted. He picks up banner. BLACK AND WHITE UNITE TO FIGHT. The shrill sound of police whistles and the approach of the patrol wagon are heard as the curtain falls*)

Politics and Social Commentary: *Angelo Herndon Jones*

Of all Hughes' plays, *Angelo Herndon Jones* receives the most consistent mention by scholars when they address Hughes' ties to the political Left. Structurally, it is not as innovative as the other plays in this study, nor does it employ their agit-prop techniques. *Angelo Herndon Jones* more closely resembles a play of social criticism that offers a political solution than a play that overtly espouses a political ideology such as Communism. In examining it, one must bear in mind that Hughes wrote it intending it for submission to a contest that sought new political plays. *Angelo Herndon Jones* is a turning point in the development of Hughes' work, his last attempt to write a serious *didactic* play with traditional dramatic structure. Except for *De Organizer*, his subsequent writings for the theater would be more in the style of popular musical drama.

Angelo Herndon the activist achieved notoriety because of his radical politics and subsequent incarceration; *Angelo Herndon Jones*, the play script, uses the character of the political leader almost tangentially. The play attracts the attention of individuals researching Hughes because it was the script with which Hughes won a national play writing contest sponsored by *New Theater*, a noted leftist publication. Hughes mentions it in correspondence, and it is one of his few leftist scripts that came to public attention. It is, however, a very short script that, to my knowledge, was never produced.

Angelo Herndon Jones, written while Hughes was in Chicago in late 1935, is a product of a period in the mid-1930s when Hughes embarked on an intensive effort to write play scripts. It met with initial literary success and buoyed Hughes' hopes of finally achieving a foothold in commercial theater or film. In a letter to Noel Sullivan in January 1936, Hughes comments on this period of his writing and on his love-hate relationship with the theater: "My life of late, creatively, has been entirely devoted to the Drama. . . . I did a play about Angelo Herndon in one act (in which Herndon doesn't appear except as a picture on a poster) which seems to have won the *New Theater* award of $50, although I haven't gotten the money yet. . . . Why I should be so devoted to the Drama, I do not know, because *Mulatto* has been nothing but a trial and tribulation since its opening, and I'm having a terrible time trying to collect the royalties." Apologizing later in the letter for the poor condition of the typing due to a typewriter bail that did not hold the paper properly, he writes, "The Drama has ruined it, as it has almost ruined me!"[1] Although several authors contend Hughes never received his payment from *New Theater,* later correspondence indicates that a check did arrive along with other payments in a fortuitous financial windfall at a time when Hughes faced mounting debts.

Hughes' interest in Angelo Herndon actually coincided with his turn to the Left in the early 1930s. The case of Angelo Herndon came to public attention in 1932, the year after the Scottsboro Boys were jailed. Herndon, a young black Communist organizer, was jailed in 1932 for causing a riot among black and white unemployed workers in Georgia. Unlike the Scottsboro defendants, Herndon was a political activist with indisputable ties to the Communist Party. Sentenced to twenty years on a chain gang, he was released in 1934, after a round of successful appeals.

Herndon remained an intriguing figure to Hughes, who went so far as to seek him out in New York.[2] His association with Herndon was both professional and personal. Angelo Herndon and Ralph Ellison edited the *Negro Quarterly,* which occasionally published Hughes' stories and poems. In 1937, Hughes went to Paris as a delegate to the Second International Writers Congress (the other American delegate was Ernest Hemingway). Another delegate known to Hughes from his earlier trip to Cuba was Nicolàs Guillén. Hughes and Guillén journeyed to Madrid as journalists, Hughes as a correspondent for the *Baltimore Afro-American* and Guillén working for *Mediodía.*[3] Hughes was staying in the quarters of the

Alianza de Intelectuales Antifascistas, when Milton Herndon, Angelo's brother, was killed in battle during the Spanish Civil War.[4]

The Scottsboro Boys and Angelo Herndon symbolized institutionalized racism for Hughes, and he referred to both cases in speeches throughout the late 1930s. The speech given at the Writer's Congress is one in which he is most critical of the American government and its relegation of the Negro to second-class status. The depression years were particularly hard on blacks in the United States. Employment in theater-related enterprises "dipped abysmally low"; a survey conducted by *Variety* in the winter of 1931 claimed that there were "twenty-five thousand unemployed workers from theater-related jobs, three thousand of whom were black artists and craftsmen."[5] The fact that Hughes persisted in his writing for the theater in such hard times speaks to his unrelenting desire to achieve success within the realm of film or theater. His comedies, not his political plays, of this period led him to achieve a modicum of success.

No record of a production of *Angelo Herndon Jones* exists, though it was offered to the Gilpin Players in Cleveland as part of a series of plays Hughes wrote for them. The Gilpin Players served as the Federal Theater Project's producing organization in Cleveland and there met with great success. The Gilpin Players evolved into the Karamu Theater Company, which remains to this day one of the most active black theater companies in the nation. Hughes' work with the Federal Theater Project is most often associated with the Karamu Theater. Karamu produced his plays *Soul Gone Home* on 27 June 1936 and *Troubled Island* in May 1937. But *Angelo Herndon Jones* was rejected because actresses objected to playing the parts of the two prostitutes in the script.

Although *Angelo Herndon Jones* was not produced by the Cleveland Federal Theater Project, Hughes' association with the FTP is worthy of comment since it was the premier political theater-producing group of the 1930s. Hughes sought out an association with the FTP through his association with Arna Bontemps, who participated in the Federal Writers' Project. Bontemps's involvement with the federally sponsored program of the New Deal proved more positive than Hughes' experience. Years later, Bontemps reminisced: "For the first time since the Harlem period of the '20s Negro writers had a chance. The greatest number of blacks worked in the New York City, Illinois and Louisiana projects, where they had been assigned to prepare histories of their race in these states."[6]

Noted black actress Rose McClendon first suggested that there be separate Negro units within the Federal Theater Project that "would in-sure the production of plays dramatizing black themes and exhibiting black talents."[7] The success of the Negro units in New York, Cleveland, Chicago, Los Angeles, and Louisiana is a telling tribute to the active par-ticipation of black artists, writers, and technicians in the cultural milieu of the 1930s. The Federal Theater Project's Negro units established the groundwork for Negro stagehands and musicians to join theatrical unions. Doris Abramson's study of the development of black playwrights in the United States sees the Federal Theater as providing an invaluable laboratory for new authors to gain experience that had been forbidden them by long-standing segregation practices.[8] Edith Isaacs shares similar sentiments in her book *The Negro in the American Theater,* maintaining that the Negro units of the Federal Theater brought more ample returns to the project itself and meant more to black actors and theater practitio-ners than any other production company except for possibly the Lafayette Theatre.[9] Similarly, Abram Hill, a participant in the Negro Theater group of FTP, claims in oral history interviews: "[T]he Federal Theater is cred-ited with having developed 15 million new theatergoers throughout the country. I would say that Harlem was far up in that number that did go to the theater in those days in the Thirties."[10]

The public success of the FTP productions in the mid-1930s should have been an inviting lure to Hughes, who continually sought commer-cial success in the theater. Yet one participant in the oral history of FTP production staff notes tersely, "Langston Hughes was making his own money so he was not too interested in the FTP."[11] In its attempt to "de-velop Negro playwrights who could write honestly about Negro life," the FTP devised a unique training program. It may well have been the col-laborative nature of the FTP writing process that caused Hughes to re-spond with aversion, since he had a long-standing wariness of collabo-rative enterprises in the theater.

In 1936, the managing directors of the Negro Theater Project 806 in New York City decided to invite one hundred Negro writers to attend "a three or four month symposium and lectures that would improve their style and form of writing plays." Fifty writers enrolled the first month and attended lectures on such subjects as script forms, research tech-niques, technical requirements, copyright laws, the need for a strong so-cial message, and Negro Theater possibilities generally. John Houseman, well known for his work with Orson Welles at the Mercury Theater and also with the Federal Theater Project, informed the group that their hope for the Negro authors was the establishment of a permanent theater.

Francis Bosworth, director of the Play Bureau of the Federal Theater, started them on a project that led to their writing a play collectively; after a month of research and criticism, the class wrote a first act. How much this approach to play writing helped the individual playwrights is difficult to judge. Large numbers dropped out during the second and third months, and by the end of the fourth month, there were only twenty-five active members. During this period, members had written and submitted to all Federal Theater production sources about eighteen full-length plays and five short ones. Three were produced, two of them by the Federal Theater and one by the commercial or Broadway theater.[12]

Hughes' assessment of the FTP was none too flattering. In a "Personal and Friendly Memorandum Not to be Forwarded to Nobody" written to Arna Bontemps, he refers to his revision of Bontemps and Countee Cullen's script, *St. Louis Women*, a FTP production in Los Angeles. Hughes, Bontemps, Cullen, and the play's director, Clarence Muse, all had their eyes on the possibility that the play might be produced as a film since the production was being mounted by the FTP Los Angeles unit. However, as with most of his collaborative efforts, Hughes found that this production was beset with collaborative problems:

> Now's [sic] to the minor details (and as a personal explanation to you)[.] Any theater is bad enough, but the F. is worse, judging from both New York and here, what with all the fighting and inner intrigue that goes on. Hallie Flanagan was just here to try and straighten out things once again, since they ran Ulmman to hell and gone, and the political gangsters are trying to upset the works. Yesterday's paper carried a story on the front page concerning some of the excitement—which included one man beaten up, another given a bottle of poison milk which killed his dog, and put him in the hospital, and is seemingly going to cause his faction of the Democratic party to lose their charter—all over F. Theater. So under the existing circumstances the fact that Muse has been able to maintain the Negro unit as a sort of little island apart—especially since it is the only unit really making any money for the cast set-up—he really has the say there, so far. And since this if your first play—and you at least have your finger now a pretty good ways into a production (which in no way would hurt your Broadway chances anyhow) whatever you choose to do about that, my personal advice would be to juggle things around someway (including Miss Salisbury and Countee) so that you won't miss out on this West Coast chance. Get them to offer some counter-proposals—which I will do my best to

get Clarence to accept—if you hurry as I have only ten more days here—and am about to go with Clarence to the ranch for the final polishing up of the script. Clarence has been working with me on this version—which is a great help—as he certainly is a good show-man, knowing how to heighten and improve a scene theatrically. So I am not speaking to him about your letter until I hear from you again, as I'd rather not have him fly up in the air right now, and withdraw his help (Which is quite aside from his job, as he's not being paid to write with me.) But he does like the show, and wants to make a big splurge with it and has so far managed to keep all factions concerned out here in a good humor toward it—in spite of some Negro opposition who want to do an OPERA next.[13]

Even with the close of the FTP in 1939, Hughes resisted attempts by individuals who had been associated with the Negro troops to regroup and start a new production company. In interviews conducted as part of the oral history collection of the Federal Theater Project, Abram Hill recounted:

After the Federal Theater went out of existence, we had no major Negro theater activity going on and there were a number of us who were desirous of continuing in the theater . . . and many of us just got together and started groups because we had gained certain ex-periences and we had gained certain techniques from the Federal Theater. . . . So we are about to enter the forties and we have no theater at all. So I did call together Langston Hughes and Ted Ward, Powell Lindsay, Frederick O'Neal, George Norford and Hughes Allison to my house for a meeting and discussed the idea of estab-lishing a theater of our own in the Harlem Community. Eventually, it was called the Negro Playwrights' Theater. . . . There were differ-ences of opinion among us who were there in that group and I couldn't see how it could be resolved. The conflicts we had could not be resolved because some of the members of that committee wanted to disqualify plays that did not have a certain political ori-entation.[14]

Although Hughes may have attended an organizational meeting, he was not intimately involved with the group or its productions. Ramper-sad characterizes Hughes' involvement with the Negro Playwrights' Theater as "nominal."[15] Others have posited various interpretations about Hughes' lack of interest and commitment to the FTP or to the groups that grew from it after its closing. Leonard DePaur's interview held in the

Federal Theater Project Collection indicates that, despite their best intentions, many of the scripts reflected decades of festering frustrations that failed to materialize. He contends that individual suspicions of the Federal Theater Project's governmental sponsorship prevented better-known and more talented writers, like Hughes, from participation:

> [I]n six months time I would have such a batch of scripts that I couldn't possibly plow through because everything they'd stored up in their craws all these years would be pouring out now because the theater would offer the opportunity for its exposure. They disappointed me in that this flood of material did not come from black writers. Langston, I often discussed it with him later on. "Why didn't you do something for us on Federal Theater?" And they had varying answers. In the first place, I don't think they were fully convinced that because the Federal Theater was a government agency, they were gonna be allowed to do anything decent, you know. There was this lack of confidence, and I think we would have had to produce a couple of successful *Turpentines* and things of that sort before they would have overcome their doubts.[16]

Hughes' back-to-back experiences with the Los Angeles FTP and the rejection by the Cleveland FTP of *Angelo Herndon Jones* were enough to cause him to reconsider his literary strengths and return to writing poetry. *Don't You Want to Be Free?*, a poetry play not included in this study, was written by Hughes in 1938 and is a montage of his poems taken from *The Weary Blues* and *The Dream Keeper*. While it touches on issues of labor and leftist politics, it is more a poetic history of social abuses directed towards blacks. Though Abramson claims hyperbolically that *Don't You Want to Be Free?* is "the best example we have of an agit-prop play produced in a little theater in Harlem," Rampersad recognizes it for what it really was: "a major step in the evolution of Hughes as an artist. Finally he had found his natural form as a dramatist."[17] Ironically, his dramatic form aligned most closely with his poetic form and with the characters found in his Simple essays. Hughes' artistic success with drama would come with his adaptations of his poems and prose. His other most notable foray into the world of political scripts came in the late 1940s when he worked with Elmer Rice and Kurt Weill on a musical version of Rice's *Street Scene*. Rampersad notes briefly that the success of *Street Scene* led to subsequent invitations for Hughes to work as a librettist on other musicals. But again, his concern about contractual arrangements, as well as demands for a cash advances, caused problems for

Hughes. Even an offer to work with John Houseman was undercut by Hughes' inflexibility on contractual matters.[18]

ANGELO HERNDON JONES

Angelo Herndon Jones dramatizes the squalor, despair, lack of opportunity, and personal and financial victimization of blacks in the cities. The characters in the play are reminiscent of the characters in the Simple stories but conspicuously lack the biting humor that carries those stories. The characters in *Angelo Herndon Jones* represent a substrata of society: prostitutes, unemployed workers, unwed mothers, corrupt police (black and white), and evicted tenants forced to leave apartments because their paltry earnings cannot pay the rent. The spirit of Herndon gives the dark and sordid lives of these characters hope and inspiration. His picture illuminates and dominates the stage at various times throughout the play. Only once is the offstage voice of Herndon heard, when Hughes again returns to the theme of a united biracial work force found in his other labor plays. Through Herndon, Hughes offers unity as the solution to the social problems confronting the nation: "I tell you, they can do what they will with Angelo Herndon. They can indict me. They can put me in jail. But there will come thousands of Angelo Herndons. They may succeed in killing one, two, even a score of working-class organizers. But you cannot kill the working class. We are the Working Class. Black and white unite to fight." All the characters place their faith in Herndon, and his story of leading a black and white coalition of employed workers in public protest is offered as a model of social revolt. The suspicions levied against such biracial support are voiced in the lines of a Detective searching an apartment for "incendiary literature." To Lank, friend of protagonist Buddy Jones, the Detective shouts: "You just stay away from them Herndon meetings, and everything like 'em, you hear? The red squad ain't gonna stand for that, niggers and white folks meeting together—to take up for niggers."

After her mother is evicted, Viola, the unwed mother, looks for Buddy, the child's father, at the Herndon rally. The rally participants join together, and with the background music of the Communist "Internationale," they defiantly carry the furniture back into the apartment from which the mother was evicted. In the closing moment of the play, Viola and Buddy, standing under the Herndon poster glowing onstage, decide to name their child Angelo Herndon Jones. The child becomes the symbol of one of "the thousands of Angelo Herndons" standing united.

The script serves as a parable for conversion to the cause of leftist labor. It is not his most radical play, nor is it the most compelling of the scripts considered here. *Angelo Herndon Jones* is another polemical script of the mid-1930s. It reiterates thematic issues and, to some extent, even uses the dialogue and closing scenes that Hughes employed in his other political plays of the 1930s. Rampersad claims that *Angelo Herndon Jones* marked a reenlisting by Hughes "even more dramatically in the ranks of the far Left."[19] From the evidence, it appears that he used leftist literary and political associations as much as they used him. It may well be that he did not reenlist but became more visible as a spokesman at various national and international conferences. Certainly, the public exposure to his political plays had not caused Hughes to become more closely identified with the Left in the mid-1930s, as they were not produced.

Angelo Herndon Jones was Hughes' last attempt to write a script that did not rely heavily on music, lyrics, or poetry to carry the production, though not his last effort to use the theater for completely didactic purposes. Hughes' literary success had come through his poems and the biting irony in his Simple stories. To some extent, he transferred the strengths of his poems and stories to the theater in the last years of the 1930s. Subsequently, he would embark upon other collaborative ventures in the American theater that would bring him some of the commercial success he dreamed of, but there would be no movie contracts, nor lucrative Broadway runs. Hughes métier was poetry: in his soul he was a lyricist more than a dramatist. With the genre of drama he would achieve success but never renown in the American theater.

Angelo Herndon Jones: A One-Act Play of Negro Life

By Langston Hughes

[The original typescript of the play, held in the Federal Theater Project Collection, contains several inconsistencies in spelling, punctuation, and capitalization. These have been retained in the script presented here. Only minor changes were made when typographical errors affecting meaning or logic were evident.]

Characters

BUDDY JONES—A YOUNG NEGRO WORKER

LANK—HIS PAL

MA JENKINS—AN OLD WASHERWOMAN

VIOLA—HER DAUGHTER

SADIE MAE—STREETWALKER

LOTTIE—STREETWALKER

A COLORED WORKMAN

A NEGRO COP

A WHITE COP

A LANDLORD

DEPUTIES

DETECTIVES

PASSERS-BY

WORKERS

POLICE

VOICES

When the curtain rises, there is a portion of a wall, three feet wide, in the center of the stage. On the wall there is a poster announcing a Herndon Meeting. The poster reproduces a large picture of Angelo Herndon, the young working class leader. On the left side of the wall there is an inner room, a poor room containing a cot and a kitchen stove. Here Ma Jenkins lives, and her twenty year old daughter, Viola. On the right side of the wall there is another inner room in another house (the rooms may be miles away since the wall is only a symbolic barrier) in which there is a cheap iron bed, a table, a stand for books. In this room Buddy Jones lives and his pal, Lank. Sometimes the light shines in both rooms at once. Sometimes in only one room. Sometimes only on the poster announcing the Herndon meeting. When the curtain rises, one sees only the poster. Out of the darkness, two girls enter. They are obviously prostitutes.

SADIE MAE: Gimme a drag, will you? Mine all run out.

LOTTIE: Draggin's mighty poor this evenin'. *(handing her a nub of a cigarette)*

SADIE MAE: So is hustlin'. I ain't made a dime tonight.

LOTTIE: Look at this hot papa's picture on the wall, Sadie Mae. I wish I had a nice young brown like that for a boy friend.

SADIE MAE: Reckon I'll keep Slug. He do get me out of jail when the need arises.

LOTTIE: I wonder who that guy is—Angelo Herndon?

SADIE MAE: I dunno. What do it say? You can read.

LOTTIE: *(reading slowly)* It say: Mass Meeting Friday. Great Speaker on Negro Rights. Clark Hall.

SADIE MAE: Is they gonna dance? (*She cuts a few steps*)

LOTTIE: It don't seem to mention it. We couldn't go nohow.

SADIE MAE: Slug'd let me go if he thought I could make a dollar.

LOTTIE: Well, I got to hug this corner.

SADIE MAE: Yonder comes a pickup, Lottie, Look!

LOTTIE: (*Peering, then disappointedly*) Yal, the cop. (*Both girls lean back against the wall, one on either side of the poster, as a Negro policeman enters*)

SADIE MAE AND LOTTIE: Hello, Sugar, Hy, Big Shot!

NEGRO COP: You sugarrin' me tonight, heh? I can't use no sugar—I'm out of cigarettes.

SADIE MAE: So is we.

NEGRO COP: (*Pointedly*) I smoke Camels. Two for a quarter.

LOTTIE: Alright, here. (*She hands him a quarter*) Now, don't forget, here's mine for the night, so leave me be.

NEGRO COP: Sweet Papa Big Billy never forgets. (*He punches her playfully in the belly with his night stick and walks on*)

SADIE MAE: A graftin' bastard! You make a quarter and they take it from you. We ain't even got smokes ourselves.

LOTTIE: You ought to be a police woman, Sadie, darlin' then you'd rake in, too, instead of givin' out. Between the cops and the pimps, we don't never have nothin. (*She turns back to the poster*) I wish I had a nice fella like this for my man.

SADIE MAE: I'm gonna keep Slug. He knows the racket. You see, it wasn't me that cop shook for a quarter, cause Slug's got me all fixed up with headquarters.

LOTTIE: Oh, yeah? Well, be careful they don't haul you and Slug both in sometime. . . . Hey, here comes a trick. (*Glances off right as footsteps approach. A colored workman in overalls passes*) Hello, baby!

SADIE MAE: What's your hurry, boy-friend?

WORKMAN: (*Going on, to exit left*) I'm C. C. Cing on S.E.R.A. time, sweetie, and my check don't come for thirty days—then I spends it all on sales-tax.

SADIE MAE: (*suggestively*) There ain't no sales tax on what we got.

WORKMAN: I'll have to tell Roosevelt. He must've overlooked you.

(*Exits, as a young man enters, left, in cap and sweater*)

BUDDY: (*to girls*) Hello!

LOTTIE: Out walkin', Jonesy?

BUDDY: No, ridin', Lottie. (*Peering at poster*) So that guy's coming! I want to hear him.

SADIE MAE: (*smiling*) How about hearin' me, lovie?

BUDDY: (*reading poster*) Friday night, tomorrow. Say he's a great guy, that Herndon. You know what he did?

LOTTIE: No, what's he do, Buddy?

BUDDY: He done get white folks and colored folks together right in the middle of the South, Lottie, and that ain't no lie.

SADIE MAE: Huh! I does that up North.

LOTTIE: Shut up, fool.

BUDDY: I mean lots of 'em, white and colored, for a good purpose—to get themselves something to eat.

LOTTIE: To eat?

BUDDY: Yes, organized people what was starvin', black and white and got them together.

LOTTIE: Then what did they do?

BUDDY: Went to the city hall to demand something to eat.

LOTTIE: Lawd, I should a-been there!

SADIE MAE: Me too.

LOTTIE: (*pointing to poster*) I told you that boy on that picture was somebody, Sadie Mae.

SADIE MAE: Yeah, but I'll keep Slug.

BUDDY: Slug Martin?

SADIE MAE: Yal know him?

BUDDY: Sure, I know that bozo. Has he ever had a job since his night club closed?

SADIE MAE: No, I'm his meal ticket. He eats, alright. (*Just then two men pass off stage left in a car. They honk the horn and call the girls*)

LOTTIE: Two white guys, Sadie Mae! Come on, honey, here's dough!

SADIE MAE: (*Waving*) Hello, dear! Sure I want a ride.

LOTTIE: Coming, pretty papa. (*The two girls rush off left and the sound of a car is heard departing*)

BUDDY: (*Staring after them*) Ain't that a hell of a way to make a living. (*Calls up the street*) Hurry up, Lank.

LANK: (*entering*) Man, I'm too tired to hurry.

BUDDY: I thought you was gonna be all night buying them two cigs.

LANK: The man didn't want to bust a package. Wants three cents for two Piedmonts.

BUDDY: They high in this neighborhood.

LANK: You would have a gal what lives in a hinety neighborhood.

BUDDY: Quit your kiddin'. There ain't no hinty slums.

LANK: How is she, Buddy?

BUDDY: Man, I'm worried. She's gonna have that baby, Viola is, sure's you born.

LANK: She is?

BUDDY: Yal.

LANK: Why didn't you buy the stuff in time?

BUDDY: I didn't have the dollar, Lank.

LANK: Then why don't you get married?

BUDDY: I ain't got no money for no license.

LANK: Then why don't you live together?

BUDDY: We ain't got no room.

LANK: You can have ours, fella. I'll move out.

BUDDY: Then where'll you stay—with my mother-in-law-to-be?

LANK: I could try it. Ma Jenkins ain't so bad for her age, I reckon.

BUDDY: Come on home, man. We got to get some sleep to turn out at five o'clock in the morning and walk them six miles cause we ain't got no carfare. If we get out yonder to that foundry on time, we might accidently get on.

LANK: Accidently is right these days and times. Yo know damn well, Buddy Jones, they ain't gonna hire no jigs around here, nohow. They must gonna let us starve to death to get rid of us. (*They continue talking as they exit right*)

BUDDY: Herndon's coming tomorrow . . . (*Their voices die in the distance. For a second the stage is empty. Then the Negro Cop enters, approaches the Herndon poster, looks at it scornfully a minute, and punches its face, tearing the paper. He goes on to exit right as the light dies out on the wall.*)

DARKNESS

(*Violent ringing of an alarm clock in the room at right. Sounds of a bed creaking and someone jumping up suddenly. A match flares weakly, an oil lamp is lighted. LANK, stands in his underwear and calls to BUDDY who is still sleeping*)

LANK: Hey, Jones get out o' that bed. It's five o'clock.

BUDDY: (*Sleepily*) Alright.

LANK: If I don't get me a job today, I really is gonna raise hell with somebody. (*Pulling on overalls as he talks*)

BUDDY: (*Sitting up*) Yal, me, too, man, cause I'm gonna have that baby to feed in no time.

(*While Buddy and Lank dress, the light dies in their room as, gradually, the dawn enters the window of the other room at the left of the stage, where an old woman and her daughter are sleeping near the stove.*)

MA JEN: (*Turning over*) Ay, Lawd! Lemme get up from here and start that white woman's clothes to boilin'. I ain't had but one washin' in two weeks. Lawd knows I needs this seventy-five cents. (*She gets slowly out of bed and begins to dress in the half-dark, muttering to herself*) Hard times, Lawdy! Lawd! (*As she puts on her clothes, she hears her daughter sobbing, with her face to the audience wall.*)

VIOLA: *(Smothering her sobs with a pillow)* Oh! Oh! Oh!

MA JEN: Honey, what's de matter with you?

VIOLA: Nothing, ma.

MA JEN: *(Bending over the bed)* Yes, they is, too. Your pillow is all wet, just like as if you been crying all night. *(Commandingly)* You tell me what's wrong, now, Viola.

VIOLA: I don't know what to do, ma.

MA JEN: Don't know what to do about what?

VIOLA: I'm gonna have a baby.

MA JEN: You and starvation's gonna have a baby, you better say. Buddy Jones ain't a-bearin' nothin! And he ain't likely to be a-feedin' nothin' neither, a young rascal! That that's why you's cryin'? I told you all to be careful! And you ain't married neither!

VIOLA: *(Bitterly)* That's all you ever tell anybody—is to be careful. Why can't you tell us how we can get married, how we can get jobs, how we can live, or something useful?

MA JEN: De Lawd'll tell you that, daughter—if you ain't too mixed up with de devil. *(She begins to make a coal fire)*

VIOLA: *(Getting out of bed)* Well, I wish the Lord would pay our rent then.

MA JEN: He will, don't worry.

VIOLA: He ain't, not for four months. And the man's coming back to collect again today.

MA JEN: Shut up doubtin' de Lawd, Viola, and get up from there and help me wash out these clothes, or go look for a job, once. I ain't been sendin' you to school all your life to lay up in bed and do nothin' but fool with Buddy and doubt de Lawd.

VIOLA: I been tryin' all summer. (*Pulling on her stockings*) I wish I'd gone in that night club of Slug Martin's when it was runnin'.

MA JEN: Yes, and you'd a-been on de streets by now, a street-walker.

VIOLA: I wouldn't a-been starvin'—me and this child I got inside me.

MA JEN: You wouldn't a-had no child.

VIOLA: Maybe I wouldn't a-wanted one! God damn it!

MA JEN: Hush up! Speakin' against God!

VIOLA: (*Almost hysterical*) There ain't no God! There ain't no God! If there was one . . .

MA JEN: Shut up, I say! . . . Shut up!

(*The light fades out, comes on again where the torn poster hangs against the wall in the pale gray dawn. The two prostitutes stagger on left, emerging from a car that drives on noisily*)

VOICES: (*Ribald shouts of men offstage in car*) So long, sweetheart! . . . So long, kid! See you in the funny paper, baby!

SADIE MAE: So long you cheap skates, you!

LOTTIE: (*Drunkenly*) Shut up, them's white folks. (*Pretending pleasure*) They paid you a quarter more'n jigs would. (*Waving to them*) Thank you darlings.

SADIE MAE: (*pathetically*) I want to get home to Slug.

LOTTIE: (*Staring at the torn poster*) I wish I had a man like that. I wish I had a baby would grow up nice like Herndon. (*Wetting torn paper and pasting it back on wall*) Honey, who punched your face and tore it all up that a-way?

SADIE MAE: (*Looking at the money in her hand*) A lousy seventy-five cents!

(They stagger off left. People start passing. The sun rises full and red. Noises of trucks in the street. An ice man yelling. Dirty children on their way to school. Two deputies and a man with papers in his hand come by. Light in the room where Ma Jenkins is alone, washing. A knock at the door.)

MA JEN: Come in.

(Enter LANDLORD and DEPUTIES)

LANDLORD: Er—Mrs. Jenkins, you've had your notice according to the law and plenty of time to move! If you can pay, pay. If you can't settle with me for your backrent, then pack up, because we're putting you out.

MA JEN: How'm I gonna pay, when I ain't got not even two cents in de house?

LANDLORD: Alright, boys, start setting the heavy pieces on the sidewalk. *(The deputies start rolling up the mattress and taking down the bed.)*

MA JEN: Here! Here! What you-all doin'? I got a washin' to get out today.

LANDLORD: Washing for who?

MA JEN: Miss Pettiford.

LANDLORD: Well you gonna get paid for that, ain't you? Take the money and get another flat.

MA JEN: *(To the men who are taking out her bed)* You ain't gonna throw me out in de cold, is you, at my age? *(They keep right on moving out the furniture)* Oh, my Laws! Help me! Wait till my daughter comes home, please. Maybe she's got work. Maybe she done found a job today. Wait, I asks you for de Lawd's sake, wait!

LANDLORD: I been waitin'. Looks like neither you, nor the Lord, nor your daughter pays their rent.

MA JEN: *(Holding the last piece of the bedstead desperately)* I tell you to put my things down.

LANDLORD: (*Grabbing her arm as men wrench the bedstead from her*) None of that now, you black wench! It's lucky I ain't had you sent to jail.

MA JEN: (*Wailing*) Take your hands off me! . . . Lawd! Oh, Lawd! Oh! Lawd!

(*Light fades out in the room, but shines on the torn poster announcing Angelo Herndon, and on the crowd passing on the sidewalk as the furniture sits beside the wall. An old black woman presently takes her place in the rocker, the tears streaming down her face. The late afternoon sun shines on the kids coming from school, on the workers coming home with their dinner pails, on the tawdry prostitutes emerging as dusk falls. Enter SADIE MAE and LOTTIE who speak to MA JENKINS as she rocks beside her meager furniture in the street*)

LOTTIE: Ain't this Mis' Jenkins? . . . Lawd, yes! . . . Ma Jenkins, ain't it kinder late to have all your things settin' out here airin'?

MA JEN: They ain't airin', honey. I's been put out o' my place.

SADIE MAE AND LOTTIE: Put out?

MA JEN: (*Weeping*) In my old age, with no place to go. And I don't know where is Viola.

LOTTIE: Where is she? . . . I know Viola ain't left you. . . . where is she?

MA JEN: Went out this mornin' to look for work and she ain't come home yet, and here's me settin' in de street. Her mama! De child'll find me settin' in de street.

SADIE MAE: Somebody else done took your room?

MA JEN: No, it's empty.

SADIE MAE: Empty?

MA JEN: Yes, empty.

LOTTIE: Well, you ought to move back in then. That landlord's got more money than you. He can [wait] with his rent.

MA JEN: He say he won't wait no longer. *(looks up)* But thank God, here comes Viola. *(her daughter enters)*

VIOLA: Mama, what's this? What you doin' out here?

(The old woman weeps)

LOTTIE: They put her out.

SADIE MAE: They ain't let her stay in.

VIOLA: You mean we're evicted?

MA JEN: I been waitin' for you, honey, to see what we can do cause we ain't go no place to stay. Is you found any little kind o' work or anything to earn a dime today?

VIOLA: No, ma, not a thing. *(Angrily)* But they're not gonna make us stay in the street. No, they won't make us do that.

SADIE MAE: Don't say what they won't do, honey. White folks don't care nothin' about you.

VIOLA: *(To Lottie)* One of you-all stay with ma, and I'm goin' and get Buddy. He's gone to the Herndon meeting, I reckon. I'm gonna find him. *(She exits right)*

MA JEN: And I'm gonna pray. *(She kneels down beside the furniture)*

SADIE MAE: And I'm gonna try and make a dollar tonight to give to this old woman so she can get herself a room.

LOTTIE: *(Looking at poster)* I wish I could go to that Herndon meeting, too.

SADIE MAE: Watch out, girl! Here come the cops, two of 'em tonight.

(A Negro Cop and a White Cop enter and walk slowly and importantly across the stage. It is almost dark now.)

WHITE COP: *(To Ma Jenkins)* You'll have to get that stuff off the sidewalk tonight or we'll run you in.

MA JEN: *(Helplessly)* Where'm I gonna take it?

NEGRO COP: To the junk heap, if nowhere's else.

WHITE COP: Just get it away from here, that's all we care.

NEGRO COP: *(Walking away)* And don't be here when we come back. *(They exit swinging their clubs)*

LOTTIE: *(calling)* Don't you need some cigarettes tonight, *(under her breath)* you bastard?

SADIE MAE: *(laughing)* Ma Jenkins don't know nothin' about payin' off the cops, does she? If she'd give them flatfeet a buck a day, she could rent the sidewalk for a speakeasy. I'll have to get Slug to fix her up at head-quarters.

LOTTIE: *(To the old woman)* Don't cry. Buddy can help you, wait till he gets back from that meeting. You seen them cops, didn't you, Ma Jenkins? Black and white cops teamed up against us! Well, if black and white can team up to keep us down—looks like we poor folks could team up, too, against them. If Herndon can bring black and white together down South, it sure can be done up North here, too, where we're just as hungry. And I tell you Sadie Mae . . . *(The lights go out, but in the darkness, growing louder and louder, there is the sound of applause, and Herndon's voice is heard speaking)*

VOICE: . . . I tell you, they can do what they will with Angelo Herndon. They can indict me. They can put me in jail. But there will come thousands of Angelo Herndons. They may succeed in killing one, two, even a score of working-class organizers. But you cannot kill the working class. We are the Working Class. *(applause)* Black and white unite to fight. *(Cries of "Herndon! Herndon! Herndon!" Applause. Then Viola's voice speaking to Buddy)*

VIOLA: And all our things are out in the street, Buddy. On the sidewalk in the night, in the cold.

BUDDY: You hear that, friends, what Viola says? She and her mother's been thrown out of their room by the landlord.

VOICES: We'll put 'em back! They won't stay out. We'll go right there, from this meeting, now!

BUDDY: Come on, Viola! Come on, honey! Now you have comrades! (*The strains of* ["T]he International[e"] *grow louder as the light comes on again and the Negro and White Workers are seen filling the stage as they carry the furniture back into the room, left, that had been emptied by the landlord and his deputies. A throng of workers fill the night. Then a cop's whistle is heard, then another. Sirens, police gongs, as patrols and squad cars arrive. Faces of black and white cops. Black and white workers. Struggle! But the furniture goes back. . . . As the noise fades away and the light dies in the Jenkin's room, loud voices are heard in the room at the right, and Lank is revealed surrounded by detectives who are searching his and Buddy's place.*)

DETECTIVES: (*Looking under the mattress, as his fellow-dicks search in drawers, etc.*) Where'd you find out about that meeting? What were you doing there? Where's this Buddy Jones who lives with you? What books do you read? Who give you incendiary literature?

LANK: What you talkin' about, man? I don't need to read no books to know I'm hungry. I don't need to read books to know I'm hungry. I don't need to read books to know I ain't got no job, to know I'm black, to know they ain't no chance for me.

DETECTIVE: Shut up! Where's Buddy Jones?

LANK: How I know where Buddy Jones is? I ain't his mammy.

DETECTIVE: Aw-right! Aw-right! Well run you in if you get too fly. You just stay away from them Herndon meetings, and everything like 'em, you hear? The red squad ain't gonna stand for that, niggers and white folks meeting together—to take up for niggers.

LANK: And how about me being hungry? You gonna stand for that?

DETECTIVE: (*Glaring*) You know what I mean? (*to the others*) Did you find anything, boys? If not, let's go. We got some more nigger houses to search tonight. (*they exit*)

LANK: (*laughing to himself*) They sure don't know how to look for nothing. (*He pulls down the window shade and out tumble several copies of various magazines, and a pamphlet life of Herndon.)* I got my life of Herndon right here! *(lights die out, come on, flooding the Herndon poster on the wall. Then in the room at the left, by the dim flicker of an oil lamp, Ma Jenkins is seen snoring in her bed, as Buddy and Viola talk in a corner.)*

BUDDY: . . . and he's right, Viola, Herndon is. I ain't, I ain't never heard nobody so right before. Black and white folks can get together and rule the whole world. That guy, Angelo Herndon, knows what he's talking about. You seen they came and put your furniture right back in the house tonight, colored and white helping us. They didn't draw no color line, did they? No sir-eee! And I'm gonna join up with them kind o' people.

VIOLA: Me, too, honey.

BUDDY: And maybe by the time our baby grows up, this country won't be like it is today—folks hungry; folks Jim-crowed, folks put out o' their houses.

VIOLA: I hope it won't be like it is now.

BUDDY: *(Positively)* Well, it won't be. We gonna change all that!

MA JEN: *(Waking and turning over)* You, Buddy Jones! Why don't you go on home to yo' bed?

BUDDY: Yes ma'am. *(To Viola)* I better go. Gee, it must be late.

VIOLA: I'll walk as far as the corner with you, honey. I need air, after so much excitement.

BUDDY: Alright, as far as the corner.

(They blow out the light and exit. The Herndon poster is bright under the street lights as the two lovers stop beneath it.)

VIOLA: Goodnight. *(As they stand close to each other.)*

BUDDY: I hate to leave you, baby, but soon's I can, we'll get a room together.

VIOLA: Alright, Buddy. We ain't got much, but we got our love.

BUDDY: Love and struggle, honey, and a baby coming! But we'll get there, don't worry. We got leaders like him (*Points to the Herndon poster*) that are gonna show us how to make a new world. He's a great guy, that Herndon, ain't he, sweetheart?

VIOLA: He sure is. (*She snuggles close to Buddy*) And so are you, Buddy. (*suddenly*) Say, listen, honey! You know what I'm gonna name our child?

BUDDY: No, what you gonna name him?

VIOLA: (*looking at the poster, then straight at Buddy*) Angelo Herndon Jones!

BUDDY: (*Slowly*) Angelo . . . Herndon . . . Jones.

(*They kiss as the curtain falls*)

A Collaboration of Jazz, Poetry, and Blues: *De Organizer*

De Organizer—or *The Organizer*, as it is sometimes called—is the last of Langston Hughes' attempts at political drama and is credited solely to Hughes in the many books that treat his life and examine his works. The play, however, is a collaborative effort between Langston Hughes and James P. Johnson. Johnson actually approached Hughes with the idea for a play in early 1937. His letter dated January puts forth the simple proposal: "I have been trieing [*sic*] for some time to locate you for the purpose of supplying me with an opera libretto. Of course providing you are willing, would like to co-operate with me . . . I have one or two subjects and plot of my own I would like to tell you about. . . . I am convinced that you and I ought to do a strong Negro opera." Hughes responded from Cleveland in late January, indicating that he would be glad to work on an opera libretto. Hughes suggested a meeting could be arranged when he returned to New York in late February or early March and concluded his letter with: "When we meet, I'd like very much to hear the ideas which you have in mind. I think we could work out something really Negro, modern, and interesting. I hope so." Johnson's subsequent letter provided more detail about the project he envisioned. He had in hand a contract to do "a grand opera" of Theodore Brown's play *Natural*

Man. Johnson explained to Hughes that the play had already been produced in California, Seattle, and other parts of the United States "as a drama using authentic spirituals." His proposition to Hughes was forthright: "I wish to have it put in blank verse so I can set it [to music] & I am willing to give you or afford you a legitimate writers share." He noted that the project should not take Hughes long and that he had "good promises and chance for production."[1]

Upon his return to New York, Hughes took a copy of the contract to his lawyer, Arthur Spingarn. A long letter to Johnson dated 8 March 1938 offers further evidence of Hughes' reluctance to enter into theatrical endeavors without an ironclad contract delineating his rights and obligations. In it he alludes vaguely to his dispute with Zora Neale Hurston, commenting toward the end, "[F]rom past experiences in the theater, I know that unless from the very beginning contracts are clearly drawn up in black and white, there may be in the end, complications and disagreements, which sometimes result badly for all concerned." In tone, his letter is a much more formal and even more demanding than the others he sent to Johnson. Hughes sidesteps his direct objections by placing the blame for his concerns on his lawyer:

> Mr. Spingarn feels that it is rather loosely drawn up and that it does not afford us any protection whatsoever on the motion picture rights to the opera, since your contract with Mr. Brown leaves him free to sell his play at any time, and should our opera be a success, he could without consulting us, dispose of the motion picture rights on the basis of the play which would, of course, then spoil any chance we might have of selling them. . . . Mr. Spingarn feels that for our own protection we should have the rights to any musical version of the play, whether it be an opera, light opera, operetta or musical play.

This, he maintained, would preclude anyone else from adapting other musical versions of the play that would be in competition with theirs.

Hughes also objected to the contractual stipulation that the play be written in blank verse: "Blank verse is the old Shakespearean form which would hardly be suitable for an entire opera libretto, although it might be used in parts." The most restrictive point of the contract, and one Hughes most probably would never have accepted had the contract been presented to him, was again placed at the request of Mr. Spingarn: "Mr. Spingarn also feels that, if we go to all the work and trouble of writing an opera version of *Natural Man* there should be a clause in our agreement with Mr. Brown that once the opera is finished, for a limited period of two or three years he would not attempt to produce his play in any first-class theater in a first-class city in competition with our joint attempts to sell the opera of the production. This, of course, would leave him still free to use his play for amateur productions and so forth." Hughes then proposed that in "light of these various defects"—which *Spingarn* found in the contract—a new contract be drawn up before they began any collaboration, "especially since on the point of the movie rights we have no protection at all." Ultimately, an agreement was reached and the collaboration progressed.[2]

Johnson's initial letter to Hughes can be characterized as polite and differential, yet Johnson was a prominent musical figure in his own right. Blues and jazz aficionados concur in their assessment that Johnson was the leading innovator in a style of playing called "stride piano." His music, featured in the lavish song-and-dance revues of George White and Earl Carroll, earned him a reputation for an innovative and revolutionary musical style in the 1920s and 1930s. His artistic reputation created a demand for his services, and a number of blues singers of the period, including Bessie Smith, enlisted Johnson to accompany them in their own performances. In Hughes, Johnson sought the sole writer of the Harlem Renaissance who, says Scott E. Brown, "took jazz—the new music—seriously." It is precisely the seriousness of *De Organizer* that makes it noteworthy for those researching Hughes—and also Johnson. While Hughes' concern for social reform pervades much of his work, Brown, who wrote the biography of Johnson, notes that "Johnson's interest is more difficult to characterize since a large part of his work in musical theater was not so revolutionary as *The Organizer*."[3]

In the summer of 1937, Hughes traveled to Paris at the invitation of the International Association of Writers. There, he worked on a draft of *De Organizer*, which, from its inception, was intended as a one-act musical, "radical in tone."[4] Upon returning to New York in September, Hughes found the Suitcase Theater faltering for lack of scripts and set about rectifying the situation with a spate of scriptwriting, with uneven results. *Young Man of Harlem*, written with both the Harlem Suitcase Theater and the Gilpin Players at Karamu Theater in mind, was rejected by both. Hughes gamely countered with five political parodies, which the Suitcase Theater subsequently produced successfully. Faced with considerable debts, Hughes increased his literary productivity proportionately. Ironically, his debts were theater-related: expected royalties for the tour of *Mulatto* failed to materialize, and he sought legal recourse through the

166 A COLLABORATION OF JAZZ, POETRY, AND BLUES

Dramatists' Guild, asking them for assistance in securing his rightful fees.

The fall of 1938 found Hughes deluged with self-imposed theatrical obligations. While overseeing a revival of *Don't You Want to Be Free?*, he also wrote and produced satirical skits, coordinated a fund-raising program for the Suitcase Theater, and wrote *Young Man of Harlem*, whose rejection led him to commit to writing another three-act play, *Front Porch*, for the Gilpin Players. He completed *De Organizer* with Johnson, and Rampersad's research indicates that during this period, Hughes had also "quietly applied for work with the New York Federal Theater." It seems that he intended to use *De Organizer* as a sample of his dramatic works for the Federal Theater to review. The title page of the original script lists several individuals and groups who were to receive a mimeograph copy: Max Lieber, his agent; Jack Gibbs; the New Theater League; the One-Act Play Magazine Company; Jimmy Johnson; and the national office of the Federal Theater.

While engaged in the business and production affairs of the Suitcase Theater, Hughes struggled to bring *De Organizer* to fruition. He had a series of meetings with Johnson at Johnson's Long Island home. By November, the play was in rehearsal and was most probably intended for production at the Cafe Society in New York. Hughes, however, sought financial refuge in California, again working in theater and film-related enterprises, this time with Clarence Muse and Arna Bontemps.[5]

Johnson sent a progress report to Hughes when he was staying at Noel Sullivan's home in Carmel, California. The news was not encouraging: "Writing to let you know *The Organizer* is in rehearsal now but I don't know when it will be produced. . . . The Cafe Society show was called off." However, he did apprise Hughes of other opportunities, noting that he had submitted Hughes' *Class Struggle* to the Theater Arts Committee Cabaret and that he had been asked by Adelaide Bean to write the music for a new show. Johnson invited Hughes to submit "[a]nything [he] might have concerning the New Deal or politics or social [themes]," in hopes of placing Hughes' work in this new production. Another letter in mid-December 1939 indicates that Johnson had a contract in hand from Jack Bragman for a production of *De Organizer* but would not sign until Hughes was satisfied with it. His efforts on behalf of their collaborative productions were held up somewhat by Hughes' absence. Johnson declared that he would not go forward with the production at the TAC Theater until Hughes was there "in person." He assured Hughes that the Labor Stage production of *De Organizer* was "sure" even though the

ILGWU theatrical group was a "little slow." This same letter informed Hughes that Johnson had an angle for a commercial production of *De Organizer*.[6]

There is evidence of additional collaborations between James P. Johnson and Langston Hughes beyond the piece called *Class Struggle in Swing*, which Johnson submitted to the Theater Arts Committee Cabaret in October 1939. His letters indicate that they collaborated on songs: "Glad to See You Again" and "I Think It Is OK," as well as a song Hughes refers to as "The Barbecue Song," written at the request of Irving Mills in 1943. A cantata is also mentioned in the correspondence, which Johnson asks Hughes to bring back with him on his return to New York. Johnson became infirm in August 1940, two months after the performance of *De Organizer*, suffering the first of what would be eight strokes. He recovered, but his association with Langston Hughes seems to have ended. Though their collaborations dwindled in the 1940s, it was Johnson that Hughes wrote to in November 1950 with a request to set one of his poems to music: "In February I have a new book of poems coming out, *Montage of a Dream Deferred*, which contains the enclosed poem, 'Night Funeral in Harlem.' I thought, perhaps you might like to put some music to it. If so, I would be delighted, and when the book comes out we can, no doubt, get some publicity through the publishers concerning the song and perhaps get some of our better concert singers to programme it."[7]

The Hughes/Johnson collaboration held the potential for theatrical greatness. Both possessed an artistic genius that was perceived early in their careers and has since been acknowledged by academic examinations. Both were held strongly by artistic roots in their African heritage, refusing to sever them when entertaining contemporary political issues. Hughes, who endured criticism for depicting blacks in an unfavorable light, steadfastly used dialect and humor indigenous to black neighborhoods and street life. Similarly, Brown contends, Johnson held to the "grass-roots heritage of jazz, maintaining a pure style at the expense of commercial success."[8]

Hughes' love for the blues—its forms, stylistic devices, and the razor-sharp edge of its messages—finds evidence in the structure of his poems. The blues allowed him to draw from creative as well as financial wells. Steven C. Tracy, whose book *Langston Hughes and the Blues* offers a fine analysis of blues structure and influences in Hughes' poetry, comments upon the fascination with folk-based material in the 1920s. The popularity of the blues—its appeal to both white and black audiences—created numerous commercial outlets for artists. He maintains that "as a creative artist, Hughes was much like the blues composer or professional musician in seeking to draw on his folk roots not only out of pride and the need for individual artistic freedom but, sometimes, for economic reasons as well. For these reasons he did not reject more commercially oriented blues but sought to use the characteristics of those kinds of blues to express one part of the city side of the blues."[9]

Although other well-known contemporary writers such as William Carlos Williams, Richard Wright, Allen Ginsberg, and Jack Kerouac experimented with blues structures and sounds in their poetry, it was Langston Hughes who was in the vanguard of the "poetry-performance movement." As early as 1927, Hughes employed a jazz pianist to play the blues as accompaniment to his poetry readings, a technique often attributed to the Beat poets in the 1950s. By his own account, Hughes worked through the composition of his blues poems by singing them on his way to work. Like poet Vachel Lindsay, on whose table Hughes first deposited his poems while working as a busboy in Washington, Hughes provided musical directives in his works. The marginalia in his hand on the pages of *De Organizer* offer clear indications of the rhythms and musical styles he intended for the production.[10]

NEW YORK PRODUCTION OF *DE ORGANIZER*

Hughes' biographers are quick to associate the production of *De Organizer* with labor groups. *De Organizer* was, in fact, performed as part of the 1940 convention of the International Ladies' Garment Workers' Union but was not performed by Labor Stage, the organization's theatrical arm. The ILGWU had won acclaim and notoriety with its productions of John Wexley's *Steel* and the political satire *Pins and Needles,* which ran at the same time as *De Organizer.* The ILGWU cultural units performed the "concert version" of *De Organizer* in the 31 May 1940 performance at Carnegie Hall and listed it in its Convention Festival Concert program. Whether there was a purely "dramatic" version that was produced is subject to question. Clearly, though, the Hughes/Johnson collaboration was not performed by the ILGWU as a play. The concert production provides the sole evidence of *De Organizer* in any kind of performance.

The ILGWU concert version, presented by the ILGWU Negro Chorus and the ILGWU Symphony Orchestra, was part of an elaborate festival that coincided with the 1940 World's Fair. However, there is a glaring discrepancy between the prominence of the ILGWU Negro Chorus's presentation in the program and the dearth of publicity given the chorus prior to the evening's performance, even though other upcoming performances were mentioned in the New York papers. Judging from the program alone, *De Organizer* seems to be the featured performance; fully two pages are devoted to the libretto, the cast, and the listing of the Negro Chorus members.[11] But the ILGWU concert was announced only once in the music section of the *New York Times* while other more famous artists performing the same evening, 31 May, received the most attention. None of the newspapers mentioned *De Organizer* in any of the few announcements that appeared prior to the performance at the World's Fair. For all intents and purposes, in the New York papers, it did not exist. A preview announcement of the event that appeared 31 May in the *New York Times* under the heading "Music Notes" indicated that there would be a performance by soloists and other music groups of the International Workers' Union, but there is no mention of Langston Hughes, James P. Johnson, the Negro Chorus, or *De Organizer*. A review the following day indicates only that "[a]n elaborate program was applauded by a large audience." This time the Negro Chorus is credited, but there is no commentary on what they performed. The Sunday *Times* carried no subsequent reviews about the performance, despite the fact that Eleanor Roosevelt addressed the ILGWU at ceremonies at the World's Fair and that the ILGWU had purchased an advance block of 125,000 tickets to the fair for that day. James P. Johnson's opening at the Cafe Society the week of the concert was the only publicity given him in the press. The only notice of Langston Hughes came four days before the concert, announcing that he had "[p]repared the book for a spectacular Negro musical . . . that shall be presented this Summer in Chicago in connection with the American Negro Exposition there."[12]

DE ORGANIZER

At first glance, one might be willing to admit that *De Organizer* fits John Gassner's definition of an "agit-prop" play: "a short play, usually a skit of no literary value but of immediate theatrical incandescence."[13] *De Organizer* is, in fact, a short play; the copy of the original script in the Langston Hughes papers is only fifteen pages long. The verse is simplistic and heavy-handed in its moralizing and sentimentality; as literature, it does fall short. But it can be argued convincingly that this script was never intended merely as proletarian literature; it was intended as a musical performance. The stirring element in any production of *De Organizer* would be its presentation as song. Therefore, the "theatrical incandescence" of this script rests in its unique collaboration—the literature of Langston Hughes and the music of noted jazz pianist and composer James P. Johnson. As part of the body of literature that comprises the works of Langston Hughes, it merits critical examination.

The text of the play reveals an evolutionary step in Hughes' use of dramatic form. Where *Scottsboro, Limited* displayed all of the strident tendencies of early agit-prop scripts of the late 1920s and early 1930s— using audience plants and espousing Communist doctrine—*De Organizer* belongs with the scripts of other playwrights produced as part of the next phase of a theatrical movement treating labor themes. What influenced Hughes' approach to labor themes is difficult to gauge. His travels brought him into contact with writers treating the same themes in their plays, and it may be that these associations affected the scripts examined here. Hughes' 1931 lecture tour of the South placed him at the University of North Carolina at Chapel Hill at the same time Loretta and James Osler Bailey's play *Strike Song* was being produced by Fred Koch's Carolina Playmakers. Notably, their script incorporates for political ends documentary evidence concerning events of the Gastonia textile strike, and it also makes unique use of labor songs to move its audience. Hughes' speech at Chapel Hill, which was denounced in the pages of the *Southern Textile Bulletin,* received comment in the same issue that blasted the production of *Strike Song.* This in itself would not be particularly significant were it not for other evidence that indicates that Hughes, during the intervening period between writing *Scottsboro, Limited* and *De Organizer,* also visited Provincetown, Massachusetts. Coincidentally, he was there at the same time that Mary Heaton Vorse's play, *Strike!,* another treatment of the Gastonia textile strike, was being readied for production by William Dorsey Blake, who wrote the dramatic adaptation from Vorse's novel and directed the play. Vorse's diaries from this period establish that "Langston" was in attendance at parties while the play was in rehearsal or production.[14] Blake later wrote for the Federal Theater Project. As already noted, Hughes planned to send the FTP a copy of *De Organizer.* The dramatic techniques used in both *Strike Song* and *Strike!* were employed in FTP productions throughout the 1930s.

Hughes' script uses dramatic techniques and staging elements in a notably similar manner to those in both *Strike Song* and *Strike!* In its use of music, *De Organizer* more resembles *Strike Song;* yet its opening and closing follow the opening and closing of *Strike!* Both *Strike!* and *De Organizer* are written in verse and are performed as an orchestrated choral reading. *Strike Song* uses actual labor songs to create a unified voice between players and audience; *Strike!* uses poetry and choral recitation to create a scene reminiscent of classical Greek drama. Hughes merged these two artistic structural elements and created a new form that used choral recitation in the rhythm of the blues and jazz.

Steven Tracy notes, "One of the most important and obvious ways that Langston used the blues tradition, which is also the primary way critics used to identify Hughes' blues poems, was in his employment of musical and stanzaic structures."[15] The eight- and twelve-bar musical stanzas that form the basis for categorizing the blues into two major types are readily apparent in Hughes' poems; his dramatic works use this form as well. Tracy and other jazz experts recognized Hughes' use of an "inverted" blues stanza in his 1938 play *Don't You Want to Be Free?* Probably because *De Organizer* was not published, Tracy was unaware of the existence of this earlier example of Hughes' use of blues structure. From the very first line, *De Organizer* displays blues form.[16]

Tracy's *Langston Hughes and the Blues* offers lively, informed analysis of the technical variations in blues forms evident in Hughes' poetry. An important point made in his extensive study reminds the reader that Hughes was not a southerner. Even though he used the blues form and wrote about injustices found in the South, he was a midwesterner, born in Kansas. Readers should consider the influence of the Chicago Renaissance on his work and Hughes' subsequent rise as a leading figure in the Harlem Renaissance. Chicago Renaissance writers like Carl Sandburg and Vachel Lindsay set a precedent for using colloquial diction in poetry. Hughes experimented with and extended the boundaries of their work by setting this colloquial diction, used in poetic structure, against a backdrop of music.

The cultural influence of the Midwest and the Chicago Renaissance on Hughes is significant. His love of the blues grew out of his exposure to a genre known as "Kansas City Blues," a particular style that made use of a combination of blues idioms—ragtime, jazz, and orchestral music, all of which are found in his dramatic works.[17] Ross Russell's assessment of the rudiments of the Kansas City style provides an accurate description of what one finds in Langston Hughes' use of the blues and specifically in his works intended for the theater:

> Kansas City style began as a grass-roots movement and retained its earthy, proletarian character to the end. In the beginning it was plain rather stiff and crude, but aggressively indigenous, and colloquial. It drew from two main sources, folksong and ragtime. From

folksong—with its grab bag of country dances, field hollers, ballads and work songs—and from the blues—both the old country blues and the newer urban blues—Kansas city extracted must of its material. In its early stages Kansas City jazz might have been described as a folksy, raggy, blues-saturated dance music.[18]

Hughes' fascination with musical forms used dramatically extended to religious and folk music well. In *De Organizer,* the group character of the Chorus brings to the text an additional element of gospel music, interspersed with the blues.

There are pronounced religious overtones in the structural elements of the play, including the use of call-response, which provides a powerful rhetorical appeal. The purposeful use of call-response worked to unify the audience with the performers in a production that became tantamount to a religious service. According to Jack L. Daniel and Geneva Smitherman, call-response "permeates all communication, and in the Traditional Black Church it is the basis of all other communicative strategies." Daniel and Smitherman address the significance of call-response as a communication tactic, asserting that "call-response seeks to synthesize 'speakers' and 'listeners' in a unified movement." They make the point that call-response is an "interactive network in which the fundamental requirement is active participation of all individuals. . . . There is no sharp line between performers or communicators and the audience, for virtually everyone is performing and everyone is listening."

Another structural element in *De Organizer* reminiscent of traditional black church services involves the arrival of the union organizer. Daniel and Smitherman maintain that such religious services begin "with the recognition of the need for God's entrance at the outset. Because it is necessary for God to enter the service, the initial part of the service consists of everyone's making simultaneous calls-and-responses to invoke the spirit."[19] The repetition of the question posed in the opening lines—"Where is that man?"—establishes expectations of "a coming," "a leader who will show the way." This is a technique found in several other labor plays of the early 1930s. In *Strike!* and *Strike Song,* the audience also anticipates the coming of the union organizer, the savior of repressed labor groups.

De Organizer is also similar to *Strike!* and *Strike Song* in character delineation and presentation. Religion and folklore combine to make the labor leader a figure of mythic proportion in this play and others like it; he is drawn as the synthesis of the Messiah and the Conjure Man of southern black folklore.[20] As in the textile plays already noted, this script has the female union organizer, romantically linked with the Organizer, arrive prior to the protagonist. Her character heightens the tension and contributes to the religious imagery. In *De Organizer*, she refers to the title character as "little David / What threw that mighty stone" and proclaims:

> That man he travels on de wings of song
> He travels on de air.
> He travels like a cloud by night.
> That man is everywhere.

The character of the organizer enters the stage setting by way of using a religious password. Even before his appearance, his character assumes tremendous stature because of the layered descriptions of him as religious messiah and John Henry, the legendary Negro rail-splitter. The woman directly compares the union leader with John Henry in the song "Slow drag blues":

> Oh! Ma man is like John Henry.
> My man is big and strong.
> Nothin' in this world can scare him.
> Nothin' makes my man do wrong.
> Yes, ma man is like John Henry.
> He's a hero in de land.
> And folks deep in troubles
> Comes lookin' for ma man.
> Yes, they comes lookin' for ma man,
> Cause ma man is like John Henry 'cept he's
> Put his hammer down.
> Now, just like John Henry, he
> Goes from town to town.
> Oh! Ma man is like John Henry, but he
> Don't drive steel no more.
> What ma man is doin' now is
> Organizin' de poor—

John Henry is not the only prominent folkloric character in Hughes' script. John, the Old Man, initiates the sharecropper chant early in the play and bustles hen-like about the meeting room interjecting comments and questions until the meeting actually begins, then demands the floor and delivers a recitative rationale on the need to organize. In the black folkloric tradition, he is a descendant of the John-and-Old Marster cycle. John in these tales is the "militant slave of black folklore." In *De Organizer,* Brother John commandeers the gun from the Overseer and orders, "If you want to 'tend this meeting, / You behave yourself!" He is a character who appears in other guises in Hughes' work. Susan L. Blake makes a convincing case that the Jesse B. Simple character of Hughes' essays, short stories, and later plays is "the migrant descendant of John." Her characterization of old John as being "neither big nor strong, . . . more than clever" and "a political analyst" transfers readily to Brother John in this text.[21]

The musical styles indicated by Hughes in his stage directions reveal the rhythmic shifts and crescendos that help move the play forward and allow it to gain power. It begins softly with the Chorus and moves to the sharecroppers' chant, which then evolves into a variation of the "Hungry Blues" led by Brother Dosher. Though Hughes' libretto exists, James P. Johnson's score for the music of *De Organizer,* according to Scott Brown, has disappeared except for two versions of "Hungry Blues" recorded in 1939. By his estimation, "If the other numbers are as well written as 'Hungry Blues' then the entire work might well represent Johnson's greatest 'serious' achievement."[22] "Hungry Blues" is followed by "The Organizer Song," sung by the female union counterpart and ending with choral recitation of labor injustices and an urging of all to "Organize!"

The character of the Organizer arrives after the blues. Once he has been properly identified through use of a religiously inspired password, Hughes indicates the Chorus is to break into a "swing shout" singing "De organizer's here and / We's feelin' mighty glad!," repeating the refrain "Mighty glad!" The female organizer then takes center stage to sing her "Slow drag blues" about John Henry. Here the Organizer takes over with a series of interrogatories and assertions reminiscent of call-response patterns of religious revivals. Daniel and Smitherman explain the culturally unifying nature of call-response: "Call-response . . . embodies communality rather than individuality. Emphasis is on group cohesiveness and cooperation; the collective common good and spiritual regeneration is reinforced by the visitation of the Spirit, and the efforts of all are needed to bring this about."[23] Old John follows with his recitation on the need to organize.

Once the Overseer interrupts the meeting, Hughes' directions indicate that the lines "The landlord don't allow no organizing here" should be delivered in a manner that should call to mind "Mamma don't 'low no piano playin' here." This culminates in a swing rendition in which the cast takes up flashlights that illuminate their faces with up-lighting (devil lights) in a grotesque jack-o'-lantern-like display as they demand in song "Take a look at me!" A repetitive choral background of "Be free!" highlights the short exchange between Old John and the Overseer and transforms into a syncopated chant chronicling the trials of the field workers and their desire for freedom. The play moves quickly to closure with a combination gospel/blues shout and a final exultant refrain of "Fight! . . . Fight!" and "We organized a union here tonight!" accompanied by dancing and waving of placards announcing a newly formed sharecroppers' union.

The play is designed to have the audience on their feet singing "Fight! Fight! We organized a union here tonight!" While the participatory elements are not so bold as those evidenced in *Scottsboro, Limited,* they are revealed structurally in those passages that lend themselves to traditional audience call-response patterns, verbal affirmations, and group refrains. The script combines many of the elements of an enacted religious ritual with folkloric conventions. The character of Overseer takes on the proportions of the devil, a personification of wickedness. Routed by the justice, righteousness, and courage of the union organizer, the Overseer withers in the face of the power of labor. The character of the Organizer, like the legendary John Henry, is willing to fight the system and conquer the mountain, or die trying. Like the "Conjure Man," he is a mysterious character of extraordinary power.

Stylistically, *De Organizer* is easily categorized with Hughes' blues poems. By today's standards, these are recognized and praised for their departure from traditional poetic norms and their incorporation of music into the line and the reading of them. However, it was because of his blues poems that Hughes became the object of criticism. While poems like "The Negro Speaks of Rivers" were accepted because of their roots in the tradition of spirituals, his blues poems were "vehemently rejected" by the same critics who asserted they lacked metaphor and poetic imagery. They were dismissed as "doggerel."[24] *De Organizer* offers evidence of both the blues and gospel traditions. It provides the meditative laments and reflective social commentary of the blues while prompting the audience to persevere, rise above adversity, and fight the evil in their lives with the gospel songs. It offers yet additional evidence of how Hughes envisioned art as a forum for protest and persuasion.

Though the play has been forgotten, it stands as one more commentary on the political efficacy of dramatic performances. Its place in the evolution of American labor plays is an important one. It combines the efforts of two American artists, James P. Johnson and Langston Hughes, to rally American labor. The assumed power of Johnson's music coupled with Hughes' politically inspired lyrics make for a unique and captivating combination of rhythms and styles culminating in an art form used for political end. The script remains an unheralded example of compelling political plays in American theatrical and cultural history.

De Organizer: A Blues Opera in One Act

By James P. Johnson and Langston Hughes

Characters

THE ORGANIZER—BARITONE
THE WOMAN—CONTRALTO
THE OLD MAN—BASS
THE OLD WOMAN—SOPRANO
BROTHER DOSHER—TENOR
BROTHER BATES—TENOR
THE OVERSEER—BASS

SCENE: *Interior of a cabin on a backward plantation in the South. Night. Lanterns and flashlights. The room is full of ragged sharecroppers, men and women.*

WOMEN:	Where is that man?
MEN:	He ought to be here now!
CHORUS:	De Organizer! Organizer!
WOMEN:	Where is that man?
MEN:	He ought to be here now!

CHORUS:	De Organizer! Organizer!
	Where is that man? He ought to be here now!
OLD WOMAN:	Brother Dosher, it's gettin' late.
DOSHER:	Sit down, sister, you got to wait.
OLD WOMAN:	Brother, I'm tired o' waitin'.
	He ought to be here now.
DOSHER:	You might be tired o' waitin'
	But we's got to wait anyhow!
	You didn't get your freedom in one day.
	You can't get a union by hurryin' this a way.
OLD WOMAN:	Well, then, where is that man?
CHORUS:	He ought to be here now.
BATES:	Yes, where is that man?
CHORUS:	He ought to be here now.
BATES:	Organizing a union is all right,
	But damn if I can organize all night!
OLD WOMAN:	Yes, where is that man?
CHORUS:	He ought to be here now!
	The good Lawd knows,
	He ought to be here now.
BATES:	Yes he ought to be here now!

(End of opening chorus)

DOSHER:	Don't worry! He'll be here.
	He's a sharecropper, too,
	Just like me and you.
OLD MAN:	Sharecropper!
OLD WOMAN:	Sharecroppers! . . . Oh!
CHORUS:	*(Chants)*
	Plantin', plowin', hoein'!
	Gettin' up early in de mornin'.
	Plowin', plantin', hoein'!
	Out in de fields at dawnin'.
	Always watchin' cotton growin'.
	Plowin', plantin', hoein'!
	Wonder where that cotton's goin'?
	Plantin', plowin', hoein'!
	Wonder where my life is goin'?
	Plowin', plantin', hoein',
	Wonder where my life is goin'?

OLD MAN: Just poor sharecroppers,
            That's all we is:
CHORUS: Plantin', plowin', hoein'!

(End of chant)

DOSHER: *(Blues)*
            Just poor sharecroppers, yes!
            But we ain't gonna be always.
            We gonna get together
            And end these hongry days.
            Folks, I've got them hongry blues—
            And nothin' in this world to lose.
            People's tellin me to choose
                'Tween dyin',
                and lyin',
                and keepin' on cryin'—
            But I's tired o' them hongry blues.
            Listen! Ain't you heard de news?
            There's another thing to choose:
            A brand new world, clean and fine,
            Where nobody's hongry and
            There's no color line!
            A thing like that's worth
            Anybody's dyin'—
            Cause I ain't got a thing to lose
            But them dog-gone hongry blues!
CHORUS: We ain't got a thing to lose
            But them dog-gone hongry blues!
OLD WOMAN: I done washed so many clothes
            My hands is white as snow.
            Done got to de place that I
            Don't want to wash no more.
            I'm going up to heaven,
            Say, good Lawd, here am I!
BATES: But Sister Mary, de Lawd's gonna say:
            You can't come in here till you die.
CHORUS: You can't come in here till you die!
OLD WOMAN: Well, I've got them hongry blues.
CHORUS: But nothin' in this world to lose!
DOSHER: Folks, ain't you heard de news.

There's another thing to choose:
A brand new world, clean and fine,
Where's nobody's hongry and
There's no color line—
A thing like that's worth
Anybody's dyin'—

CHORUS: Cause we ain't got a thing to lose
But them dog-gone hongry blues!

(End of Blues)

OLD WOMAN: Where is that man? He ought to be here now.
OLD MAN: Yes, where is that man?
BATES: Where is that man?
OLD MAN: Maybe I better go and take a look once more.
DOSHER: Shade de light, brother, 'fore you open de door.
OLD WOMAN: Yes, shade that light, so's the boss won't see.
BATES: And when you hits de pike, walk quietly.
OLD MAN: I'll walk quietly.
But that man, which way'll he come?
From de East or from de West?
DOSHER: He's comin' from de West,
Where de union's best.

(A WOMAN's voice giving the password outside)

WOMAN: Jerico! . . . Jerico!
CHORUS: Shsss-ssss-ss-s! Who can that be?
WOMAN: Jerico!
DOSHER: One!
WOMAN: Jerico!
DOSHER: Two!
WOMAN: Jerico!
DOSHER: Three!
Then she's due to be!
Open de door, let's see.

(The OLD MAN opens the door. The WOMAN enters, bringing leaflets.)

WOMAN: Folks, it's me!
DOSHER: Yes, she's due to be!

> She brings us news about that man.
> And something here for us in her hand.

CHORUS: Strange woman, where is that man?

OLD WOMAN: That organizing man?

CHORUS: Yes, where is that man?

[Notations in text indicate "Song: 'Organizer'"]

WOMAN: That man is comin' by a secret way.
That man is comin' all alone.
That man is like little David
What threw that mighty stone—
Cause he's de organizer!

CHORUS: He's de organizer! He's de organizer!

WOMAN: That man he travels on de wings of song.
He travels on de air.
He travels like a cloud by night.
That man is everywhere.—
Cause he's de organizer!

CHORUS: He's de organizer! Organizer!

WOMAN: He's gonna help us build a union,
Build it of white and black,
Cause de people that works in de fields all day
Is tired of de landlords on our back.

CHORUS: Yes, we's tired of de landlords on our backs.

(End of Song)

WOMAN: Folks, I bring you leaflets!
Folks, read 'em well.
This little bit of paper here's
got a lot to tell.
It says: *(Recitative)*
Ten thousand bales of cotton to de landlord!
How much was ours?
Ten thousand acres of cane to de big boss!
How much was ours?
A million water melons on de market!
How much was ours?
How can we get them things
That should be ours?

              Here, take this little leaflet, folks,
              And read it well.
              This little bit of paper's got
              A lot to tell.

OLD MAN: What does it say?

CHORUS: How can we get them things that should be ours?

OLD WOMAN: Which is de way?

BATES: Them things we plant and plow and hoe for
              Underneath these southern skies?

DOSHER: How can we make a living?

WOMAN: Organize!

CHORUS: Organize! . . . Organize!

OLD WOMAN: This here little leaflet says, Organize!

CHORUS: Organize! . . . Organize!
              O-R-G-A---N-I-Z-E!
              O-R-G-A---N-I-Z-E!

OLD MAN: Who ever wrote this paper sure must be wise!

CHORUS: Cause this here little leaflet says ORGANIZE!

OLD WOMAN: But where is our man?

BATES: Yes, where is that man?

OLD MAN: Maybe something's happened to our man?

OLD WOMAN: Woman, now you tell us where is that man?

WOMAN: He'll be here soon.
              He travels on de air.

DOSHER: He travels like a cloud by night.
              That man is everywhere.

WOMAN: He'll be here.

OLD WOMAN: He's your man?

WOMAN: Yes, he's my man. I love him, too.

OLD WOMAN: But ain't you scared for your man? Ain't you?

WOMAN: No, he'll be here soon. He's coming to you.
              He's helping us all. And I can't be selfish
              About him. Of course,
              Sometimes I miss him because
              My man's an organizer.
              My man's an organizer
              He moves from place to place.
              I guess I wouldn't be human
              If I didn't miss his loving face.
              So I admit:

Sometimes I'm lonely when he's gone away,
But I keep thinking there will come a day.
When this man of mine will do
All the things he wanted to,
And the better world he's dreamed of will come true.
Then what will it matter all these
Days we've spent apart,
There'll be a future bright with joy
Blooming in my heart,
All the poor folks in the world
Will be poor no more,
For my man's an organizer and
That's what he's working for.
And although I'm lonely when he's gone away from me,
Tomorrow he'll be with me and tomorrow we'll be free,
You and I, my man and me, we'll be free!

OLD WOMEN: I believes you. You sure do love him.
But when's he coming here.

OLD MAN: We can't wait! It's gettin' late!

BATES: We got to go. Where is that man?

WOMAN: Listen!

(A MAN's voice heard without [that is, outside] giving the password)

ORGANIZER: Jerico! . . . Jerico!

DOSHER: Now, I reckon you'll stay.

BATES: Yes, I'll stay! Get out o' my way.

ORGANIZER: Jerico!

DOSHER: One!

ORGANIZER: Jerico!

DOSHER: Two!

ORGANIZER: Jerico!

DOSHER: Three!
It's de organizer! Glory be!

CHORUS: It's de organizer! Yes, it's he!
It's de organizer! Thank God a-Mighty!
It's de organizer! Lawd! De organizer!
Thank God a-Mighty! It's de organizer!

(The door opens and the ORGANIZER enters)

DOSHER: Jackson, where you been so long?

ORGANIZER: I been organizing.

DOSHER: Where you been organizing?

ORGANIZER: Been way cross Mississippi organizing.

DOSHER: Who you been organizing?

ORGANIZER: I been organizing black folks!
And organizing white folks!
And organizing peoples on de land!
I been tellin' everybody
In de cotton and de cane fields,
Been tellin' everybody they's a man!

OLD MAN: And de white folks, what they sayin'?

ORGANIZER: De poor white folks is with us.
De rich white folks is mad.

WOMAN: But, baby, how you feelin'?

ORGANIZER: Lawd, I'm feelin' mighty glad!

CHORUS: Mighty glad! Mighty glad!

ORGANIZER: Oh, I'm feelin' mighty glad! (As he mounts a box to speak)

CHORUS: (Swing shout)
De organizer's here and
We's feelin' mighty glad!
Mighty glad! Mighty glad!
Yes, de organizer's here and
We feelin' mighty glad!

(Mighty glad! Mighty glad! continues softly as the WOMAN lifts her voice in praise and love. [Additional notations indicate "Slow drag blues—John Henry."])

WOMAN: Oh! Ma man is like John Henry.
Ma man is big and strong.
Nothin' in this world can scare him.
Nothin' makes my man do wrong.
Yes, ma man is like John Henry.
He's a hero in de land.
And folks deep in troubles
Comes lookin' for ma man.
Yes, they comes lookin' for ma man,
Cause ma man is like John Henry 'cept he's
Put his hammer down.

Now, just like John Henry, he
Goes from town to town.
Oh! Ma man is like John Henry, but he
Don't drive steel no more.
What ma man is doin' now is
Organizin' de poor—
And when he gets done organizin' we
Can take this world in hand.
Cause ma man is like John Henry and
John Henry was a man!

CHORUS: John Henry was a man, Lawd!
John Henry was a man!

(End song)

ORGANIZER: *(Begins Organizer)*
Folks, you is hongry!
Folks, you need bread!
What you gonna do, folks?

CHORUS: Get mad! Get mad!

ORGANIZER: Folks, that ain't de way!
Folks, that ain't right.
The way to get what we all need's
Unite! . . . Unite!
You don't get mad at de rain, do you?
You don't get mad at de sun?
Ain't no use to get mad then
At a big boss with a gun!
De rain you stores in cisterns.
De sun gives de berries their juice.
De union can take any old boss
And turn him every way but loose!
When we got a big strong union, folks,
A union of black and white,
There'll be more difference in this old South
Then there is twixt day and night.
So to organize is right!

CHORUS: Yes, to organize is right!
Right! . . . Right! . . . Right! . . . Right!
Yes, to organize is right!

ORGANIZER: Sharecroppers all over Dixie,
Farm hands and tenants as well,
De union is de only way
To free ourselves from hell.

CHORUS: To free ourselves from hell!
Yes, to free ourselves from hell!

(End song)

ORGANIZER: Then, Brother Dosher, take de chair,
And let's get de meetin' started here.

OLD WOMAN: Yes, let's get de meetin' started here.

OLD MAN: Brother Dosher, I wans de floor.
I has a word to say.

DOSHER: Wait a minute, Brother John,
Till de meetin's underway.

OLD MAN: *(Recitative)*
Well, when de meetin's underway,
I has a word to say. And it is this:
The sooner we on this plantation organizes,
the better, because the way things is going now,
if we don't organize, we is gwine to get put off,
and if we get put off we's got no place to go,
and no work, and to get relief is hell, and I
don't want relief nohow! I likes to work, so
let's get together and organize and pertect ourselves
and these here fields and this here state
and our country, because . . .

(Loud shots are heard outside)

OLD WOMAN: Uh-oh! That's de overseer!

BATES: De overseer!

DOSHER: Put out that light!

ORGANIZER: Keep quiet! Don't run!
Let him in if he knocks!
We might as well face him now
And tell him what we've made up our minds to.

CHORUS: Face him! Tell him! Yes, that's true!

(A commanding voice is heard outside)

OVERSEER:	You John! . . . You Mary!
	You must think I can't see that light!
	You'll hold no meeting here tonight!
OLD WOMAN:	That's de overseer!
OVERSEER:	You-all croppers think you're wise,
	Sneaking off to the woods to organize!
	(Knocking loudly)
	Open up that door!
OLD MAN:	Come in, if you want to come in!
OVERSEER:	*(Kicking in door)*
	I'll come in all right!
	What's going on in here tonight?
ORGANIZER:	We's organizing!
OVERSEER:	What? . . . That's a damned disgrace!
	You'll have no union on this place!
	(Like "Mamma don't 'low no piano playin' here.")
	Don't you know
	The landlord don't allow no organizing here?
CHORUS:	What?
OVERSEER:	The landlord don't allow no organizing here!
	I've got my whip and I've got my gun—
	And you'll get no organizing done!
	The landlord don't allow no organizing here!
CHORUS:	But there's gonna be some organizing here!
	Yes, there's gonna be some organizing here!
	We don't care what de landlord don't 'low
	We gonna organize anyhow.
	There's gonna be some organizing here!
OVERSEER:	What? What's that? What's that I hear?
CHORUS:	We said there's gonna be some organizing here!
ORGANIZER:	In spite of your whip
	And in spite of your gun,
	We gonna get some organizing done!
CHORUS:	There'll be some organizing here!
	Yes, there'll be some organizing here!
OVERSEER:	Who are you dogs? Say!
	Who's talking back to me?

CHORUS: *(Swing)*
              Look in Alabama, man, and you will see!
              Look in Mississippi! Look in Tennessee!
              Take a look at Dixieland and you will see!
ORGANIZER: *(Lighting up his face with a flash-light)*
              Take a look at me!

(Others light up their faces, too, until the OVERSEER is surrounded by a sea of faces glowing in the night.)

OTHERS: And me!
              And me!
              And me!
OVERSEER: *(Cracking his whip angrily)*
              But I said there'd be no organizing here!
              I mean there'll be no organizing here!
CHORUS: You may crack your whip!
              You may shoot your gun—
              But we's made up our minds
              To get some organizing done.
OVERSEER: I said NO!

(He shoots four times. Quickly, the SHARECROPPERS surround him and take his gun.)

ORGANIZER: All the bullets in the world
              Can't shoot me!
OTHERS: Nor me!
              Nor me!
              Nor me!
CHORUS: We're four million croppers
              Determined to be free!

(The keep up refrain of "Be free!" in the background)

OLD MAN: Mary, take that gun and put it on de shelf.
              (To the OVERSEER)
              If you want to 'tend this meeting,
              You behave yourself!
ORGANIZER: We've got too much business here tonight

	To be interrupted by outsiders
	Who want to start a fight.
	Brother John, while you're over in that corner,
	Bring the flag along.
OLD MAN:	I will.
	This here flag I carried up San Juan Hill.
	My son followed it in France when he was killed.
ORGANIZER:	It's your flag, Mister Overseer,
	And my flag, too.
	So listen what us croppers have
	to say to you:
VOICE:	*(Syncopated chant)*
	I've chopped de cotton all my life long.
CHORUS:	So to want a little freedom now can't be wrong.
VOICE:	I've worked in de sun all day long,
CHORUS:	So to want a little freedom now can't be wrong.
VOICE:	I've plowed with old Jennie all my life long.
CHORUS:	To want a little freedom now can't be wrong.
VOICE:	I got up at sunrise all my life long.
CHORUS:	To want a little freedom now can't be wrong.
VOICE:	Plowing, planting, hoeing, all life long.
CHORUS:	To want a little freedom now can't be wrong.

(End song)

OVERSEER:	You-all say *freedom*?
	Don't look at me.
	I work for the landlord, too.
	I ain't free!
WOMAN:	Then take this little leaflet.
	Read it and be wise.
	If you want to be free,
	Organize!
CHORUS:	Organize! Organize!
	If you want to be free
	Organize!
OVERSEER:	How many's in this union?
CHORUS:	Everbody's here!
OVERSEER:	I'm going back and tell the landlord.
OLD WOMAN:	Huh! We don't care!

ORGANIZER: *(Shout)*
                All we want is, be sure to get it right.
                Tell him we organized a UNION here tonight!
CHORUS: Yes, we organized a union here tonight!
OVERSEER: Lemme out of here! *(He rushes out)*
CHORUS: We organized a union here tonight!

(Everybody dances, joins hands, exultant with joy. Happy movement. Large signs are lifted, SHARECROPPERS UNION.)

MEN: Fight! . . . Fight!
WOMEN: Fight! . . . Fight!
CHORUS: We organized a union here tonight!

Curtain

Conclusion:
Hughes' Lost Legacy

The poetry, short stories, essays, autobiographical writings, and popular plays of Langston Hughes have attracted the close scrutiny of literary scholars. Yet few have focused their attention in any depth on Hughes' labor plays. Reasons for their neglect may stem from the fact that they were difficult to find, having never been published. Perhaps it was the taint of Communism in the plays or Hughes' connection with leftist politics that made academics reluctant to expose these writings to public examination. Others may have feared that Hughes' literary reputation as America's premier black poet might be adversely affected, or even ruined, if his Communist connections were made known. The careers and reputations of other writers had been so ruined in the Communist witchhunts of the 1930s and 1950s. But the early nineties saw the demise of Soviet Communism, and the years of blacklisting because of real and alleged Communist affiliation are long over. Hughes' reputation as an American literary figure is secure. But some aspects of his career require further scholarly examination, such as his connection with radical political groups and his association with individuals like Whittaker Chambers, with whom Hughes founded a theater to produce Hughes' plays.

His political plays of the 1930s are important for several reasons. First, they offer a unique perspective on American labor and organizing efforts. There have been studies of plays that dramatize American labor, but Hughes' plays not only dramatize American radical politics and labor but also offer clear evidence of a movement by the American Communist Party to attract blacks and other minorities through the promise of better labor conditions. These plays provide insight into a political movement directed towards minorities in the unionizing efforts in the 1930s. While other labor plays of the period might allude to the targeting of minorities, no one is able to speak with as much authority about the issue as Langston Hughes. His ethos made him influential in supporting various labor and political causes.

The United States government certainly appreciated who Hughes was—a member of the American Communist Party and an activist willing to lend his name and growing prominence in the literary community to social and political causes. Hughes' associations were enough to merit the scrutiny of federal agents. The political Left of the 1930s courted Hughes. His poems sympathetic to the "Red" cause were published in magazines considered subversive. And when he boldly embarked on a trip to Russia, federal agents followed him through Europe, Russia, and Asia building a file of spurious evidence against him.

The U.S. State Department closely monitored Hughes' association with the political Left beginning in 1932 when he began his trip to Russia and ending in 1952 when he was called to testify before the Senate Committee on Permanent Investigations headed by Senators McCarthy and McClellan. First indications of official interest in Hughes occurs in a letter from the American embassy in London dated 22 October 1932, in which the writer includes a copy of the September/October 1932 *Negro Worker* containing a poem by Hughes entitled "The Same." The letter refers to the poem and concludes, "About Langston HUGHES, . . . our friends should be much indebted for any information that could be given them regarding this individual."[1]

The *Negro Worker,* published in Britain, described Hughes as "the young revolutionary novelist and poet. . . . He has recently written a play on the infamous Alabama case, called the 'Scottsboro Express.'" Such identifications with revolutionary causes coupled with the publication of his poem "The Same," which played to the revolutionary pieties of the Party, intensified government surveillance of Hughes throughout his tour.

The Same

It is the same everywhere for me:
On the docks of Sierra Leone,

In the cotton fields of Alabama,
In the diamond mines of Kimberley,
On the coffee hills of Haiti,
The banana lands of Central America
The streets of Harlem,
And the cities of Morocco and Tripoli.

Black:
Exploited, beaten, and robbed,
Shot and killed.
Blood running into
Dollars
Pounds
Francs
Pesetas
Lire
For the wealth of the exploiters—
Blood that never comes back to me again.

Better that my blood
Runs into the deep channels of Revolution,
Runs into the strong hands of Revolution,
Stains all flags red,
Drives away from
Sierra Leone
Kimberley
Alabama
Haiti
Central America
Harlem
Morocco
Tripoli
And all the black lands everywhere
The force that kills,
The power that robs,
And the greed that does not care.

Better that my blood makes one with the blood
Of all the struggling workers in the world—
Till every land is free of
Dollar robbers

> Pound robbers
> Franc robbers
> Peseta robbers
> Lire robbers
> Life robbers—
> Until the Red Armies of the International Proletariat,
> Their faces black, white, olive, yellow, brown,
> Unite to raise the blood Red Flag that
> Never will come down![2]

The information about Hughes requested in the London embassy's letter was sent in a confidential memorandum 15 November 1932. It indicated that the government had been fully aware of Hughes' associations with leftist figures from 1930 onwards and provided the following assessment of Hughes and his controversial activities up to 1932:

> Mr. James Langston Hughes, or Mr. Langston Hughes as he is more generally known, among the intellectuals in the communist movement within the past two years . . . is one of the regular contributors to the New Masses, a monthly magazine published in New York City which is definitely sympathetic with the communist movement. The latest publication of Mr. Hughes is entitled "Scottsboro, Limited." It consists of four poems and a one-act play devoted to the so-called Scottsboro case.
>
> Mr. Hughes accompanied a group of American Negroes to Moscow last June. The group was to participate in the production of a film, the title of which was to be "Black and White." It is understood that this film, which was to be made in Russia under the auspices of the workers' International Relief, was to portray from a communist viewpoint the life and struggles of Negro workers throughout the world. Production of the film was subsequently postponed. While no definite reasons for the postponement have ever been given, an article in the New York AMSTERDAM NEWS, a leading Negro paper published in Harlem, stated that the film was not postponed but was definitely canceled at the request of American engineers in Russia. This article, written by two members of the group, has aroused much comment in Negro circles in the United States. The communist press is devoting much space to the refutation of that charge, and has printed many articles by Mr. Hughes, who is still in Russia. In his contributions, Mr. Hughes attacks the accuracy of the AMSTERDAM NEWS article and states that the production of the film was postponed and not canceled. (In

connection with this matter, reference is made to R.A. memorandum No. 1465 of November 2, 1932)

Mr. Hughes is at present the bearer of Department passport No. 352769, which was issued on March 25, 1931. In his application for that passport, he stated that he was born at Joplin, Missouri on February 1, 1902; that he resided at 4800 Carnegie Avenue, Cleveland, Ohio; that he was an author by occupation; and that the passport was desired for a period of six months for the purpose of traveling in the West Indies and South America.[3]

Subsequent memoranda referred to Hughes as "the Communist Negro in Moscow" and document Hughes' travels and associations. Embassy letters from London indicate that Hughes and his traveling companions, Mildred Jones and Dorothy West, were being watched, and there was speculation about whom they might contact. The memo notes that "Langston Hughes is evidently in fairly close touch with Walt Carmon, who is believed to belong to the International Union of Revolutionary Writers."[4] A memorandum of 19 July 1933 provided biographical information about Jones, West, and Carmon. Carmon's information contained more evidence of Hughes' political predisposition: "With reference to Mr. Walt Carmon . . . it may be stated that there is no record of any American passport having been issued to a person of that name within recent years. It is possible that Mr. Carmon may be a Canadian citizen. It is known that he is one of the most important members of the John Reed Club of the United States, which is affiliated with the International Union of Revolutionary Writers."[5] Additional memoranda of 26 September 1933, 28 November 1933, and 1 February 1934 indicate that the government agents spent some time trying to track and identify the elusive Walt Carmon.

On his return to the United States by way of China and Japan in July 1933, authorities detained and questioned Hughes in Tokyo. According to State Department communiqués, "Because of Hughes' alleged connection with known members of Red organizations in Tokyo he had been taken to police headquarters and questioned on July 23. He was detained a short time and released the same afternoon."[6] There are two extant accounts of what happened to Hughes during the interrogation by Japanese police; both should be read with an eye to the biases and distortions they may contain. The first is the official report provided by Japanese police to the American Consul General in Shanghai and was submitted under the heading "Movement of James Langston Hughes, American Nigger

Writer in Japan." In it one finds an itinerary of Hughes' travels and visits with individuals connected with the Writers League; this association provided all the rationale needed for the police to take him into custody. "As his connections with the members of the League became more and more intimate he was summoned to the Tokyo Metropolitan Police Board where he made the under-mentioned statement following which he was released on condition that he would leave Japan at the earliest possible date." Hughes' statements transcribed in the interview sufficiently warranted his continued surveillance by government agents for years to come. After some brief biographical information, Hughes listed for the police his associations as being with the International Revolutionary Writers League, the International Revolutionary Plot Writers League, the Authors League, the Dramatist Guild, the National Association for Advancement of Colored People, and the Laborers Cultural League. He followed this by stating:

> Being a Negro I have been struggling for the emancipation of the Negroes and of the oppressed masses and will continue my struggle forever. Communism aims at the emancipation of the oppressed masses but I still doubt whether or not complete freedom can be secured through the realization of communism. I do not claim to be a communist but I do not object to be regarded as a sympathizer because I sympathize with and support all Communist movements and also the oppressed people. After all I am a liberalist who is interested in communism and the struggles for the emancipation of the oppressed. The object of my visit to the U.S.S.R. was to inspect the conditions there in order to publish a book on Russia. . . . During my stay . . . I inspected factories, schools, shops, farms, museums, theaters, etc. I attended in the capacity of an observer to the dramatic olympiad which was held for two days (May 5 & 6) in Moscow but did not attend the conference of the International Revolutionary Plot Writers League (Molto). I was not associated with any politicians in Russia but had several meetings with persons who were connected with arts and cinematography. . . . I bore the cost of all my expenses which amounted to Gold $1,000.00 and 3,000.00 rubles. During my visit to Shanghai . . . [o]n the night of July 16 I was invited to dinner by Madam Sun Yat Sen. As she had lived several years in a district where Negroes live in large numbers during her stay in the U.S.A. I had a great pleasure in discussing with her because she understands how the Negroes are oppressed in that country. I also had meetings with many leftist writers but I do not remember their names.[7]

Another version of the incident appears in the Noel Sullivan Papers and seems to have been part of the publicity for a meeting of the National Committee for the Defense of Political Prisoners. According to this account:

> On his way back from Russia Mr. Hughes arranged to spend a couple of days in Tokio [*sic*]. A group of Japanese writers there had planned a luncheon for him. Within twelve hours of his arrival, and an hour or so before his hosts were to meet him at his hotel, Mr. Hughes was "requested" to visit Police Headquarters. There he was detained and questioned; he was refused permission to telephone to the American Consul. After *seven hours* of questioning had satisfied the police authorities that he had no intentions against the Japanese government Mr. Hughes was allowed to go "free." That is, he was allowed to leave the police station. But he was warned against communicating with any Japanese persons before his departure; his luggage was searched, and two police detectives accompanied him until he left Tokio [*sic*]. All this because Mr. Hughes had been in Russia, and also was known to have contributed poems to radical magazines in America. At his hotel, after the examination, Japanese reporters who came to interview him, told Mr. Hughes that 11 of the writers who were to have been at the luncheon in his honor had been arrested too.[8]

The final word from the U.S. government on this incident notes that Hughes "was detained a short time and released the same afternoon. He then proceeded to Yokohama where he voluntarily sailed from Japan on a steamer for which he had already purchased passage. He made no complaint to Consul General or to the Embassy. The action of the police seems to have been in accordance with Japanese laws and to provide no reason for representations."[9] It helped Hughes' cause with the U.S. government not at all that upon his return he moved to Carmel and kept the company of Lincoln Steffens and Ella Winter. His participation in the activities of the local John Reed Club and willingness to travel as a firsthand observer to one of the most virulent labor disputes in California agricultural history did not go unnoticed by federal agents. Hughes may have suffered from a naïveté regarding his active pursuit of literary opportunities afforded by leftist publication outlets. He clearly underestimated the resolve of government forces to limit the influence of what they considered "Red" threats. Even our own government programs came under suspicion. Successful programs of the New Deal, like the

Federal Theater Project, the closest this country has ever come to a nationally supported theater that reached all classes in all states, did not escape the Red paranoia. The Federal Theater was closed in 1939 under an act of Congress.

In examining political theater in the 1930s, many theater historians stop with the Federal Theater Project. When considering black playwrights of this period, the focus again rests primarily on the Negro troupes of the Federal Theater Project and occasionally on Federal Theater-related production companies like Karamu House in Cleveland. In 1969, Doris Abramson wrote as an introductory rationale for her book, *Negro Playwrights in the American Theater: 1925–1959*, "Very little has been written about Negro playwrights specifically. The several studies that have been made of the Negro in dramatic literature and theater emphasize characters and performances in plays about Negro Life." From 1969 to 1998, there have been several more studies of the contributions of black writers, playwrights, and poets to American letters. But also needed are studies examining the political influences upon these same writers and how those influences were manifested in their works. Labor historians have long understood the collective influence of various ethnic groups on American culture and their radicalization from the turn of the century to the 1930s. This period, marked by internecine strife, protest movements, industrial strikes, and reactionary politics to those strikes, has come to be known as the "Labor Wars." The plays considered here address one aspect of that struggle through the eyes of one of America's foremost literary figures. The political Left profoundly influenced Langston Hughes, and this is evident in his plays of this period.

American industry used rhetorical strategies that appealed to the public with sterile metaphors of technological progress. Conversely, American labor organizers used rhetorical appeals to sway rural and urban laborers that spoke to the solidarity of brotherhood and economic and emotional prosperity. This rhetorical strategy is evident in Hughes' plays as well. In his political and labor plays, Hughes makes use of strong religious metaphors as well as labor rhetoric that call for a biracial army to conquer institutionalized racism and the poverty endemic in a capitalistic system. Salvation would be found in the group, not in the machine. This is a humanistic predisposition found in any number of labor plays of the 1930s and evidenced clearly in the plays by Langston Hughes. His labor/leftist scripts speak powerfully of the political idealism of minority labor and of their hopes and disappointments in the system.

Ironically, this segment of Hughes' writing has been ignored. Webster Smalley's 1963 compilation of Hughes' plays brought to public attention Hughes' social and humorous plays but not his political plays. Smalley's introduction discounts Hughes' attempts to treat these political issues artistically: "The position of the Negro in the United States is one of the facts that any Negro must face if he is to write at all. No one has more faith in the strength and dignity of his people than does Hughes, but only a few of his works can be called militant or didactic. Some few readers might wish that he were more belligerent, but he is an artist, not a propagandist."[10]

The evidence overwhelmingly suggests that Smalley is not correct in his assessment of Hughes. Hughes seems to have been following assiduously guidelines for the development of a serious indigenous Negro theater company laid out by leading black writers. From 1919 and continuing through the 1920s, black writers addressed the formation of such a theater group in journals of the day. Hughes was well aware of the public literary discussion and contributed his own essay, "The Negro Artist and the Racial Mountain," published in the *Nation* in 1926. In an article that same year, the *Crisis* editor W. E. B. Du Bois outlined four fundamental principles of a Negro theater: "The plays of a real Negro theatre must be: 1. *About us.* That is, they must have plots which reveal Negro life as it is. 2. *By us.* That is, they must be written by Negro authors who understand from birth and continual association just what it means to be a Negro today. 3. *For us.* That is, the theatre must cater primarily to Negro audiences and be supported and sustained by their entertainment and approval. 4. *Near us.* The theatre must be in a Negro neighborhood near the mass of ordinary Negro people."[11]

Seven years earlier, Willis Richardson articulated a call for support to develop the "Negro drama" as part of an artistic movement that would address issues pertinent to Negro life and issues. His article of 1919, again in the *Crisis*, defines his vision: "When I say Negro plays, I do not mean merely plays with Negro characters. . . . Miss Grimke's 'Rachel' is nearer the idea; still even this, with its Negro characters, is not exactly the thing I mean. It is called a propaganda play, and a great portion of it shows the manner in which Negroes are treated by white people in the United States. . . . Still there is another kind of play; the play that shows the soul of a people; and the soul of this people is truly worth showing." Hughes echoed these sentiments as late as 1961 in an interview at the Karamu Theater in Cleveland.[12] In another interview, nearly a decade earlier, Hughes himself commented on the perception of him as a protest writer: "I have every so often been termed a propaganda or protest writer. . . . That designation has probably grown out of the fact that I write about what I know best, and being a negro in this country is tied up with difficulties that cause one to protest naturally. I am writing about human beings and situations that I know and experience and therefore it is only incidentally protest—protest in that it grows out of a live situation."[13]

Contrary to Smalley's position, Langston Hughes *was* a literary propagandist in the 1930s, and he employed the literary form used repeatedly by politically inspired artists—the drama. Through drama, through the representation of character, through their speeches before an audience, one finds a seductive means of making political ideology available to the uneducated, the nonliterary, and the underprivileged. Hughes advocated the precepts articulated by Du Bois and others regarding the development of an indigenous black theater movement. His plays provide evidence of his attempts to employ intrinsic cultural linguistic and social elements in his labor plays. The use of dialect, call-response, and documentary detail of abuses in the Scottsboro case and the agricultural strikes was artistically innovative. The experimentation of the documentary style of *Harvest* revealed itself in his poetry as well. "Ballad of a Landlord" incorporates newspaper headlines within the verse. According to James A. Emanuel, Hughes refined this technique so that "almost twenty years later in 'Neon Sings' (in *Montage of a Dream Deferred*) [he creates] a poem almost totally comprised of the names of Harlem bars and night clubs."[14]

Similarly, Hughes takes the dramatic depiction of labor organizer Caroline Decker as Jennie in *Harvest* and refines and recasts it into the militant characters of Joyce, Lynn Clarrise, and Minnie in *Simple's Uncle Sam*. Hughes is credited with providing "the most strikingly realistic descriptions of black female freedom fighters" in the literature of black American writers.[15] The blending of secular and religious forms of language and music with the secular abuses of racism, prejudice, and work conditions and religious appeals to hope, faith, and pride in self offered a radical departure in theatrical form. While radical for the theater of the 1930s, it was a form understood by Hughes and his intended audience in the black community. Call-response, which he employed in *Scottsboro, Limited* and *De Organizer*, somehow essentializes Hughes' approach to his audience. It is what two rhetorical critics call "the manifestation of the cultural dynamic which finds audience and listener or leader and background to be a unified whole. . . . Black communicative performance is

concentric in quality—the 'audience' becoming both observers and participants in the speech event."[16] This "oneness" or "wholeness" of audience and performance is clearly something Hughes understood from his
cultural experience and intended to recreate through his plays.

There is a great deal more to be done to analyze all of the dramatic
works of Langston Hughes. His radio scripts, historical pageants, operas,
and other theatrical collaborations require serious academic attention.
Twenty years ago, Gloria T. Hull comprised a list of questions critics
might consider when analyzing Marxist influences on Langston Hughes.
The study presented here moves closer to providing answers to a few of
the questions posed. Though Marxist criticism is not currently fashionable among literary critics and the questions Hull asked were intended
as starting points for the analysis of Hughes' poetry, they are still worth
noting for subsequent considerations of his dramas that treat political
and labor themes:

> 1. How do Hughes' identifiably Marxist poems compare with/differ
> from his non-Marxist ones? Which are better? Why? According to
> what/whose standards? Answering these questions would require
> textual analysis and could also include some discussions of Hughes'
> literary lineage and of the personal/historio-cultural reasons why
> he chose the particular forms he did. One would also keep in mind
> that Hughes' 1930's poems are usually deemed inferior and either
> explicitly or implicitly speak to this judgment.
> 2. What . . . is the effect of Hughes' radical ideology upon his art—
> both its content and form, and above all, the two in relationship
> to each other? . . . [D]o the answers to these questions tell any-
> thing . . . about the influences of politics on poetry (a subject with
> ramifications also for the new Black Poetry of the 1960s)?
> 3. [D]oes it make any difference in the finished product whether or
> not Hughes is writing from a Marxist and/or revolutionary point of
> view?
> 4. What new light is shed on his total canon?[17]

Arnold Rampersad began answering this last question in his 1986 article
"Langston Hughes and His Critics on the Left" but did so as a narrowly
focused response to Lydia Filatova.[18] Similarly, my analysis attempts to
heighten public awareness, again, of a narrow segment of the canon,
Hughes' leftist plays of the 1930s.

Langston Hughes' stature as an American poet and social critic is un-
deniable and well deserved. Unfortunately, he remains virtually un-

known as a dramatist of any literary importance in American theater history. The primary and secondary sources of this investigation reveal that there is more to Hughes as an American political dramatist than has been addressed by other scholars. Previous scholars had cleared a path that, I believe, this study has been able to extend. In turn, it is my fervent hope that researchers will take up where this book ends, to begin investigations of the dramatic works of Langston Hughes focusing on their political and cultural insights. His associations with the theater companies that he helped to found to produce his plays merit similar in-depth explorations. In these, investigators may find new and intriguing information about Hughes' political affiliations. They may come to discover the motivations that caused him to cultivate left-wing associations that posed a clear commercial liability for him. The analysis of his dramatic works is of undoubted importance to American letters and American theater history. Few American artists were as articulate and as attuned to the political leanings of minority groups in the United States in the 1930s as Langston Hughes.

Notes
Bibliography
Index

Notes

INTRODUCTION: CHASING THE DREAM

1. Edward J. Mullen, ed., *Critical Essays on Langston Hughes* (Boston: G. K. Hall and Co., 1986), 15–16. See also Donald C. Dickinson, *A Bio-bibliography of Langston Hughes, 1902–1967* (Hamden, CT: Archon Books, 1967), 59.

2. Hughes' personal and professional interest in the theater is documented in several sources. Readers are encouraged to seek their own support for these assertions beginning with Arnold Rampersad's *The Life of Langston Hughes*, vols. 1 and 2 (New York: Oxford University Press, 1986). The first chapter notes that "Langston was his mother's son in his passion for the theatre and the road" (12). Scores of references to Hughes' theatrical projects inserted throughout both volumes attest to this interest in theatrical success. Additional verification can be found in Reuben and Dorothy Silver's interview conducted with Hughes on 6–7 May 1961 at Karamu Theater, Cleveland, while Reuben Silver served as the director of the theater; see Susan Duffy, Transcription, "Interview with Langston Hughes," *Artist and Influence* 13 (1994): 107–28. The audiotape is held in the Schomburg Collection for Research in Black Culture and the Hatch-Billops Collection, both in New York.

3. Rampersad, 1:184, 193–213, and Duffy, Transcription, 107–28.

4. Margaret Larkin, "A Poet for the People," *Opportunity* 5 (March 1927): 84–85.

5. Alain Locke, "Outstanding Books of 1932," *Opportunity* 11 (January 1933): 14–18.

6. Langston Hughes to Noel Sullivan, 24 October 1934, Noel Sullivan Papers, Box 40:1, Bancroft Library, University of California, Berkeley (hereafter cited as Bancroft NSP).

7. Doris Abramson, *Negro Playwrights in the American Theater: 1925–1959* (New York: Columbia University Press, 1969), 68.

8. Langston Hughes to Noel Sullivan, 29 January 1936, Box 40:1, Bancroft NSP.

9. Eric Homberger, *American Writers and Radical Politics, 1900–1939: Equivocal Commitments* (New York: St. Martin's Press, 1986), 129.

10. Homberger, 123–31.

11. Daniel Aaron, *Writers on the Left: Episodes in American Literary Communism* (New York: Harcourt, Brace and World, 1961), 224.

12. *New Masses* (September 1931): 21, cited in Rampersad, 1:216, 356.

13. Aaron, ix.

14. Rampersad, 1:182–210 provides detail of Hughes' fall from grace with Mrs. Charlotte Mason. Pgs. 211–41 offer important and detailed information about Hughes' shift toward leftist political activities.

15. Mordecai Gorelik, "Theater Is a Weapon," *Theater Arts Monthly* 18 (June 1934): 420.

16. Morgan Himmelstein, *Drama Was a Weapon: The Left-Wing Theater in New York 1929–1941* (New York: Rutgers University Press, 1963), 218.

17. Langston Hughes to Noel Sullivan, 29 January 1936, Box 40:1 Bancroft NSP.

18. Duffy, Transcription, 125. Harold Clurman articulates a similar rationale in his introduction to *Famous American Plays of the 1930's* (New York: Dell Publishing, 1959).

19. Harvey Teres, *Renewing the Left: Politics, Imagination, and the New York Intellectuals* (New York: Oxford University Press, 1996), 206–7.

20. Wendy Smith, *Real Life Drama: The Group Theatre and America 1931–1940* (New York: Alfred A. Knopf, 1990), 124. George Lewis, "We Need Anti-War Plays," *Workers Theater* (August 1932): 6; Himmelstein, 230. For a more complete discussion of anti-Nazi and anti-war plays of the period, see Susan Duffy and Bernard K. Duffy, "Anti-Nazi Drama in the United States 1934–1941," *Essays in Theater* 4 (November 1985): 39–60.

21. Umberto Eco, *The Role of the Reader: Explorations in the Semiotics of Texts* (Bloomington: Indiana University Press, 1979), 21, 55, 222.

22. Smith, xi.

23. See Susan Duffy, *American Labor on Stage: Dramatic Interpretations of the Steel and Textile Industries in the 1930's* (Westport, CT: Greenwood Press, 1996).

24. For an additional discussion of this assertion, see Duffy, *American Labor on Stage.*

25. Alain Locke, "Steps Toward the Negro Theatre," reprinted in *Lost Plays of the Harlem Renaissance 1920–1940,* ed. James V. Hatch and Leo Hamalian (Detroit: Wayne State University Press, 1996), 442.

26. Margaret A. Reid, "Langston Hughes: Rhetoric and Protest." *Langston Hughes Review* 3.1 (Spring 1984): 13–20.

27. Langston Hughes, "I Wonder as I Wander," in *The Langston Hughes Reader* (New York: George Braziller, 1958), 405, 416.

28. Langston Hughes, "Jazz as Communication," in *The Langston Hughes Reader,* 492–94.

29. Langston Hughes, "The Negro Artist and the Racial Mountain," reprinted in Hatch and Hamalian, 408–12.

30. Jay Williams, *Stage Left* (New York: Charles Scribner's Sons, 1974), 130–31.

31. Langston Hughes to Noel Sullivan, 29 January 1936, Box 40:1, Bancroft NSP.

32. Dudley Fitts, "A Trio of Singers in Varied Keys," *New York Times Book Review,* 29 October 1961, 16, in Mullen, 88.

33. Thomas Millard Hinery, Letter to the editor, *Messenger* 7 (June 1925): 239, in Mullen, 5.

34. This is from Hughes' interview with Reuben and Dorothy Silver of May 1961, which I transcribed for *Artist and Influence.* See Duffy, Transcription, 120–21.

35. His long battle with Zora Neale Hurston over authorship of *Mule Bone* is outlined revealingly in a recent book by the same title, edited by George Houston Bass and Henry Louis Gates Jr. In my research I discovered an anecdote related by Hughes in his interview with Reuben and Dorothy Silver that, to my knowledge, does not appear in any of the discussions about the Hughes/Hurston feud. In the interview, Hughes relates a trick he played on Hurston when he saw her for the last time before her death. I offer it here so that there is a record of it for other studies:

> Well, there's nothing more except a little anecdote that might be amusing. The last time I saw Zora Neale Hurston was in Washington, perhaps five or six years ago, at George Everett Johnson's home and she was staying with George Johnson, which I did not know. The Washington writers, those who were left around, including Mr. Johnson were giving a party for me and it was to be a benefit at Johnson's home. She (Mrs. Johnson) decided she couldn't clean up her house, cause she's about 75, and they gave the party somewhere else. Meanwhile, I went to Mrs. Johnson's home to go to the party with her and she had gone. And she had told me that day that Zora Hurston was staying there and she was coming to the party. But when I got to her house they had already gone ahead to get things ready. Now, laying on the living room table, where Ms. Hurston was working and writing, was the script of a play—I've forgotten the name of it now, a play, and I saw it sitting there, opened it, looked at it, saw it was by Zora Neale Hurston—and just out of devilment, as she had once rubbed my name off of *Mule Bone,* I took the page out of the script and put it in the typewriter and typed "And Langston Hughes" except that I put my name at the top, "By Langston Hughes and Zora Neale Hurston." I put it back in the script,

so I never knew what she might have said when she saw it, but I imagined she laughed because she had a very good sense of humor. So anyway at the party she was very courteous here and we were very cordial, but we didn't mention *Mule Bone,* of course. (113–14)

36. See Duffy, Transcription, 118.

37. Donald Ogden Stewart, *Fighting Words* (New York: Harcourt, Brace and Co., 1940), 62.

38. *The Langston Hughes Reader* (New York: George Braziller, 1958), 483–85. See also Langston Hughes to Arna Bontemps, 22 December 1946, in *Arna Bontemps, Langston Hughes: Letters, 1925–1967,* ed. Charles H. Nichols (New York: Dodd, Mead and Co., 1980), 213.

39. Duffy, Transcription, 107–8.

40. Duffy, Transcription, 108–20.

41. Duffy, Transcription, 120–21.

HUGHES' MOVE TO THE LEFT: *SCOTTSBORO, LIMITED*

1. Rampersad, 1:216.

2. Rampersad, 1:217.

3. Rampersad, 1:219.

4. John Gassner, "Social Realism and Imaginative Theater: Avant-Garde Stage Productions in the American Social Theater of the Nineteen Thirties," *Theater Survey* 3 (1963): 12. See also Duffy and Duffy, "Anti-Nazi Drama," 41, and Himmelstein, 10–15.

5. Himmelstein, 10.

6. For an examination of agit-prop form in Federal Theater Project plays, see Susan Duffy and Bernard K. Duffy, "Theatrical Responses to Technology During the Depression: Three Federal Theater Project Plays," *Theatre History Studies* 6 (1986): 142–64.

7. Rampersad, 1:235.

8. Telegram, Noel Sullivan to National Committee for the Defense of Political Prisoners, 2 December 1933, Box 134: 1933-Oct.-Dec., Bancroft NSP. A letter from Langston Hughes to Gilmore Millen, 2 November 1933, includes Hughes' name at the top of the letterhead along with Sherwood Anderson, William Rose Benet, Malcolm Cowley, Floyd Dell, John Dos Passos, Theodore Dreiser, Waldo Frank, Michael Gold, Suzanne LaFollette, Melvin P. Levy, and Edna St. Vincent Millay. Among the list of "Members in California" are the names of Noel Sullivan, Lincoln Steffens, Ella Winter, and Upton Sinclair. Noel Sullivan Papers, Box 40:1, Bancroft NSP.

9. "John Reed Club Told of Valley Cotton War," *Carmel Pine Cone,* 10 November 1933. See also Rampersad, 1:283.

10. Rampersad, 2:5.

11. Lydia Filatova, "Langston Hughes: American Writer," *International Literature* 1 (1933): 105.

12. Rampersad, 1:236, 238.

13. Langston Hughes, "A Chant for Tom Mooney," in *A New Song: A Collection of Poems* (New York: International Workers Order, 1938), 13–14.

14. Eugene Gordon, "Negro Novelists and the Negro Masses," *New Masses* (July 1933): 20.

15. Langston Hughes, "To Negro Writers," in *American Writers' Congress*, ed. Henry Hart (New York: International Publishers, 1935), 139–41.

16. Eugene Gordon, "Social and Political Problems of the Negro Writer," and Eugene Clay, "The Negro in Recent American Literature," in H. Hart, 141–53.

17. Michael Gold, "Introduction," in *A New Song: A Collection of Poems*, by Langston Hughes (New York: International Workers Order, 1938), 7–8.

AN AMERICAN DOCUMENTARY PLAY: *HARVEST*

1. Biographical notes on Noel Sullivan, TS, Local History Department, Harrison Memorial Library, Carmel-by-the-Sea, CA. Virginia W. Stone, "The Master of Hollow Hills," *Noticias del Puerto de Monterey: A Quarterly Bulletin of Historic Monterey,* Monterey History and Art Association (June 1986): 9–11. "In Appreciation of Noel Sullivan," *Carmel Pine Cone,* 20 September 1956.

2. Langston Hughes to Noel Sullivan, 31 January 1933, Box 40:1, Bancroft NSP.

3. Rampersad, 1:277. The chapter "Waiting on Roosevelt," 276–305, offers interesting insights about Carmel and Hughes' position as one of the few black residents in the area.

4. Homberger, 128.

5. Homberger, 128, 129, 130, 228.

6. Ella Winter to Joseph Freeman, 3 June 1932, Joseph Freeman Papers, Box 149, Hoover Institution, Stanford University.

7. "Residents Blush on Realizing They Are of Communist Party," *Carmel Pine Cone,* 24 June 1932.

8. Faith Berry, *Langston Hughes, Before and Beyond Harlem* (Westport, CT: Lawrence Hill and Co., 1983), 152.

9. Cletus E. Daniel, *Bitter Harvest: A History of California Farmworkers, 1870–1941* (Ithaca: Cornell University Press, 1981), 141.

10. *Carmel Pine Cone,* 20 October 1933; 27 October 1933.

11. *Carmel Pine Cone,* 13 October 1933, 10; 20 October 1933; 27 October 1933, 1; 10 November 1933.

12. Ella Winter, *And Not to Yield, An Autobiography* (New York: Harcourt, Brace and World, 1963), 286.

13. *Carmel Pine Cone,* 26 January 1934, 3.

14. Winter, 190–97.

15. Paul Taylor, *On the Ground in the Thirties* (Salt Lake City: Gibbs M. Smith, 1983), 17–158. The best historical synthesis of this material can be found in the U.S. Senate's *Hearings Before a Subcommittee on Education and Labor,* 76th Cong., 3rd sess., 1939–41.

16. Rampersad, 1:290–91.

17. Rampersad, 1:281.

18. Taylor, 51.

19. Langston Hughes to Noel Sullivan, July 1934, Box 40:1, Bancroft NSP.

20. Berry, 211–12.

21. Bonnie Gartshore, "Langston Hughes and the Vigilantes," *Monterey Herald,* 25 October 1990, 1–D.

22. Berry, 215.

23. John Thompson, "Langston Hughes," *Coast Weekly,* 24 May 1990, 30.

24. Langston Hughes to Maxim Lieber, 8 August 1934, Beinecke LHP.

25. The members of the Executive and Advisory Committee of the Theater Union included Joseph Freeman, Manuel Gomez, Charles R. Walker, and Liston M. Oak; dramatists Paul Peters, Sherwood Anderson, John Howard Lawson, Sidney Howard, and Elmer Rice; writers Countee Cullen, H. W. L. Dana, and John Dos Passos; actress Rose McClendon; and social critic Lewis Mumford. Margaret Larkin served as the executive secretary. See also Rampersad, 1:296.

26. Winter, 199.

27. Berry, 212.

POLITICS AND SOCIAL COMMENTARY:
ANGELO HERNDON JONES

1. Langston Hughes to Noel Sullivan, 29 January 1936, Box 40:1, Bancroft NSP.

2. Berry, 210.

3. Barbara Dale May, "Poetry and Political Commitment: Alberti, Guillén and Hughes," *Studies in Afro-Hispanic Literature* 2.3 (1978–79): 20.

4. Rampersad, 2:30, 41.

5. *Variety* survey reported in Abe Green and Joe Laurie, *Show Biz* (New York: Holt and Co., 1953), 336, subsequently cited in Errol Hill, ed., *The Theater of Black Americans* (Englewood Cliffs, NJ: Prentice Hall, 1980), 2:34.

6. Monty Noam Penkower, *The Federal Writers' Project: A Study in Government Patronage of the Arts* (Urbana: University of Illinois Press, 1977), 67.

7. Hill, 2:37.

8. Abramson, 46.

9. Edith Isaacs, *The Negro in the American Theater* (New York: Theater Arts, 1947), 106. See also Abramson.

10. Interview with Abram Hill (Brown), tape recording (first tape, side 1), 27 February 1977. Oral history interviews, Theater of the Thirties Collec-

tion, Fenwick Library, George Mason University, Fairfax, VA (hereafter cited as Fenwick TOT).

11. Abstract of interview with Anderson, 24 May 1978, Fenwick TOT.

12. Abramson, 48.

13. Langston Hughes to Arna Bontemps, ca. 1936, in Nichols, 70.

14. Interview with Abram Hill (Brown).

15. Rampersad, 2:18.

16. Interview with Leonard DePaur, tape recording (first tape, side 2), 28 December 1976, Fenwick TOT.

17. Abramson, 48, and Rampersad, 1:359.

18. Rampersad, 2:154.

19. Rampersad, 1:321.

A COLLABORATION OF JAZZ, POETRY, AND BLUES: *DE ORGANIZER*

1. James P. Johnson to Langston Hughes, ca. January 1937; Langston Hughes to James P. Johnson, 24 January 1937; James P. Johnson to Langston Hughes, ca. February/March 1937, Langston Hughes Papers in the James Wendall Johnson Collection, Beinecke Rare Book and Manuscript Library, Yale University (hereafter cited as Beinecke LHP).

2. Langston Hughes to James P. Johnson, 8 March 1938, Beinecke LHP.

3. Scott E. Brown, *James P. Johnson: A Case of Mistaken Identity* (Metuchen, NJ: Scarecrow Press, 1986), 110, 221.

4. Rampersad, 1:363.

5. Rampersad, 1:360–67. See also Langston Hughes and James P. Johnson, *De Organizer* TS, f. 829–30, Beinecke LHP.

6. James P. Johnson to Langston Hughes, ca. fall 1939; James P. Johnson to Langston Hughes, 14 December 1939, Beinecke LHP.

7. James P. Johnson to Langston Hughes, n.d. and 14 December 1939; Langston Hughes to James P. Johnson, 8 November 1950, Beinecke LHP.

8. Brown, 245.

9. Brown, 245. See also Steven C. Tracy, *Langston Hughes and the Blues* (Urbana: University of Illinois Press, 1988), 48–49, 123.

10. Tracy, 8, 112. See also Langston Hughes, *The Big Sea* (New York: Alfred Knopf, 1940), 21, and Roderick C. Hart, "Black-White Literary Relations in the Harlem Renaissance," *American Literature* 44 (January 1973): 612–28.

11. See the International Ladies' Garment Workers' Union Papers, Labor Management Documentation Center, M. Catherwood Library, Cornell University, Ithaca, NY, for the concert program. Leonard De Paur served as musical director for the ILGWU production while Paul Creston received the task of trying to recreate James P. Johnson's innovative jazz piano style. Of anecdotal interest is the inclusion of Earl Jones as the understudy for the part of the union

organizer. Robert Earl Jones, also referred to by Hughes as Earl Jones, was the father of contemporary actor James Earl Jones. Robert Earl Jones was a member of the IWO (International Workers' Order) and of Hughes' Suitcase Theater Group from its inception and had been previously cast by Hughes as the lead in his play *Don't You Want to Be Free?*

12. *New York Times,* 26 May 1940, sec. 9, p. 2; 31 May 1940, 15; 1 June 1940, 7; 2 June 1940, 43, 47, sec. 9, p. 2.

13. Gassner, "Social Realism," 12.

14. See Duffy, *American Labor on Stage,* 18, 35, 61, 140.

15. Tracy, 144.

16. Tracy, 72–73.

17. Tracy, 107, 143.

18. Ross Russell, *Jazz Style in Kansas City and the Southwest* (Berkeley: University of California Press, 1971), 321.

19. For a discussion of call-response, see Jack L. Daniel and Geneva Smitherman, "How I Got Over: Communication Dynamics in the Black Community," *Quarterly Journal of Speech* 62.1 (February 1976): 26–39.

20. For a discussion of the role of the "Conjure Man" in southern black literature, see J. Lee Greene's entry on black life and literature and James R. Curtis's entry on Charles W. Chestnutt in Charles Reagan Wilson and William Ferris, eds., *Encyclopedia of Southern Culture* (Chapel Hill: University of North Carolina Press, 1989), 172–74, 202–3. See also the introduction to *Conjure Tales* by Charles W. Chestnutt, retold by Ray Anthony Shepard (New York: E. P. Dutton and Co., 1973), ix.

21. Susan L. Blake, "Old John in Harlem: The Urban Folktales of Langston Hughes," in Mullen, 168, 170.

22. Brown, 220.

23. Daniel and Smitherman, 34.

24. Mullen, 5.

CONCLUSION: HUGHES' LOST LEGACY

1. Letter, No. 1462, 22 October 1932, Declassified State Department Records, 800.00B, Hughes, Langston/2, National Archives, Washington, DC. (Unless otherwise specified, all citations contained here refer to file 800.00B, Hughes, Langston. Collection hereafter referred to as National Archives.)

2. Langston Hughes, "The Same," *Negro Worker* 9–10.2 (September/October 1932): 31–32. In National Archives.

3. Memorandum no. 493, 15 November 1932, National Archives.

4. Memorandum no. 1590, 29 May 1933, National Archives.

5. Memorandum no. 493, 19 July 1933, National Archives.

6. Telegram, Grew to Secretary of State, 15 September 1933, State Department files, 394.1121-Hughes, Langston, National Archives.

7. Report to American Consul General at Shanghai, China, 28 August 1933, regarding "Visit to Orient of Mr. James Langston Hughes," National Archives.

8. TS, Noel Sullivan Papers, Box 40:1, Bancroft NSP.

9. Telegram, Grew to Secretary of State, 15 September 1933, State Department files, 394.1121-Hughes, Langston, National Archives.

10. Webster Smalley, ed. *Five Plays by Langston Hughes* (Bloomington: Indiana University Press, 1963), vii.

11. W. E. B. Du Bois, "Krigwa Players Little Negro Theatre: The Story of a Little Theatre Movement," in Hatch and Hamalian, 447.

12. Willis Richardson, "The Hope of a Negro Drama," in Hatch and Hamalian, 438. See also Duffy, Transcription, 107–28.

13. David D. Britt, "The Image of the White Man in the Fiction of Langston Hughes, Richard Wright, James Baldwin and Ralph Ellison" (Ph.D. diss., Emory University, 1968), 25.

14. James A. Emanuel, "The Literary Experiments of Langston Hughes," *College Language Association Journal* 11 (June 1968): 343.

15. Rita Dandridge, "The Black Woman as Freedom Fighter," *College Language Association Journal* 18 (December 1974): 273.

16. Daniel and Smitherman, 39.

17. Gloria T. Hull, "Notes on a Marxist Interpretation of Black American Literature," *Black American Literature Forum* 12 (Winter 1978): 150.

18. Arnold Rampersad, "Langston Hughes and His Critics on the Left," *Langston Hughes Review* 8.5 (Fall 1986): 34–40.

Bibliography

Aaron, Daniel. *Writers on the Left: Episodes in American Literary Communism.* New York: Harcourt, Brace and World, 1961.

Abramson, Doris. *Negro Playwrights in the American Theater: 1925–1959.* New York: Columbia University Press, 1969.

Berry, Faith. *Langston Hughes, Before and Beyond Harlem.* Westport, CT: Lawrence Hill and Co., 1983.

Blake, Susan L. "Old John in Harlem: The Urban Folktales of Langston Hughes." In *Critical Essays on Langston Hughes,* edited by Edward J. Mullen. Boston: G. K. Hall and Co., 1986.

Britt, David D. "The Image of the White Man in the Fiction of Langston Hughes, Richard Wright, James Baldwin and Ralph Ellison." Ph.D. diss., Emory University, 1968.

Brown, Scott E. *James P. Johnson: A Case of Mistaken Identity.* Metuchen, NJ: Scarecrow Press, 1986.

Chestnutt, Charles W. *Conjure Tales.* Retold by Ray Anthony Shepard. New York: E. P. Dutton and Co., 1973.

Clay, Eugene. "The Negro in Recent American Literature." In *American Writers' Congress,* edited by Henry Hart. New York: International Publishers, 1935.

Clurman, Harold. *Famous American Plays of the 1930's.* New York: Dell Publishing, 1959.

Dandridge, Rita. "The Black Woman as Freedom Fighter." *College Language Association Journal* 18 (December 1974): 273.

Daniel, Cletus E. *Bitter Harvest: A History of California Farmworkers, 1870–1941.* Ithaca: Cornell University Press, 1981.

Daniel, Jack L., and Geneva Smitherman. "How I Got Over: Communication Dynamics in the Black Community." *Quarterly Journal of Speech* 62.1 (February 1976): 26–39.

Dickinson, Donald C. *A Bio-bibliography of Langston Hughes, 1902–1967.* Hamden, CT: Archon Books, 1967.

Du Bois, W. E. B. "Krigwa Players Little Negro Theatre: The Story of a Little Theatre Movement." In *Lost Plays of the Harlem Renaissance 1920–1940*, edited by James V. Hatch and Leo Hamalian. Detroit: Wayne State University Press, 1996.

Duffy, Susan. *American Labor on Stage: Dramatic Interpretations of the Steel and Textile Industries in the 1930's*. Westport, CT: Greenwood Press, 1996.

———. Transcription. "Interview with Langston Hughes." By Reuben and Dorothy Silver. *Artist and Influence* 13 (1994): 107–28.

Duffy, Susan, and Bernard K. Duffy. "Anti-Nazi Drama in the United States 1934–1941." *Essays in Theater* 4 (November 1985): 35–60.

———. "Theatrical Responses to Technology During the Depression: Three Federal Theatre Project Plays." *Theatre History Studies* 6 (1986): 142–64.

Eco, Umberto. *The Role of the Reader: Explorations in the Semiotics of Texts*. Bloomington: Indiana University Press, 1979.

Emanuel, James A. "The Literary Experiments of Langston Hughes." *College Language Association Journal* 11 (June 1968): 343.

Filatova, Lydia. "Langston Hughes: American Writer." *International Literature* 1 (1933): 105.

Freeman, Joseph. Papers. Hoover Institution, Stanford University.

Gassner, John. "Social Realism and Imaginative Theater: Avant-Garde Stage Productions in the American Social Theater of the Nineteen Thirties." *Theater Survey* 3 (1963).

Gordon, Eugene. "Negro Novelists and the Negro Masses." *New Masses* (July 1933): 20.

———. "Social and Political Problems of the Negro Writer." In *American Writers' Congress*, edited by Henry Hart. New York: International Publishers, 1935.

Gorelik, Mordecai. "Theater Is a Weapon." *Theater Arts Monthly* 18 (June 1934): 420.

Green, Abe, and Joe Laurie. *Show Biz*. New York: Holt and Co., 1953.

Hart, Henry, ed. *American Writers' Congress*. New York: International Publishers, 1935.

Hart, Roderick C. "Black-White Literary Relations in the Harlem Renaissance." *American Literature* 44 (January 1973): 612–28.

Hatch, James V., and Leo Hamalian, eds. *Lost Plays of the Harlem Renaissance 1920–1940*. Detroit: Wayne State University Press, 1996.

Hill, Errol, ed. *The Theater of Black Americans*. Englewood Cliffs, NJ: Prentice Hall, 1980.

Himmelstein, Morgan. *Drama Was a Weapon: The Left-Wing Theater in New York 1929–1941*. New York: Rutgers University Press, 1963.

Homberger, Eric. *American Writers and Radical Politics, 1900–1939: Equivocal Commitments*. New York: St. Martin's Press, 1986.

Hughes, Langston. *The Big Sea*. New York: Alfred Knopf, 1940.

———. "A Chant for Tom Mooney." In *A New Song: A Collection of Poems*. New York: International Workers Order, 1938.

———. "I Wonder as I Wander." In *The Langston Hughes Reader.* New York: George Braziller, 1958.

———. "Jazz as Communication." In *The Langston Hughes Reader.* New York: George Braziller, 1958.

———. *The Langston Hughes Reader.* New York: George Braziller, 1958.

———. "The Negro Artist and the Racial Mountain." In *Lost Plays of the Harlem Renaissance 1920–1940,* edited by James V. Hatch and Leo Hamalian. Detroit: Wayne State University Press, 1996.

———. Papers. James Wendall Johnson Collection, Beinecke Rare Book and Manuscript Library, Yale University.

———. "To Negro Writers." In *American Writers' Congress,* edited by Henry Hart. New York: International Publishers, 1935.

Hull, Gloria T. "Notes on a Marxist Interpretation of Black American Literature." *Black American Literature Forum* 12 (Winter 1978): 150.

International Ladies' Garment Workers' Union. Papers. Labor Management Documentation Center, M. Catherwood Library, Cornell University.

Isaacs, Edith. *The Negro in the American Theater.* New York: Theater Arts, 1947.

Larkin, Margaret. "A Poet for the People." *Opportunity* 5 (March 1927): 84–85.

Lewis, George. "We Need Anti-War Plays." *Workers Theater* (August 1932): 6.

Local History Department. Harrison Memorial Library, Carmel-by-the-Sea, CA.

Locke, Alain. "Outstanding Books of 1932." *Opportunity* 11 (January 1933): 14–18.

———. "Steps Toward the Negro Theatre." In *Lost Plays of the Harlem Renaissance 1920–1940,* edited by James V. Hatch and Leo Hamalian. Detroit: Wayne State University Press, 1996.

May, Barbara Dale. "Poetry and Political Commitment: Alberti, Guillén and Hughes." *Studies in Afro-Hispanic Literature* 2.3 (1978–79): 20.

Mullen, Edward J., ed. *Critical Essays on Langston Hughes.* Boston: G. K. Hall and Co., 1986.

Nichols, Charles H., ed. *Arna Bontemps, Langston Hughes: Letters, 1925–1967.* New York: Dodd, Mead and Co., 1980.

Oral history interviews. Theatre of the Thirties Collection, Fenwick Library, George Mason University, Fairfax, VA.

Penkower, Monty Noam. *The Federal Writers' Project: A Study in Government Patronage of the Arts.* Urbana: University of Illinois Press, 1977.

Rampersad, Arnold. "Langston Hughes and His Critics on the Left." *Langston Hughes Review* 8.5 (Fall 1986): 34–40.

———. *The Life of Langston Hughes.* 2 vols. New York: Oxford University Press, 1986.

Reid, Margaret A. "Langston Hughes: Rhetoric and Protest." *Langston Hughes Review* 3.1 (Spring 1984): 13–20.

Richardson, Willis. "The Hope of a Negro Drama." In *Lost Plays of the Harlem Renaissance 1920–1940,* edited by James V. Hatch and Leo Hamalian. Detroit: Wayne State University Press, 1996.

Russell, Ross. *Jazz Style in Kansas City and the Southwest*. Berkeley: University of California Press, 1971.

Smalley, Webster, ed. *Five Plays by Langston Hughes*. Bloomington: Indiana University Press, 1963.

Smith, Wendy. *Real Life Drama: The Group Theatre and America 1931–1940*. New York: Alfred A. Knopf, 1990.

State Department records. National Archives, Washington, DC.

Stewart, Donald Ogden. *Fighting Words*. New York: Harcourt, Brace and Co., 1940.

Stone, Virginia W. "The Master of Hollow Hills." *Noticias del Puerto de Monterey: A Quarterly Bulletin of Historic Monterey,* Monterey History and Art Association (June 1986): 9–11.

Sullivan, Noel. Papers and correspondence. Bancroft Library, University of California, Berkeley.

Taylor, Paul. *On the Ground in the Thirties*. Salt Lake City: Gibbs M. Smith, 1983.

Teres, Harvey. *Renewing the Left: Politics, Imagination, and the New York Intellectuals*. New York: Oxford University Press, 1996.

Tracy, Steven C. *Langston Hughes and the Blues*. Urbana: University of Illinois Press, 1988.

Williams, Jay. *Stage Left*. New York: Charles Scribner's Sons, 1974.

Wilson, Charles Reagan, and William Ferris, eds. *Encyclopedia of Southern Culture*. Chapel Hill: University of North Carolina Press, 1989.

Winter, Ella. *And Not to Yield, An Autobiography*. New York: Harcourt, Brace and World, 1963.

Index

SUSAN DUFFY is a professor in the liberal studies department at California Polytechnic State University where she teaches courses on literature in performance. She has published more than twenty articles as well as four books, including *American Labor on Stage: Dramatic Interpretations of the Steel and Textile Industries in the 1930s* and *The Political Left in the American Theatre of the 1930s: A Bibliographic Sourcebook.* Duffy is the recipient of the 1993 Cal Poly Distinguished Teaching Award and the 1998 Faculty Woman of the Year Award.